Practicing Narrative Mediation

Practicing Narrative Mediation

Loosening the Grip of Conflict

John Winslade

Gerald Monk

JOSSEY-BASS
A Wiley Imprint
www.josseybass.com

Published by Jossey-Bass
A Wiley Imprint
989 Market Street, San Francisco, CA 94103-1741—www.josseybass.com

Readers should be aware that Internet Web sites offered as citations and/or sources for further information may have changed or disappeared between the time this was written and when it is read.

Limit of Liability/Disclaimer of Warranty: While the publisher and author have used their best efforts in preparing this book, they make no representations or warranties with respect to the accuracy or completeness of the contents of this book and specifically disclaim any implied warranties of merchantability or fitness for a particular purpose. No warranty may be created or extended by sales representatives or written sales materials. The advice and strategies contained herein may not be suitable for your situation. You should consult with a professional where appropriate. Neither the publisher nor author shall be liable for any loss of profit or any other commercial damages, including but not limited to special, incidental, consequential, or other damages.

Jossey-Bass books and products are available through most bookstores. To contact Jossey-Bass directly call our Customer Care Department within the U.S. at 800-956-7739, outside the U.S. at 317-572-3986, or fax 317-572-4002.

Jossey-Bass also publishes its books in a variety of electronic formats. Some content that appears in print may not be available in electronic books.

Library of Congress Cataloging-in-Publication Data

Winslade, John.
    Practicing narrative mediation : loosening the grip of conflict/John Winslade, Gerald Monk. — 1st ed.
        p.   cm.
    Includes bibliographical references and index.
    ISBN 978-0-7879-9474-7 (cloth)
        1. Conflict management.   2. Mediation.   3. Storytelling.   4. Discourse analysis, Narrative. I. Monk, Gerald, date.   II. Title.
    HM1126.W58   2008
    303.6'9—dc22   2008018496

Printed in the United States of America
FIRST EDITION
HB Printing   10 9 8 7 6 5 4 3 2 1

Contents

Preface   vii

1   How to Work with Conflict Stories: Nine Hallmarks of Narrative Mediation   1

2   Negotiating Discursive Positions   40

3   Tracing Discursive Positioning Through a Conversation   64

4   Working with Cultural Narratives in Mediation   99

5   Divorce Mediation and Collaborative Practice
with Chip Rose   129

6   Outsider-Witness Practices in Organizational Disputes
with Allan Holmgren   166

7   Employment Mediation
with Alison Cotter   185

8   Restorative Conferencing in Schools   215

9   Conflict Resolution in Health Care   242

Epilogue   283

References   289

About the Authors   299

Index   303

For Michael White
(1948–2008)
In appreciation for his incalculable contributions to the
development of narrative practice

Preface

In 2000, we published *Narrative Mediation: A New Approach to Conflict Resolution*. This new book began with the idea that we might update that text. However, as we discussed with Jossey-Bass the idea of a second edition containing a number of revisions and also new concepts growing out of our experience over the last seven years, it rapidly became clear that we were talking about more than a few changes and additions. The idea of preparing a completely new text was the logical result. This book is the result of that decision.

This book covers new ground in several directions. One direction has led us to examine the development that has been taking place in narrative practice in general in the last ten years. In particular, we have drawn from the wide field of practice of narrative family therapy and community work. In addition, a growing number of practitioners have taken up the practice of narrative mediation, and we have sought to represent that growth through inviting some of these practitioners to participate in writing this book. Finally, we have considered the development that has occurred in our own work through the teaching and practice we have undertaken in the last ten years.

When we wrote our 2000 book, we were both living in New Zealand and had been doing mediation primarily in family and organizational contexts. Since 2000, we have both, at different times, relocated to California and widened our familiar domains of practice. Many of the developments recorded here derive from the widening of our contexts of reference for the practices discussed.

We have also taught conflict resolution practice to students in a number of different universities: the University of Waikato in New Zealand; San Diego State University, California State University-San Bernardino, and California State University-Dominguez Hills in the United States; and the Conrad Grebel University College at the University of Waterloo in Canada. In addition to teaching these formal courses, between us we have taught workshops at many sites in many countries: New Zealand, the United States, Australia, Canada, the United Kingdom, the Netherlands, Austria, Denmark, Sweden, Cyprus, Russia, and Israel. The more we teach about narrative mediation, the more we explore the ideas involved and learn from the responses of workshop participants, who ask questions, probe our assumptions, query cultural leanings, get excited about different aspects of this approach, and often apply concepts in different arenas of practice. All this is both gratifying and stimulating. It also works on us to develop our own understanding of what narrative mediation is about. In pursuit of constant improvement in the clarity of our teaching, we have designed new teaching tools and exercises, and the practice has changed in our own minds along the way. To us it has seemed to become simpler and clearer, and we hope that is the experience of workshop participants.

In the general field of narrative practice, the work of Michael White and David Epston continues to be important, and there are many others who have thrown their lot in with the narrative movement and contributed to what is now a robust and growing literature. In this book Michael White's notions of the *absent but implicit* (discussed in Chapter One), *double listening* (Chapter One), and *outsider-witness practices* (Chapter Six) are examples of concepts that we have drawn from new developments in narrative family therapy work.

From the work of Bronwyn Davies and Rom Harré, among others, we have featured the notion of working with discursive positioning, which was mentioned in our 2000 book but not with the same degree of elaboration as here. John's own work on a thesis for his PhD degree (completed in 2003) applied the idea of discursive positioning to mediation practice. Some of his thinking has been published in article form and now this book draws more extensively on his work. Our book is also indebted particularly to the collaboration of Wendy Drewery and her inspiration and theoretical groundwork. She was also the chief supervisor for John's PhD degree study at the University of Waikato. John is also grateful to Terry Locke for his perceptive support and careful attention to John's work on the PhD degree project.

In our earlier book we made particular use of the poststructuralist theorizing of Michel Foucault. Much more of Foucault's work has been translated into English since then, particularly his later emphasis on the technologies of the self and the concept of governmentality, and this book has benefited as a result.

Now let us look at this book chapter by chapter. In Chapter One we have fashioned a restatement of the whole idea of narrative mediation. Chapters Two and Three then explore in some depth the leverage that can be gained from applying the concept of discursive positioning. In Chapter Four we focus on culture and mediation, taking a constructionist approach to thinking about culture. This chapter is influenced by the work we did in writing a textbook (published by Sage) on cultural issues in the counseling field. In the second half of the book we explore the penetration of these ideas into a range of practice contexts. The intention is to show how conflict resolution work in different contexts can take on a narrative spirit.

Since moving to the United States, one new domain of practice is collaborative divorce, which we discuss in Chapter Five. We have now taught several workshops on this subject in California and in Canada. We would especially like to thank Peggy Thompson for inviting us to introduce narrative mediation ideas into the collaborative divorce movement. Peggy has been a staunch supporter of narrative perspectives and has had the vision to see the strong connection between the underpinnings of narrative practice and collaborative divorce. Gerald, especially, has become connected with this movement and has worked as a coach in the collaborative divorce model. We are grateful for the enthusiasm with which those responsible for starting this invigorating new set of conflict resolution practices have welcomed the ideas we have been exploring. It was Gerald's connection with Chip Rose that led to Chip's contribution to Chapter Five. Chip is a highly experienced family law attorney, mediator, and trainer in collaborative divorce, and we were pleased to include his creative and helpful contributions. It is especially good to be able to add to our psychological perspective the perspective of a lawyer who appreciates the aims of narrative mediation.

For four years John has been a regular visitor to Denmark at the invitation of the DISPUK organization. The DISPUK community of psychologists and organizational consultants offers professional development programs in family therapy and organizational development and management, and teaching to DISPUK course participants working in a second language has given John a new appreciation for the clear articulation of ideas. DISPUK director Allan Holmgren has been a champion of narrative and social constructionist practice. His work with organizations and managers led John to ask him to join in coauthoring Chapter Six, on narrative practice in organizational conflicts. Allan is indebted to Australian therapist Michael White, whom he regards as his "close friend and ally" and without whom "the work presented here couldn't be done."

Alison Cotter was part of our original group at Waikato Mediation Services in the 1990s. In 1997, she and John coauthored a chapter in our *Narrative Therapy in Practice: The Archaeology of Hope* (also published by Jossey-Bass), one of our first ventures into print on the subject of narrative mediation. In 1999, Alison, Gerald, and John coauthored an article on narrative mediation in the *Negotiation Journal.* Alison then moved from private practice mediation to a position as a mediator with the mediation services of the New Zealand Department of Labour. Her work there has continued to develop the practice of narrative mediation in employment mediation. We honor that work in Chapter Seven, which discusses employment mediation and which Alison coauthored with us. (The accounts of actual mediations in this chapter have enough details changed to ensure the anonymity of the participants.)

The work on restorative conferencing described in Chapter Eight began while we were still in New Zealand and owes a great deal to our partnership with a team that at various times included Wendy Drewery, Donald McMenamin, Stephen Hooper, Timoti Harris, Angus Macfarlane, David Paré, Helen Adams, Brian Prestidge, and many others in the schools that were part of the two pilot projects for the New Zealand Ministry of Education with which we were involved. These ideas continue to be carried forward in New Zealand schools by Kathie Cronin-Lampe, Ron Cronin-Lampe, Kerry Jenner, Maria Kecscemeti, and many others. We all still owe a debt to Margaret Thorsborne in Queensland for her initiatives in restorative conferencing and to those who have made the New Zealand version of the family group conference such a potent tool. Alan MacRae deserves special mention in this regard, as do Judges Fred McElrea and David Carruthers.

In addition to becoming involved in introducing narrative mediation in the area of collaborative divorce, Gerald has been invited to work in the domain of conflict in health care organizations. He would like to thank Barbara Filner and Carole Houk for helping him to introduce narrative mediation into the health care field. Along with other members of the National Conflict Resolution Center in San Diego, Gerald has been involved for several years in training health care ombuds and managers in conflict resolution work. Again, these groups of people have taken enthusiastically to narrative mediation, and this work has led to the discussion of this field in Chapter Nine of this book.

At the end of a movie, there is usually a long list of credits that honors all those who have had a hand in the production. Writing a book presents a similar requirement, although the number of people involved is much smaller. If you think of this as a list of credits, there are still some others who need to be credited for their contributions. Alan Rinzler at Jossey-Bass encouraged the project at its beginning and made a point of keeping us to our deadline. We would also like to mention Seth Schwartz, who works as an assistant editor at Jossey-Bass, Carol Hartland, who managed the production process for us, and Elspeth MacHattie, who provided careful copyedits.

In Chapters One and Two we have used some excerpts from conversations that were role-played and recorded for that purpose. Lucy Vail was responsible for recording these conversations, and we are also indebted to the following current and former students who volunteered to take part: Lisa Lopez, Michelle Myers, Gina Portillo, and Brenda Forsse. Thanks are also due to Sara Chavez for generously allowing us to use her writing on border identity oppression in Chapter Four. John taught an online course for California State University-Dominguez Hills in the summer of 2007, and several students in that course have allowed us to use pieces of their work as examples of narrative practice. Amanda Bowers and Paul Shantic contributed a conversation that appears in Chapter One, and Laurie Frazier contributed the narrative letter used as an example at the end of Chapter One.

In addition we are grateful to Pete Roussos for his generous sharing of his creative materials developed for the San Diego Family Law Group. We are grateful too to Linda Solomon for her contributions on the neutral coach model, developed with her colleagues in Texas. We would also like to thank Louise Aguilar and Leny Ambruso for generously sharing their conflict prevention chart, developed during their work as health care ombuds and mediators.

Finally, Gerald owes a great deal of thanks to his dear wife and loving partner of nine years, Stacey Sinclair, for all her assistance with reading and editing drafts and offering helpful suggestions. John's wife, Lorraine Hedtke, has also been a solid supporter of this book and has made helpful suggestions at many points. Writing is a personally demanding task, and it requires lots of encouragement and backup. Giving loving attention to words cannot happen easily without a context of loving support in many tangible ways. John is deeply grateful to Lorraine for offering this loving support, and fortunate to be able to say so publicly in these lines.

June 2008

JOHN WINSLADE
Redlands, California
GERALD MONK
San Diego, California

Practicing Narrative Mediation

Chapter One

How to Work with Conflict Stories: Nine Hallmarks of Narrative Mediation

This book is about taking stories seriously in the practice of mediation. Taking stories seriously, to us, means treating them as having the power to shape experiences, influence mind-sets, and construct relationships. It also means seeing them as having something of a life of their own, as embarking on a mission that sometimes seems to drag people along behind. It means inquiring into the work being done by such stories in conflict situations, particularly into whether the protagonists in a conflict are happy with the direction that a story is taking them and whether they would prefer to go somewhere else.

Even in these few words, we have departed from some other common ways in which people understand stories. From time to time you may hear people say, "Oh, that's just a story," in a way that disparages the truth value of what has been said. The implication is that the account given is not fully accurate or that it is a deliberate distortion or that it is not very objective and therefore not worth much. In some forms of professional practice, stories are regarded as suspect versions of the truth of what has happened, and the job of the professional is conceived of as penetrating beneath the surface to the underlying truth. From this perspective, mediators might hear the different versions of what disputants tell them as layers of camouflage that cover over the facts. If mediators can only see through the stories to those hidden facts then they will be in a better position to help

1

the parties deal with the substantive issues that divide them and move toward resolution.

It is not really surprising that this suspicious perspective is commonplace among professionals. It is, after all, the standard approach in most of social science to search for underlying patterns, foundational facts, or solid, verifiable, or even generalizable truths. Jerome Bruner (1986) refers to this as the *paradigmatic* approach. So when mediators undertake this search, they are doing what many others in many other branches of the human sciences have done.

Our concern is with the opportunity that might be missed in the process of quickly dismissing stories as unreliable. What might be missed is the work done by stories to *construct* realities, not just to *report* on them, apparently inaccurately. Rather than moving as quickly as one can away from stories and toward an emphasis on what is factual, objective, and patterned, we believe there is much to be gained by staying with the stories themselves, inquiring into the work that they do, and experimenting with how these stories might be reshaped in order to transform relationships.

In this first chapter we explain how we have been going about doing this kind of exploration. And we summarize what we see as the hallmarks of a narrative practice of mediation. We have written about narrative mediation before, and this book is intended to develop what we published eight years ago (Winslade & Monk, 2000). Since then we have tried out many ways of describing the practice of narrative mediation, seeking the way that will make it easier for practitioners to entertain embracing this practice. This chapter is in many ways a distillation of that experience.

Some years ago we read an article by Joseph P. Folger and Robert A. Baruch Bush (2001) on the hallmarks of a transformative perspective in mediation. We found this article helpful because it specified some ethical and theoretical commitments and also clearly pointed to some particular practices. Although we have many sympathies with what the transformative mediators are endeavoring to do, we also have some different emphases in our own work. This article sharpened our understanding of a transformative approach and made us notice places of difference in how we think about doing mediation. It also prompted us to identify the hallmarks of a narrative approach to mediation and to consider how we might state these hallmarks in succinct and accessible ways. We are grateful to Folger and Bush for cuing us to follow this line of inquiry.

This chapter results from that inquiry. For those who have not read our previous book, this chapter will introduce you to a narrative perspective relatively quickly. For those who have read our previous book, this chapter distills that work into a briefer statement.

Here then are nine hallmarks of a narrative practice in mediation. We shall list them all together and then expand on each one in turn.

1. Assume that people live their lives through stories.
2. Avoid essentialist assumptions.
3. Engage in double listening.
4. Build an externalizing conversation.
5. View the problem story as a restraint.
6. Listen for discursive positioning.
7. Identify openings to an alternative story.
8. Re-author the relationship story.
9. Document progress.

The first two hallmarks are about the assumptions that a mediator brings with him or her into the room. They therefore involve some preparatory work, reading about the background to these ideas and thinking through the implications of these assumptions. The other seven hallmarks are practices built on the foundation of these assumptions. They involve practice and rehearsal to develop facility with their use.

Hallmark 1: Assume That People Live Their Lives Through Stories (Stories Matter)

This hallmark is about the adoption of the narrative perspective in mediation. Some people who have not come across narrative mediation before respond to the concept by assuming that its focus is on fostering the telling of stories, or on the analysis of stories or on the autobiographical impulse. There is nothing wrong with these focal interests, but they are not what we mean by a narrative perspective. We are referring to the idea that narratives serve a shaping or constitutive purpose in people's lives.

What do we mean by a *narrative*, or *story*? In the first place, we are speaking about the stories that people tell themselves or tell each other. In many social interactions people respond to the presence of the other(s) by telling a story. "How was your day?" is usually followed by the telling of a story. "What have you been doing lately?" produces a different response but still a story. When a lawyer in a courtroom asks, "What did you see happen?" the witness tells a story in response. When a police officer says, "Is there any reason why I should not give you a speeding ticket?" the driver might construct a justificatory story. When a spouse asks, "Why are you so late?" the husband or wife so questioned is less likely to respond with a list of rationally enumerated reasons than with an explanatory story. As people tell stories they establish for themselves, as well as for others, a sense of continuity in life. Stories give people the reassuring sense that life is not just a series of events happening one after the other without rhyme or reason. In terms of individuals' sense of themselves, stories enable people to have a sense of coherence about who they are. However, as Sara Cobb (1993) has pointed out, some stories are more coherent accounts than others. Some retellings are more rehearsed than others. These differences can influence what happens to the stories that people tell in the context of mediation.

We are also using the word *story* to refer to the background stories with which each person's cultural world is redolent. People do not just make up from nothing the stories they tell each other. From the cultural world around them, they draw on a range of resources and borrow ready-made narrative elements, and then they fashion these elements into a format intended to meet a communicative purpose. These narrative elements include plot devices (such as a beginning in medias res; a sudden turn of events; an act of God, or deus ex machina; a complicating action; a related subplot; or an expected or unexpected denouement); story genres (such as comedy, tragedy, melodrama, soap opera, or slice-of-life story); characterizations (such as victim, villain, rescuer, saintly hero, objectified target, flawed genius, powerful controller, or disempowered recipient); contextual settings, each with its typical conflict format (such as the workplace dispute, domestic dispute, community or neighborhood dispute, organizational dispute, commercial dispute, school conflict, or landlord-tenant dispute); and thematic driving forces (such as racism, sexism, homophobia, disability, power, recognition, authenticity, or employee rights).

As narrative mediators observe these narrative elements at work, they often hear the playing out of background cultural scripts of which the protagonists are not the original authors. Seyla Benhabib (2002) recommends, in fact, thinking of culture primarily in narrative terms. For example, if a person refers to a character such as the schoolyard bully, the controlling husband, the punitive boss, or the noisy neighbor, there are a number of stock story lines that will come easily to his or her mind. It is much easier for disputants to attempt to fit themselves and their fellow disputants into one of these well-known story lines than it is for them to make up a completely new plot. Apart from any other consideration, using stock narrative elements makes it easier to garner the recognition and support of third parties (friends, relatives, and even mediators).

Along with these background scripts come built-in assumptions about how the world is, how people should be, and how people should respond when the "rules" are broken. It is for these assumptions that we find it most useful to employ the terminology of discourse theory. The word *discourse* can be used in a variety of ways. We are using it to refer primarily to the conceptualizations of Michel Foucault (1972, 1978, 1980, 2000), who emphasized the function of discourse as repetitive practice out of which people form their understandings of the world they live in. These understandings then work in turn to inform the practices (both linguistic and behavioral) that people engage in. The motion of discourse is thus circular and works to seal off the possibility of thinking otherwise. Discourse is a function of the way that people use recursive patterns of language to embody social norms and to establish taken-for-granted understandings about how things are in the world. Discourses can be represented as statements of meaning about the ordinary and everyday aspects of life: eating fruit is good for you; it is polite to say thank you when offered something; family loyalty is of primary importance; it is important to stand up for yourself when attacked; hard work brings rewards; infidelity ends a marriage; and so on. Behind each of these statements lies a story that people have heard repeated many times or that they can slot into when it applies to their life circumstances. Many of these pieces of discourse are not at all contentious, but some are strongly disputed: for example, a man should be the head of the household; white privilege is based on natural superiority; homosexuality is not natural; disabled persons should be grateful for the charity they receive. Each of these meanings serves an organizing function in a power relation. It sets up exchanges between people as individuals and as social groups. Notice how the word *natural* is used in some of these statements. This illustrates the way in which discourses work to make some assumptions appear to have such undisputed ordinariness that they can scarcely be questioned. They appear to be, and come to be treated as, part of the natural order of the universe.

Hallmark 2: Avoid Essentialist Understandings (It's Not All in the Natural Essence)

Essentialism is the habit of thought that invites people to always look for explanations in the intrinsic essence of things or of persons rather than in cultural influences like narratives. This has been a tradition of thought in Western culture since the time of the ancient Greeks. In recent times, however, it has come under constant critique, and alternative perspectives that are more dialogical, more relational, and more constructionist are being promoted.

Essentialist, or inside-out, approaches to conflict ascribe people's behavior to their nature, whether this nature is thought of as personality or as an internal state involving emotion, attitude, and mood. "He's an aggressive person!" "She's manipulative by nature"; "He's a victim type"; "Those two have a personality conflict"; "She is disturbed"; "He is ADHD." Rather than understanding people as motivated by internal states, instinctual drives, forces immanent in the core self, or personality, we prefer to start from a different psychology, one that is built on an outside-in approach. From this perspective, we can see people's interests, their emotions, their behaviors, and their interpretations as produced within a cultural or discursive world of relations and then internalized.

Thinking this way leads to a study of how power operates through discourse to produce expectations of people's places in the world. It also leads to an understanding of narratives as setting up positions in a conflict, as constructing relations, as producing the feelings and emotions in these relations. This approach to emotional experience does not make a person's feelings any the less real or any the less painful, but it might alter how others conceptualize their responses. Rather than assuming that a person's feelings or thoughts are essential to *who he or she is,* one might think of them as essential to *a narrative in which the person is situated* and, therefore, when the story shifts, or the person's position within the story shifts, the emotions will follow.

There is a delicate distinction here that needs to be stated with care. We are not suggesting that people's strongly held feelings should be ignored. We agree with the emphasis in other approaches to mediation on empathetically acknowledging feelings and on encouraging disputing parties to recognize each other's perspectives. But at the same time we want to be careful in how we think about just what is being recognized or empathized with. It is a position in a narrative rather than an essence of who the person is. It is constructed more than natural. It is real in its effects but it may be subject to change. Any one individual may be part of more than one narrative, may shift tracks to another line, may become something other than "who he is" or "who she is." This leads us into the next hallmark, which is built on the rejection of the assumptions of essentialism. It is the beginning of a narrative practice in mediation.

Hallmark 3: Engage in Double Listening (There's Always More Than One Story)

Double listening starts from the assumption that people are always situated within multiple story lines. It is a recognition of the complexity of life. We do not have a bias in favor of *integrating* a person's multiple story lines into a singular or congruent whole, as some psychologies would argue one should. We do not believe that the integration of disparate narratives is a worthwhile goal for social practice. It is sometimes assumed that integration is necessary to combat confusion. In practice, however, people are well used to shifting seamlessly from one narrative to another, as they go from home to school, from home to work, from the peer group to the family, or from one relationship to another. Far from being confusing, multiple narratives often give people a range of narrative options within which to situate themselves and from which to respond. They are a resource to be treasured, rather than a complication to be integrated away.

In mediation we are, on the one hand, particularly interested in the conflict-saturated relationship narrative in which people are often stuck. And we are, on the other hand, also interested in the alternative relationship story out of which people would prefer to relate to each other, if they could. We do not assume that the conflict story will lead us and the disputants through the narrow ravine of negotiation to arrive eventually at the peaceful plain of resolution and agreement. Rather, we assume that the two stories may continue to run parallel to some degree. In narrative mediation, we are first interested in inviting people to switch tracks to the path of the alternative story. This story might feature their preferred ways of interacting about their differences, their unexpressed hopes that brought them to mediation, themes of cooperation or understanding or respect. They may also involve actions that shift the power relations onto a more just footing, or intentions to make things better, even when one is unable to carry through on these intentions.

Double listening hears both of these stories. It does not acknowledge just the pain of the conflict story but also the hope of the other story that sits alongside. It allows mediators to acknowledge and recognize, at the same time, feelings of anger and pride, hope and despair, hurt and recognition. As we engage in double listening we hear certain aspects of what people say more richly. We listen for the pieces of information that are commonly glossed over, and we hear them as indications of the existence of another story, one that is currently lying subjugated. We hear the word *but* in the middle of a sentence as a hinge around which two stories are swinging. Take this utterance for example: "I was really angry at the time but I calmed down later." The remark is made up of two statements that may refer to two different positions in two different stories of events: one in which outrage and strong feeling shape the response and one in which considered reflection takes the response in a different direction.

Double listening may also cue us to notice the contradictions between people's words and their nonverbal expressions. Think of the person who says yes to a proposal but the voice is hesitant and the expression on the face is strained. The nonverbals say no while the verbalization says yes. Which is correct? If we are double listening, they may both be correct and consistent responses, but each may have meaning within a different narrative.

Deconstruction

Once essentialism is eschewed then the meaning of what people say in a mediation does not have to be assumed to be obvious or single-storied. Following the deconstructive method of linguistic philosopher Jacques Derrida (1976), in narrative mediation we are often seeking to open up new meanings in the parties' utterances, in the hope that they can provide openings to new story lines. Derrida approaches deconstruction by identifying the negative as well as the positive meaning of any word or concept. A word is treated not as having intrinsic meaning in itself but as having meaning in the context of its relationship with other words, especially with its binary opposite. Each side of the binary relies to some extent on the other side to support its meaning. There is, for example, a binary relationship between concepts like aggression and passivity, love and hate, problem and solution, grievance and redress, remorse and forgiveness, employer and employee, landlord and tenant, and victim and villain. Derrida's deconstructive inquiry aims to release meanings from the rigidity of binary opposition and to search out surplus meanings that might give rise to new forms of living.

This idea is of importance to mediation because the practice of mediation has been built on a setup that assumes the two parties in a dispute are in some form of binary opposition. The very purpose of negotiation might be considered to be the development of surplus meaning, beyond the parties' encapsulated stories about the conflict. In the hustle and bustle of practice, however, mediators do not have the luxury of engaging in the detailed philosophical inquiries that someone like Derrida develops. What they can do, though, is to maintain a stance of naïve inquiry that treats meanings as curios to be respectfully turned over and examined, rather than accepted at face value.

Michael White has developed Derrida's idea into a further version of double listening. This version attends to an "absent but implicit" story (2000, p. 153) and enables the mediator to hear the story that lies hidden or masked in the background of a conflict story. Every expression about an event can be seen to be built on a contrast with its opposite. If mediators engage in doubly listening to an expression of strong anger at being wronged, they can also hear in the background a statement of what the speaker values, believes in, hopes for, cherishes, or desires to protect. Double listening enables them to do more than acknowledge the experience of being angry and feeling wronged; it also opens up the possibility that they can listen to the story of what the speaker values and holds important.

Let us illustrate this idea with an example. Suppose someone says in a mediation, "I am upset about being spoken to in that way. It is offensive and wrong, and I am not going to sit and listen to it." We can hear the anger and outrage and can acknowledge it, as many mediators are taught to do, through reflection and paraphrase. But we can also hear something else. What is absent from the words but implicit in them is that this person is expressing a preference for the opposite to what has been happening. It may be a preference for more inclusive conversation, for an ethic of speaking that is not offensive, or for a valuing of relationship in a certain respectful mode. Double listening enables us to inquire into this implicit, preferred story of relationship, rather than stopping at acknowledging the anger and pain. We are often struck in mediations by the fact that on the one hand, people are sitting there talking about things they are upset and angry about, that they find really painful, and yet on the other hand, they are sitting there with some implicit hope that this will make a difference. The hope may not be expressed openly but it is implicit in their presence in the room. Mediators can give this story of hope for something better a chance if they first of all hear this absent but implicit hope and then begin to inquire into the story that it is a part of. This story may often be subordinate to the story of the outrage and pain, but it perhaps speaks to the person's better intentions in relation to the other party. If given the chance for expression, these better intentions can give rise to a different story in the future.

Ury's Positive No as an Example of Double Listening

William Ury (2007) has recently pointed to a form of double listening. In his account of "the power of a positive no" in the process of negotiation, he advocates that when people want to say no, they should also identify the underlying principle of what they are saying yes to and couch the no in the context of that yes. As he puts it, "Saying No means, first of all, saying *Yes!* to yourself and protecting what is important to you" (p. 16). The resulting no is more respectful and less provocative than a no that does not contain an indication of what the negotiator is saying yes to. Not everyone, however, will be in the position to make such a positive no without some assistance. That is where mediators who engage in double listening can help. When they hear a person saying no, they can ask questions to bring forward the implicit yes statement that explains the value positions that are being protected.

Double listening, then, is a practice that consistently hears not just one story but at least two, and often more. It opens up complexity rather than closing it down. When mediators use it to draw out the differences between different stories, then they are in a position to invite people to make choices about which story they want to live from in this context. Making this choice is an exercise in agency and goes a long way toward forgoing positions of helplessness in mediation.

Here is a small example of double listening in action. It comes from a role-played mediation that addressed a conflict between two coworkers in a residential facility for adults with intellectual disabilities.

> *Lisa:* I don't want to come off as overprotective or overbearing. I guess that's just my personality. I don't mean to be like that.
> *Mediator:* So it's important to you not to come across as overprotective . . .

    Lisa: Overprotective or overbearing to the residents, because they are over the age of eighteen and I do want them to develop life skills. It's just the way we do it.

Mediator: So am I right in understanding that one thing this conflict is doing is that it has you concerned about how you are coming across to Michelle and to the residents.

    Lisa: Mmhmm, exactly.

Mediator: And maybe it's distorting, would that be fair, it's distorting how you come across.

    Lisa: I think it is. It is distorting. I don't want her to think that.

The mediator's responses here do not hear just Lisa's sense of displeasure at how she is being represented as overprotective and overbearing by Michelle, her coworker, in the conflict. Nor do they discredit Michelle's experience of Lisa in those terms. Instead, Lisa's negative response to how she is represented is also heard in positive terms. The flip side of her rejection of being thought of as overprotective is that she cares about how she comes across in her relationship with Michelle. This is a positive concern, not just a negative expression of anger at what another disputant is saying. Such double listening also opens up grounds for an inquiry into what might be "distorted" by the conflict story, which might be a desire for a working relationship that embodies concern for the other rather than just anger at what the other has said. It is also noticeable that Lisa embraces this version of events with some enthusiasm. Double listening, in our view, often produces an experience of being heard to have and be respected for quite complex nuances of thought and emotion.

Hallmark 4: Build an Externalizing Conversation (The Person Is Not the Problem; The Problem Is the Problem)

In the stress of conflict situations, it is not uncommon for one party to develop a conviction that the other party is in fact the problem, that this person is by nature a bad person in some way. In private moments this first party might also harbor musings about himself. "Am I just too stubborn?" he might wonder.

Or he may feel a degree of ongoing guilt about things he has said or done in the heat of the conflict. The thought that therefore "I am a bad person" may persist. Such convictions are built on essentialist assumptions about the origins of conflict. These assumptions often establish a position from which it is not easy to negotiate in good faith. How can you do a deal with the devil? Or how can you trust your own devilish nature to do such a deal? As people tell conflict stories, they often reinforce their internalized convictions and sink further into them.

Externalizing conversations provide an antidote (White, 2007, p. 9) to these convictions by attributing the pain and suffering to the conflict itself, rather than to the nature of either of the parties. Building externalizing conversations is central to narrative practice. Externalizing is a mode of language use that shifts the relational ground between a person and a conflict. It invites people to see the conflict as a third party (one that has a life of its own) and as leading them along a path (willingly or unwillingly) that may or may not suit them. Externalizing creates a linguistic space in which people can notice the effects of the conflict itself, rather than its causes, and assess whether they like those effects or not. It assists people to step out of positions of blame or shame and enables them to save face by ascribing problems to the conflict itself, rather than to themselves or to the other party. Therefore externalizing language helps people separate from the conflict story and makes room for alternative stories to emerge. Here are some examples of externalizing questions that mediators might ask:

Examples of Questions Using Externalizing Language

- What might we call this thing that we're up against? Is it an argument? A dispute? A disagreement? A situation? Or what? What would you call it?
- How long has it been around? How has it grown in importance?
- What effect is it having on you?
- How does it get you to feel? To speak? To behave?
- How does it persuade you to think about the other person?
- What is it costing you?

- Does it follow you into all the domains of your life? Work, home, finances, friendships, customer relations, staff morale?
- If it was to keep on getting worse, where might it end up taking you?
- How much power does it have over you?
- Does it interfere with your best intentions? Your hopes for something else? Your preferences for how things could be different?

People often report that externalizing conversations open up new spaces in their thinking. Some report the effect as almost physically tangible. They can feel the weight of something experienced internally as oppressive and painful shifting as they respond. Others talk about the advantages of taking a different perspective from which the conflict itself does not feel so intense and that affords them some reflective space to consider anew what is important to them.

Mapping the Effects of a Conflict

As mediators learn to use externalizing conversations, they often feel awkward for a while, as if the words do not fit easily in their mouths. Some start to get the hang of it and enjoy the first few exhilarating moments of externalizing and then quickly run dry and wonder where to go next. One externalizing utterance does not, of course, make for a conversation. We therefore advise that it is useful to build on an initial foray into externalizing language by moving directly to the process of *mapping the effects* of the externalized problem. The parties may be invited to give the conflict a name, or a name may arise spontaneously out of the conversation. Or if no name seems to emerge, the conflict can be referred to simply as "it." Then the mediator can ask, "So what effect is *it* having on you and on your relationship?" The mediator needs to persist with this inquiry, so that enough of the effects of the conflict are mapped out and noticed.

The effects of the conflict story on the persons embroiled in it can be mapped across a range of domains. There will clearly be emotional effects, which most people can easily talk about, but it is a mistake in narrative mediation to stop with the emotional effects. To do so risks isolating people in their individual emotional responses. There will also be relational effects, which will take different forms according to the context in which the conflict takes place. In family mediation the relational effects influence the communication patterns and trust displayed between family members or in the care of children. In organizations, relational effects may be manifest in the formation of cliques, in dysfunctional meetings that achieve little, in declining membership participation, in complaints from the general public, and so on. In businesses, relational effects may be experienced in problems between departments, in expressions of lowered employee morale, in increased customer dissatisfaction, or in decreased income through sales, and so on. In schools, relational effects may affect student learning opportunities. In hospitals, relational effects may affect the quality of patient care. Mapping the effects of a conflict benefits from being extended beyond the mind of the individual to what is happening in the context of the dispute. As a result, disputants get to experience their own feelings about the dispute as embedded in a wider context. People are commonly surprised by what emerges from this inquiry into a conflict story's effects and are galvanized into a determination to change things.

Example of an Externalizing Conversation

Here is an example of the development of an externalizing conversation; it also includes some mapping of the effects of the problem.

Mediator: I'm wondering if we can take your problem here and give it a name if that's OK. Can we call it something like "procedural situation"? Just to give it a name so that we all know what it's about. If you don't like that or have a better name then we can think of something else, is that OK?

Participant: "Registration problem" would work with me.

Mediator: OK, great. How has this registration problem made you feel and think in relation to yourself, home, and the university?

Participant: Well, it has made me think about how I approach issues that I have a problem with. I don't want to appear combative.

Mediator: So that's important to you and how you want people to see you at work?

Participant: Yes. I am not someone who goes out of her way to get into conflict and this thing makes me appear that way. Or at least I am concerned that it does. But I do also think I have a right to ask those questions and have them answered.

Mediator: Any other effects the registration problem is having, on you or on anyone else?

Participant: My husband is probably tired of me complaining about it at home and I think that within the university it creates a lot of tension between our Enrollment & Financial Aid Department and the program administrators.

Mediator: So, a lot of people are affected by this problem, in your mind. Where do you think this will lead? In other words, if nothing changes and the registration problem persists, what do you think this will do to you and the university and your family?

Participant: I don't think it will have a very big impact on my family but I think the university could have a lawsuit filed against it for breaching the law. It's not like we're some Joe Schmo university, it's a very reputable university and if people knew the practices that go on, they wouldn't see it as very reputable anymore.

Mediator: So this registration problem has affected your relationship with your coworkers, your boss, and at home in terms of your husband who has listened to you vent.

Hallmark 5: View the Problem Story as a Restraint (How Is the Problem Holding You Back?)

This hallmark is built on the idea that what people talk about and the way they talk about it construct the world that they live in. This is a basic assumption of social constructionism. In this sense all talk is constructive. It sets the ground for people's experience. If people talk differently or talk about something different from their usual subjects, they will experience the world differently. It therefore matters very much what people say and how they speak.

If this is true, then consider the first thing that people in mediation often spend their energy talking about. Many approaches to mediation stipulate that the first task of mediation is to define the problem. In response many mediators spend due time asking the parties to define the problem and to expand upon their different perspectives on it. By the time this task has been completed the problem has not only been defined but has grown in proportion in people's minds. A pile of problem talk has been built up in the middle of the room, and for the rest of the conversation, it dominates what can be talked about. The more people focus on it, the more it grows in significance. In order to deal with the problem people have to climb the mountain of the problem to reach the downhill slope on the other side. The first part of the mediation conversation has, moreover, added height to the mountain that they have to climb.

Accessing a Story of Hope

An alternative approach is to resist the temptation to start by defining the problem. We have experimented sometimes with starting by inviting people to talk about the counterstory to the problem. Later we seek to build on and grow this counterstory into a fully fledged account of clients might go forward in life without the conflict being so dominant. At the start of the conversation, parties have already made a small commitment, however tentative, to this counterstory. They are in the room. They have come along to participate. To do so they must have some hope in mind for something useful to come of the mediation. We can therefore invite them to speak to this hope early on. "What is your hope for what might come from this meeting?" we might ask. Or, "How do you hope we might talk about things here today?" These questions invite people to speak from their most noble selves. Many will respond by speaking about a desire for respectful conversation or for an outcome that honors both parties or some variation on such themes. Some will hear the question as asking them to speak about what Fisher and Ury (1981) have called their own positions with regard to outcome. That is, they will respond not so much from a position of inclusive hope as from a position of "what I want." In this case we might need to repeat the questions in slightly different words.

The effect of asking about people's hopes as the first topic of conversation in mediation is that people's best intentions, their noblest desires, and their ideal values (and not the most painful parts of the conflict) are placed in the forefront of attention. The intention is not to be Pollyannaish about the problem, to focus only on positive thinking or to avoid facing the conflict story, but simply to frame it differently. From this opening we can then move on to ask about the problems that seem to be standing in the way of people's hopes. The problem story then gets constructed as an obstacle to the forward movement of their most hopeful story, rather than as the mountain to be climbed before they even get to that cherished story. The forward momentum of a hopeful story is established early on, and the conflict story is constructed as a restraint that holds it back. Thinking of a conflict as a restraint is different from thinking of it as a mountain to climb. It orients the conversation differently, and we believe it opens up a different quality of talk that leads in different directions.

Example of Accessing a Story of Hope

Here is an example of a piece of conversation from early in a mediation built on the assumption that it is worth bringing out stories of hope before focusing on the problem story.

> *Mediator:* As you came long here today, I'm imagining that you both had some hopes for the kind of conversation you might have. Do you have anything that you would like to put out about the kind of conversation that might be useful?
>
> *Michelle:* I was hoping that I would be heard and I'd be given a chance and that Lisa would listen to the ideas that I'm trying to share.

Mediator: [*Noting down what she says*] So you'd be given a chance and you'd feel listened to.

Michelle: Mmhmm.

Lisa: I just hope that she understands that this is the way it's always been. I'm not picking on her. This is just the way I have always done it. I've been here twelve years and this is the way I like to work and I just want her to realize that I'm not picking on her. This is just the way that it has always been.

Mediator: OK. So for you what you would hope for would be that the conversation that we could have here would be one that increased that understanding. So what you're both expressing here is a desire for a conversation that involves hearing, listening, and understanding.

Lisa and Michelle: [*Together*] Right.

Mediator: Anything else that you would hope for?

Lisa: Maybe that we would come to some type of agreement.

Mediator: [*Noting this down*] Come to agreement.

Michelle: I was hoping that we would come to some agreement too.

Mediator: So we've got that as another hope for this conversation, that it would bring us to some kind of agreement. And in a minute I'll ask you, "About what?" But first is there anything else that you hope this conversation will feature?

Lisa: I'd like to resolve this issue and move on.

Mediator: [*Noting this down*] That you would resolve this issue and move on.

Lisa: Mmm.

Mediator: [*To Michelle*] Does that fit for you too?

Michelle: Yeah, I just want to have a pleasant work environment.

Mediator: [*Noting this down too*] A pleasant work environment. That's what you are hoping for. [*To Lisa*] How's that sound to you?

Lisa: It sounds OK.

Mediator: So you've got these ideas about what a good conversation would be about. That it would be about hearing, listening, understanding, reaching agreement, resolving issues, and establishing a pleasant working environment. But my understanding is that there have been some problems that have been getting in the way of these things. And I guess it would be a good time now to tell me and to tell each other just what have been the issues that have been getting in the way of the pleasant working environment.

In this exchange, hints of what the problem story is about are slipped into the participants' responses. But there is also remarkable agreement about what the participants want from the mediation. This is by no means a universal occurrence, but it is also not uncommon. If people come into a mediation feeling a degree of apprehension and tension, the positive emphasis of such an exchange can often help to ease this tension and to free up the conversation that follows. Having noted carefully the words that the participants have used in this exchange, the mediator is also able to return later to elements of this incipient alternative story and to revisit them as contrasting themes to the themes of the conflict story. For example: "You said earlier that you wanted to feel listened to and understood. Does what Michelle is saying now sound a bit more like that?" Or, "You said earlier that you were hoping for the reestablishment of a pleasant working environment from this conversation. Do you think that what Lisa is proposing now would help create that?"

Hallmark 6: Listen for Discursive Positioning (Words Can Break Your Bones Too)

The proverbial saying "Sticks and stones can break your bones but words can never hurt you" does not take account of the concept of discourse. Discourse theory demonstrates powerfully how the words people employ, or more accurately the discourses in which they engage, have very powerful material effects on their own and others' lives. Words do participate in the breaking of bones.

The alternative to an essentialist position is to think in terms of discourse. If conflicts do not originate out of persons' intrinsic nature, then they must come from what has been internalized into people through the course of living. In other words, they come from the cultural world, or the world inhabited by discourse. As people use discourse they construct utterances that draw on particular discourse patterns. The web of discourse usages that they draw on, even as they engage in conversations that perform a conflict, make up a worldview. This view of the world is a building block for the construction of personal identity and of relationships with others. Sometimes a single sentence, or even a single word, can call into being, if one slices all the way through the discourse in which it is situated, a world complete with story lines, identities, and relationships.

Discursive Positioning

The term that has been coined to describe this phenomenon is *discursive positioning*. Positioning theory (Davies & Harré, 1990; Harré & van Langenhøve, 1999) is the branch of general discourse theory that addresses this phenomenon. It is important to stipulate that the *positions* of discursive positioning are different from the positions discussed by Fisher and Ury (1981). Fisher and Ury are referring to the initial desired outcomes that parties bring into the mediation process and that are in contrast to their underlying interests. We are referring to something different when we speak of a person's discursive positioning. *Positioning* in our sense is a relational term. When individuals make an utterance, they call into place a form of relation through their very choice of words. They set things up in a certain way and thus implicitly call the other person(s) in the conversation into position in a relation of some kind. Conversations, including mediation conversations, can be seen as ongoing negotiations of these positions. The material out of which these positions are constructed is discourse. If the discourse out of which people are speaking is laced with, say, sexist or racist discourse, then the position that they will establish for themselves, and the position into which they call their interlocutor, will be constructed in this sexist or racist discourse. The other person may be implicitly called upon to support a sexist position or may be called into an objectified position by racist discourse. In this way the parties in conversation move each other around. Each sets the conditions for her own and the other's speech. Each also limits the range of positions from which the other can speak.

Because we are interested in the relational conditions in which new stories can take root, we are particularly interested in the ways in which people position each other. Positioning theory promises to be a tool for making sense of how relationships are constructed and, therefore, of how changes to existing constructions can be made. It is a story-building tool.

In Chapters Two and Three we are going to explore the potential of discursive positioning much further than we did in our previous book on mediation, so we will not go much deeper into this subject here. But we shall give a couple of examples to illustrate the idea.

Imagine that someone says, in a mediation between neighbors, "I tried talking to him nicely about it but he wouldn't listen." How might we hear this statement in terms of discursive positioning?

Even without a great deal of context, we can hear how the speaker is seeking to establish a position with the mediator of rationality and culturally appropriate behavior, however this might be defined. In the relation between the two disputing parties, the speaker is intent on creating legitimacy for his own actions: I spoke "nicely," therefore I should be seen as a sane and reasonable person and my viewpoint should be given credence. It might even be understandable and legitimate in this context if I were to lose control in the next moment in the story because I am justified by my earlier efforts to be reasonable. In contrast, the other party to the dispute is positioned in a place of illegitimacy as the one who wouldn't listen, who does not respond to cool rational behavior, who is perhaps a little crazy, and who does not observe the normal rules of cultural exchange. If this person is to respond, he must now do so from the place in which he has been positioned as the irrational one. He may choose to take up this position and demonstrate irrational and emotional behavior, or he may refuse the position in which he has been placed and respond in a way that also claims for this moment a rational and reasonable identity. He may dispute the "talking nicely" claim of the first speaker and reposition him as the crazy one from the start.

Being rational, speaking "nicely," keeping one's emotions under control, and disparaging others' behavior as crazy or inappropriate are not intrinsic aspects of any person. They can be defined very differently by different people. An individual's understanding of each of these ideas is produced in a cultural context. There is a long history in the discourse of Western cultures of privileging rational control over emotional expression, and that history lies in the background of this exchange. Without an implicit acceptance of this background discourse by all the parties to the conversation, the words used and the positioning work these words do would not make sense. There are also gendered expectations of the positions people establish in this exchange. Imagine if one or both of the participants were women. Expectations of what might be appropriate or normal behavior in a given situation might be different for women. Therefore there is a sense in which all of this background discourse is being called on in the instant that a person makes the statement, "I tried to speak nicely to him." A whole moral order is set in place in that moment.

In the course of a conversation there are many such instances of positioning. People establish a range of positions for themselves, calling on a range of discourses in the process. They also call each other into position in these discourses. There may be patterns that repeat themselves many times in the course of a mediation conversation, but there will also usually be variety within these patterns. By its very nature a discourse is established over the course of many conversations between many people in a particular cultural context. Therefore an established discourse cannot be changed as a result of one conversation. Positions, in contrast, are being shifted and negotiated all the time. In mediation, people can and do change their positions in relation to a discourse, and they change the ways in which they call each other into position. Hence, we are interested in describing what happens in mediation as, in many senses, a process of negotiation of discursive positions. We are not referring just to the negotiation that works out the final outcome of the mediation. We are talking about the little, moment-by-moment negotiations over meaning. These we understand as negotiations over positioning, and believe that they contribute in important ways to the outcomes of mediation conversations.

Example of Discursive Positioning in a Conversation

Here is a section of a mediation conversation that illustrates the function of discursive positioning in the production of a conflict.

Michelle: The most recent example is a concert that I coordinated with the adults in the home. They're gonna perform for the community. A holiday concert. And she has a problem with that.

Mediator: So tell me about the concert a little bit. I'd like to understand what that's about.

Michelle: Well, when we went to the plaza, we found fliers about a concert and people from the community could sign up and they could play instruments and sing. It's just a holiday gathering for the community, and I thought it would be a really good way for the adults in our home to show their skills and just have a really good time like everyone else, and Lisa thinks that that's not a good idea.

Mediator: So what was your thinking behind this? Why did it appeal to you?

Michelle: Well, ever since I have been there, I've noticed that the adults in our home are segregated from the whole community. It's almost like we're trying to hide them from the community. And I just want to integrate them into everything. I don't know why we have to keep them separate. We should have them integrated into the parades and the concerts and they should be able to go on outings with the neighbors and the other young adults.

Mediator: So is that like a value that's important to you? About not hiding people with disabilities away. I'm interested in knowing your relationship with that value. It sounds important to you. Is it something you have always believed, or . . . ?

Michelle: I think it's something I've always believed. But through school, I just graduated in June, I read a lot of articles and books and it's just the perspective I agree with, that we should integrate people with disabilities with typical people and they shouldn't be sheltered away and hidden. I think it will help them to grow in their skills and reach their potential if we help them to be around other people. And she thinks there is something completely wrong with that.

Mediator: So, Lisa, I'm interested in how these issues have appeared to you?

Lisa: Well, she mentioned that the residents are being hidden. I wouldn't call it hidden or segregated from the community. I just want to protect them. You know, we are a family. And we go places together. I just want to see that we are a family and not possible dating material. We are a family and I just want to protect that.

Mediator: So does the word *family* suggest some values about how you go about your work that are important to you? Tell me about that.

Lisa: Yes, I value families and relationships. . . . And then this concert that she's coordinating. We hadn't talked about that. I hadn't officially approved it and I don't think the residents are capable to be out there in an environment where they would not feel safe.

Mediator: That's your concern. That they would not feel safe?

Lisa: Yes, and all the people coming and stopping to look. . . . I'm just not comfortable with her coming in and trying to make changes right from the start. I've been here long enough to know how I like things.

Lisa's final comment suggests that the dispute is partly a matter of a different sense of timing in relation to changes and new ideas. But it has developed in the context of some wider discursive debates about how people with disabilities are to be constructed in the world. References to concepts like segregation and integration allude to the use of human rights discourse in these debates. Michelle mentions the way that she has been influenced in her thinking by the reading of academic literature on these subjects. Lisa has perhaps come from an older discourse tradition of constructing people with disabilities within a discourse of charity and protection. Neither of the disputants made up the terms of these discursive debates on her own. But they are both seeking to establish positions in their relationship on the basis of these discourses. Each also experiences being positioned by the other. It would hardly be sufficient to reference these positions back to their personal needs or interests or to their essential personalities without taking account of the larger cultural field of play in which they are participating. In this cultural field of play, dominant and alternative discourses of disability jostle for attention and shape the relations between people and shape too the utterances that people make in conversation. They play a role in the production of this conflict. They position Lisa and Michelle in different places in ways that neither individual is wholly responsible for creating (although each still does have choices about how she will take up positions in relation to these discourses).

Hallmark 7: Identify Openings to an Alternative Story (What Would You Prefer?)

After narrative mediators have mapped out the problem story and developed an externalizing conversation about it, they are interested in identifying an opening to a different relationship story. If they have been doing the double listening we described earlier, they might already have heard a number of possible openings to this alternative story. The story of a conflict is always only one possible story out of a range of stories that may be told about a relationship. Because most relationships are made up of hundreds and thousands of events, inevitably the parties will be able to marshal many events together to support a story of the relationship that presents the conflict in bright lights. Equally inevitably, however, other events will be left in the shadows simply because they do not fit with the brightly lit story of the conflict. There does not have to be any deception involved in the omission of these events. They are left out simply because it is necessary to select plot elements (out of the many possible events) and to string them together in order to form a coherent story.

Narrative mediation takes advantage of this phenomenon. The mediator can develop an alternative story by paying attention to the plot elements that are being left out of the conflict story and then seeking their reinclusion. In the shadows of a story of angry exchanges, there are often moments of reflection and remorse or of quiet calmness. In the shadows of a story of despair, there are moments of hope. In the shadows of a story of obstinacy, there are moments of willingness to negotiate. In the shadows of a story of the failure of empathy, there are moments of recognition. In the shadows of a story of ruthless competition, there are moments of cooperative teamwork. In the shadows of a story of denigration, there are instances of respect. The skill of the mediator lies in catching these moments and inquiring into them. This inquiry is not conducted in the spirit of seeking to reveal inconsistency, contradiction, or hypocrisy and then saying, "There, your story is not true!" It is conducted in the recognition that inconsistency and contradiction are to be expected and can be valuable resources for constructing narratives to fit the complexity of life.

In the gaps opened up by externalizing conversations, many openings can be found. These openings might be exceptions to the escalation of the conflict. They might be unheralded moments of cooperation or goodwill. They might be intentions to do better. They might be expressions of hope for peaceful relations. They are always present if mediators are alert to them, if they seek them out, if they join them together into a story line.

Starting Points for Opening an Alternative Story

Mediators who are alert to the opportunities that lie cast aside on the edges of the stories that disputing parties tell can find a number of possible starting points for opening an alternative story. We list some of them here.

1. Ask the parties if they like what the conflict is doing to them and if they would prefer something different. Although the answer to this question may seem obvious, having it stated out loud can make a difference. Very often people express preferences for greater peace and understanding and cooperation

and teamwork. A question like, "Can you help me understand more of the reasons for your preference for coopera- tion?" takes this inquiry further into a rich vein of story construction.

2. Hear the pieces of information often dropped into a conver- sation as asides and typically not treated as having much sig- nificance because they do not fit with the conflict story. These are potential plot elements for an alternative story of the rela- tionship, but they are easily glossed over and currently remain unavailable because they have not been included in any story. Inquiring into these plot elements can rescue them from the oblivion that is the destiny of unstoried events: "Excuse me, but did I just hear you say that, despite all the tension between you both in the office, you actually worked on that project without difficulty. How did you do that? What vision of a pos- sible relationship between you was implicit in that instance?" An inquiry may start here into the know-how and preferences the parties may have for cooperative relationship—a resource for dealing with the issues in dispute.

3. Build on the absent but implicit values that lie hidden behind the expressions of anger or outrage in the dispute, as discussed earlier. For example, a mediator who hears a complaint about the presence of injustice might inquire into either of the parties' interest in combating injustice in the world. Or a denial of an accusation of racism might contain within it an absent but implicit principled objection to the discourse of racism that might be explored. Exploring this objection as a positive value might open up a story of shared commitment between the parties to work against racism.

4. Ask directly for exceptions to the conflict story. For example, you can say: "I know you have been living under the cloud of resentment that has been settling around you over several months, but I am wondering if there have been times when this cloud has lifted, even for a brief time. Have there been any such moments? And how did you respond to each other at those times?"

5. Ask for examples of different behavior admired in others. This approach was documented in a recent book by Michael White (2004). White avowed that it was not a practice of

mediation per se, but we think it fits within the broader context of conflict resolution. In an account of a conversation with two gay men who were experiencing a high degree of conflict in a relationship, White described interviewing one of the men, while the other listened, about the relationship models he was drawing upon. Was there anyone he could think of in his background whom he admired for an ability to deal with conflict differently? The man thought of an uncle who was no longer alive. White then interviewed him for a few minutes about this uncle and what was special about him. How might this uncle have responded in the situations that his nephew was experiencing? What transpired was the opening of some new considerations for dealing with the current conflict.

6. Explore the intentions to act on an instinct that has never yet materialized in deed. All individuals have many more intentions in life than they manage to act on. In a conflict situation these may include a desire to reach out in understanding to the other person. The conflict story itself may often overwhelm this desire, and yet it exists as a possible response that might make a difference to the relational conditions in the mediation conversation. A mediator who gets a sense of the existence of such an intention may inquire into the imagined action that this intention would, if acted on, give rise to. Making this intention explicit and elaborating a description of it may make the expression of this understanding more likely to have some effect. Even the declaring of an intention without it being carried out can introduce a new plot element into a rigid story of oppositional and angry relationship.

There are potentially many more approaches to opening up an alternative story of relationship. Once openings are identified, the challenge is to grow these expressions into a viable story that has a chance to compete against the dominant, conflict-saturated story. The most useful tool the mediator has when these openings appear is the application of respectful curiosity. Being curious about the gaps or exceptions to the dominance of the conflict story can prise these exceptions loose from the grip of the conflict.

Example of Opening an Alternative Story in a Conversation

Here is a piece of conversation that exemplifies creating an opening to an alternative story.

Mediator: Do you have any sense of what would happen if this conflict were to keep on going and maybe get even worse?

Lisa: It would be very uncomfortable for myself and for the residents.

Michelle: It would be horrible because I really love my job and I want to stay there. I love the residents. I love what I do. And it would be horrible if I had to keep fighting or justifying why I want to integrate them into the community.

Mediator: And would it be sustainable for very long or not?

Michelle: If it keeps going, I don't know how I'd be able to stand it. And I don't want to leave.

Mediator: [*To Lisa*] Would it be similar for you?

Lisa: I think she has some great ideas and I don't want to see her go either.

Mediator: OK. You've both spoken about a number of the effects of this problem. You've spoken about how it affects you personally, how it's affecting others, how it could get worse and create an even more uncomfortable situation if you didn't deal with it. Is that fair enough [*both nod*]? I guess I'm hearing you both say, but I just want to check this. . . . Are you happy that it keeps going like this? I hear you both saying that you really want it to change and I just want to be sure about that.

Lisa: I do.

Michelle: Something has to change.

Lisa: I want to be able to work together. Not to be best friends but to be able to be civil and to work side by side.

This piece of conversation marks a move by both parties away from the conflict story. Both take up a position more against the conflict than against each other. In this exchange they are repositioning themselves in a shared preference for a better working relationship. The mediator may think the answers to these questions are obvious by this stage. But the purpose of asking these disputants to evaluate their conflict and its effects is not so much to discover their inner experience as to construct it. They are being asked whether they are ready to take a stand here. The stand is in relation to the externalized problem. Do they want it, or would they prefer something different? Their responses constitute a step toward a different future. The detail of what this future might entail is not yet clear. But these two individuals are now relationally aligned where they can negotiate this detail while standing on the platform of a large slab of goodwill.

Hallmark 8: Re-Author the Relationship Story (Let's Build a Story of Cooperation)

There is an old English proverb that says, "One swallow does not a summer make." Equally, one exception does not make a viable story. A moment of difference needs to be built upon and connected with other moments of difference and with substantial themes if an alternative story is to be capable of sustaining a relational shift in the face of the conflict story. In order to enhance the likelihood that disputants can make this shift, a mediator can provide the scaffolding (Vygotsky, 1986) for the construction process. This involves asking a series of carefully constructed questions that invite parties to step forward into their own preferred story of relationship and to use that story as the foundation for the formulation of an agreement or resolution, if that is needed.

The goal of a narrative mediation process, however, is not necessarily the reaching of an agreement. We agree with Folger and Bush's (1994) critique of making reaching and signing off on an agreement the target of all mediation practice. This idea is too limiting and instrumental for the wide range of possible mediation outcomes. Folger and Bush (1994) argue for the achievement of greater empowerment and the development of heightened recognition (defined in specific ways) as the goals for mediation. Our emphasis is slightly different. Consistent with the narrative ideas we have been outlining, we think the goal of mediation needs to be constructed in terms of a story. A story is not a one-time event but something that moves through time.

Rather than trying to resolve the conflict to form a different basis for relationship, we favor re-authoring the relationship story to form a basis for people going forward from a conflict situation. In Wittgenstein's (1958) words, a mediation may be considered successful if people "know how to go on." The path forward may feature a range of possible outcomes. An agreement or written resolution may be one such outcome, but we would expect even the best possible agreement to fail if it is not incorporated into an ongoing story. For a start, any agreement is only as good as the actions taken to implement it. On other occasions, as Bush and Folger point out, mediation may lead to shifts in understanding between people that make the drawing up of an agreement redundant. Our focus is therefore on the creation of a sustainable, forward-moving narrative. One feature of stories is that they move through time according to a plot sequence. Therefore, if there is to be an agreement, we are interested in the relational story that might give rise to it and in the further elaboration of this story after the signing of an agreement. The agreement itself is thus contextualized differently from the way it is in a problem-solving mode.

So how does this story get built? In discussing Hallmark 7 we identified a number of possible points where mediators could open such a story. Having found one such opening, a mediator may then ask questions to establish further instances of exception to the dominance of the conflict story. For example, the mediator can ask, "Are there other occasions you can recall when you did not allow the cloud of resentment to dominate things?"

Once two or three instances of the alternative story have been found in the relationship history, they can be linked together as an alternative relational story. It can then be named for its preferred themes. It may be a story of cooperation or teamwork or of understanding, mutual respect, collaboration, or justice, and so on. This naming gives the story an identity, adds narrative coherence, and serves to summarize all the details together in a memorable chunk.

Construction of an Alternative Story Through Asking Questions

An important principle here is that the alternative story should be produced by the parties to the dispute, not out of a mediator's brilliant insight. There is always a danger of imposition. Imposed stories violate the ethical principle of democratic sovereignty, and they are also less likely than others to work in practice. Relational practices that are not generated by the parties themselves may have a poor ecological fit in the living context of the persons affected by them, and the skills to implement them may not exist in the parties' repertoires. At the same time, mediators should not abandon all the influence possible in their role for fear of imposing something. They should instead restrict their role to that of asking questions and building the scaffolding that the parties can use to construct the relational structure they must later inhabit.

In order to strengthen the sense of a alternative story moving through time, a mediator can inquire into the history of the story of, say, cooperation.

For example, the mediator may ask, "How long has cooperation been part of your relationship? When has it been present in the past?"

The same inquiry can then be pursued into the future: "If you were to grow this story of cooperation that you both say you prefer into the future, how might it help you deal with these issues you have been struggling with?"

This ongoing inquiry supplies the alternative story with the movement through time that it needs if it is to compete with the conflict story. Once established, the spirit of this alternative story can be invoked to negotiate through issues that remain outstanding between the parties: "In the spirit of the teamwork we have been talking about, what suggestions do you have for making arrangements for the care of your children? What would you like to ask of or offer to each other?" When this question is asked in the context of a relational story that expresses preferred values for both parties, then the negotiation phase (if needed) can go much more smoothly.

Example of the Construction of an Alternative Story

Here is a piece of conversation that illustrates the development of an alternative story of relationship. It comes from a mediation between two sisters who are in a dispute over the terms of a will after their mother's death.

Mediator: I'm wondering if you want these things to continue and perhaps develop further, or whether you would perhaps prefer things to be in a different place?

Brenda: I'd much rather have a better relationship.

Gina: Mmmm.

Brenda: And to really use each other for support and really be like . . . like sisters I guess. Yeah.

Mediator: [*Noting down these words*] . . . have a better relationship . . . use each other for support . . . and what was that last thing?

Brenda: Act like sisters.

Mediator: [*Noting again*] . . . act like sisters. . . . What's the history of you supporting each other? You've described differences between you over the years but I'm just interested in the history of that?

Brenda: I think we've intended to be there for each other. You know, we've had intentions but I think we could do a lot better.

Mediator: So you would describe it as an intention that has sometimes not been carried as far as you would like it, preferably?

Brenda: Yeah.

Mediator: So has that intention ever been made manifest? Is there any way in which you have had a sense of offering your support to Gina or experiencing her offering support to you?

Brenda: Well, you know, I'll come over and I'll watch Joey or I'll hang out with Joey or she'll help every now and then with me getting into my photography and . . .

Mediator: Yeah? How has she done that?

Brenda: Well, she came with me when I was looking at different studios and spaces to rent. So she was actually there for that.

Mediator: OK and what did that mean to you?

Brenda: That it was actually important to her. You know, I'm not married and I don't have kids and still what I do is . . . you know . . . worthwhile. I guess she realized that it was important to me. Other people might not see that as important.

Mediator: OK. So that was somehow validating for you that she took seriously something that some other people may not have taken seriously and saw how important it was for you.

Brenda: Yeah.

Mediator: And does that qualify as acting like sisters?

Brenda: I guess so.

Mediator: It did at the time and that's what you would prefer to have more of?

Brenda: Yeah.

The conversation went on to document more of the history of "acting like sisters," now from Gina's point of view. This was a story of the sisters' relationship that had been somewhat neglected. It was not immediately obvious to either of them because of the influence of a dominant story of different lifestyles and of resentment between them that had reached boiling point over the disagreement about the will. As Brenda thinks about it, all she can recall at first are the "intentions" for something better. She has to work to reconstruct a memory of events that contradict the dominant story. When she does recover one such memory, the mediator asks questions to build meaning around this event. This needs to be repeated several times, perhaps, and to include both parties before it can constitute a viable story that can be lived out. When such a story has been established, it can serve as the basis for a negotiation over outstanding substantive issues that can be conducted in the spirit of "acting like sisters."

Hallmark 9: Document Progress (What's Written Down Lasts Longer)

A feature of narrative practice that Michael White and David Epston (1990) introduced into the family therapy field is the principle of creating written documents in order to extend the life of conversations. We think this principle is equally applicable to mediation practice. The basic idea is that writing things down gives them greater permanence for people, because conversations can easily fade in the memory over time. Given the modern cultural context, the written word also comes with greater authority than the spoken word. Hence it is often valuable to document things that were said in conversation so that they can echo longer.

Recording More Than Agreement

It has long been the practice of mediators to create written records of the agreements that people reach (if they do so) at the end of mediations. We want to be clear that we are talking about more than that. Our interest here is to document the story of relationship that has been told. Written agreements may well be part of that story. But they are never the complete story. Writing a complete story would of course be impossible. But it is possible to write and send to the parties a document, often in letter form, that is private and personal and that articulates what has transpired in conversation. It is often useful to send such a letter between meetings if the mediation has adjourned and a subsequent meeting is to be held. In this situation the letter can serve to keep the conversation alive and available for further pondering before the next meeting.

In order to produce such a document it is necessary to take notes during the mediation itself. These notes should be records of what the parties actually said, rather than records of the mediator's thoughts about the parties and their utterances. Then the document created can contain, in quotation marks, the parties' actual words quoted back to them. Because it is important to reproduce the exact words, mediators will find it hard to rely on memory. Also, if mediators are taking notes of the significant things that the parties say, then they can be seen as scribes who are underlining the importance of each person's knowledge by having sufficient respect and care to write it down. It is important that the letter should as much as possible *not* be a record of the mediator's impressions, interpretations, insights, judgment calls, advice, or brilliant logic. This is not a place for the mediator to demonstrate his or her own virtuosity! It is a place for the reproduction of the parties' impressions, interpretations, insights, judgment calls, advice to themselves and to each other, or brilliant logic.

The form of the letter is also important. It should include the following:

- A description of the conflict story, carefully written in externalizing language
- Some recognition of the effects of the externalized problem
- The words the parties have used to describe their preferences for some alternative story of relationship
- A brief description of any significant developments in that alternative story
- Some questions for ongoing consideration.

Example of a Letter That Documents Progress

Here is an example of such a letter. It was written by a mediation student about a practice mediation session done in class. It serves as an excellent illustration of the genre of document we are talking about.

June 17

Dear Chad and Shelly,

By the time you read this, Chad, you will have graduated from high school. Congratulations! I met with you two to discuss the "loyalty thing" that arose when Chad wanted to have some sort of contact with his biological father, and wanted to be able to include him in some of Chad's big life events. Initially, this just seemed like there was a lot of hurt to be seen, embarrassment to be dealt with, fear of rejection and fear of the future, that sort of thing. It was as if Chad's growing up, moving on, was causing a lot of hurt and wonderment as to what might happen in the future.

Both of you were very firm about the fact that your relationship has always been good up till now, and that David was "cool" and "no problem." It seems like it was all good until this loyalty thing reared up with Chad's impending adulthood. This loyalty thing attacked your relationship, and you reported, and demonstrated (!) just how vicious this loyalty thing could be.

When it attacked, you noticed that it "made you think that the other person was just out to hurt you!" Most surprising! When you asked the very reasonable question of why Chad would want to jeopardize your very good relationship, and Shelly, you said he was "such a good boy," no one could come up with any answer! Perhaps that intention never existed in you, Chad. What would you say? It was just such an amazing moment; we all just sort of stared at each other, remember? The loyalty thing could not stand up to searching questions, could it!

So we discovered that there was a way to move into the future without the loyalty thing attacking. You agreed that it attacks more "when I am stressed," and you've both been stressed. When you took a look forward at the future, without the loyalty thing getting in the way, both of you identically saw "barbeques and grandchildren and lots of love." So it looks like good love behind, good love ahead! That was a big agreement for you; this new way of looking at life through what you described as "a very long lens"—so the bumps seem more manageable.

This may just be a bump in the road of growing and changing—you mentioned that this was a "long view" story. You were clear that there is plenty of love to go around in the long view story.

Some questions I have for you as you move forward into these turbulent times:

- When time is precious, how will you hold onto the "long view" story? What priorities does each of you have for that time?

- Where could Chad's biological father fit into that long view story? Who else might fit into that long view story? Shelly's parents? If I listened into a family holiday dinner a decade from now, who would be there? Who would stop by?

- What benefits can you see from living the long view story? Are those benefits worth having? Why?

- Are there moments when you can more easily see the long view story?

- How will you, Chad, and you, Shelly, personally benefit from the long view story?

- Who else in your lives will benefit from the long view story?

When I see you again next week I would like to ask you some more about these questions and probably some others. I am particularly interested in ideas we can generate about how to keep the long view story from being sidelined by the loyalty thing. I'm also interested in how we can deal with Chad's interest in his biological father from the perspective of the long view story rather than from the perspective of the loyalty thing.

I'd like to thank you for your courage and openness in exploring this bump in a wonderful family with me. Chad, all the best to you in your graduation, your marriage and your naval enlistment. Shelly, you spoke about how you know you have raised "a strong, smart young man," and of how proud you are of him. It's well deserved.

Best in the future to you all.

Respectfully and in appreciation of the long view,
Laurie Frazier

Chapter Two

Negotiating Discursive Positions

The following two-line exchange occurred in a television interview between a white woman reporter and the African American boxer Mike Tyson, who carries a reputation for uncontrolled violence both in and out of the boxing ring.

Interviewer: Can you tell me where all the rage within you comes from?

    Tyson: [*Smiles*] You know, you're so white asking me a question like that.

This exchange is intriguing because of the clear communication mismatch. The two utterances are like ships sailing past each other on divergent courses that cannot easily be altered. Seen from that perspective this exchange is not unlike the often contrasting stories that disputants tell in mediation. In this chapter we want to explore what happens in such exchanges and, more specifically, to view them through the concept of discursive positioning. We first tease this particular exchange apart and then explore the theoretical concepts involved in doing so. In the second half of the chapter we apply the concept of positioning more directly to mediation practice.

How Discursive Positioning Helps Make Sense of an Interaction

In order to tease out the work being done within discourse by the two parties in this exchange one might pose the following questions about it:

- What are the assumptions built into the interviewer's question?
- In what discourse do these assumptions fit?
- What are the assumptions built into Tyson's reply?
- In what discourse do these assumptions fit?
- In each utterance, what kind of conversation is being opened up? What is likely to be emphasized in this conversation, and what is likely to be excluded?
- In each utterance, what kind of platform is being constructed for the other person to stand on in response?
- After the interviewer's question, what options does Tyson have? After Tyson's comment, what options does the interviewer have?

These questions can be expected to yield an account of the exchange in terms of discursive positioning. In such an account, each person's utterance is looked at more as an action performed upon the other person than as an expression of individual essence.

The interviewer's question can be argued to offer Tyson a position in a particular psychological discourse. This discourse provides the conversation with a particular set of assumptions (assumptions of one kind or another are necessary before a question can make sense as an utterance). For example, in this discourse, acts of violence are accounted for by postulating an individualized psychic container of rage that will spill over when it reaches a certain level. This metaphor is drawn from a psychological discourse widely known throughout mainstream, psychodynamic, Western knowledge. None of this is spelled out. It remains implicit and assumed. We would argue that the question positions Tyson within this discourse. He is instantiated into the assumptive world, complete with a set of moral imperatives, on which the question relies. From a narrow slot within this world he is asked to respond. If he were to accept this positioning and attempt to answer the question about where the "rage" comes from, he could be said to take up the position offered, in which case he would also be adopting a responsibility to find outlets for his rage that do not lead to its spilling over. If you listen carefully to the echoes of other discourses, you might also hear faint echoes of racist assumptions in the interviewer's question. For instance, there is a longstanding assumption in

European discourse that contrasts European "rationality" with the more "animal passions" of other races, particularly of blacks. An assumption of implied superiority is inherent in the terms of the contrast (see Edward Said's 1994 account of Orientalism for examples of this discourse).

In his response, however, Tyson refuses the position offered up by the interviewer. His smile seems to recognize the discourse he is being offered. In his retort he seeks to establish a position for himself and for the interviewer in a completely different discourse, with a completely different set of assumptions and moral imperatives. He situates his comment in a conversation about race, which completely reinterprets the meaning of the interviewer's question. Now she is the one who is pathologized for her inadequate (and privileged) understanding of race. By implication, she is told that she cannot possibly understand the psychological experience of a black man. Her question is relegated to an expression of naïveté, if not outright racism. At the same time, Tyson's violence is rendered more understandable in the context of a response to (violent?) racial oppression. It is implicitly contextualized more favorably against a general discursive background of race relations. He perhaps can be said to be claiming a superior moral position as a victim of racism.

Both utterances rely on an essentializing logic. The interviewer's question relies on an essentialist account of violence as an expression of the emergence of rage from within. And Tyson's reply relies on an essentialist account of the experience of race that automatically assigns victim status and oppressor status on the basis of skin color, with little room for nuanced understandings. If you step out of these essentializing discourses, however, you might see this exchange as one in which power is actually being constructed in the moment, and it is far more nuanced than either of the essentialist narratives cited. Both speakers, consciously or unconsciously, are attempting to position themselves in favored positions through their choice of discourse. And both are offering each other positions of diminished legitimacy at the same time. In a sense both are seeking power through the control of meaning. Neither is powerless. Tyson's response shows that it is possible to refuse a position offered to you. At the same time it is probably the discourse chosen by the interviewer that will be granted a greater hearing in the wider community. This exchange is an example of how power relations, in poststructuralist terms, are worked out on the ground around the control of meaning. Control of meaning can, in turn, be understood as control over which discourse will dominate. As in mediation, meaning is to some extent structured by the background discourses being called upon, but it is by no means determined. Hence it matters just which instances of positioning are picked up and which are refused or renegotiated. We think it is useful both for mediators to learn to listen for discursive positioning and for researchers into mediation to learn to analyze how such positioning is negotiated.

What Positioning Theory Is About

In Chapter One we introduced the concept of listening for and working with discursive positioning. We have written a little about this topic before (Winslade & Monk, 2000), but the subject deserves to be elaborated much more fully. It is one of the aims of this book to demonstrate the usefulness of the concept of positioning in both theory and practice. To this end we devote this chapter and the next to the application of positioning theory to mediation.

Positioning theory builds on Foucault's concept of subjective positioning, and was developed by Bronwyn Davies and Rom Harré (1990; 1999), among others. One of its advantages is that it affords people the opportunity to address the particularity of localized experiences without losing touch with the powerful social discourses within which subjective experience is built. Traditionally, the personal and the social domains of living have been divided up by the social sciences into subject matter that is proper for psychology and subject matter that is proper for sociology and anthropology. Yet individuals do not live their lives in separate personal and social domains. In practice these domains are of a piece. It is in the conjunction of the personal and the social that people experience the conflicts that they bring to mediators. The concept of positioning is useful in the conceptualization of the mediation task because it focuses on this very relationship.

Think of each utterance as situated in discourse simply because it uses discursive material (words and meanings) in order to make sense. Any utterance calls on a discursive background that, if followed back far enough, is formulated in a view of the world. Moreover, according to Bakhtin (1986), each utterance can make sense only in response to other utterances in a dialogue or in the history of dialogues in a particular genre of conversation. Furthermore, an utterance is not just a representation of discursive meanings that have their existence somewhere else. It is also where the event of discourse production takes place. It is a response to another utterance and it anticipates a subsequent response. As people speak, they create and exchange pieces of discourse and in the process structure and give shape to their own and each other's worlds. It is this moment-by-moment process of construction of the world that the analysis of positioning seeks to describe.

This productive function of discourse was also an important concern for Foucault. In his analysis of power relations elaborated through discourse, he was careful to show that people are not just recipients of the influence of social discourse. They are also producers of it, as they participate in conversational exchange. They use discourse as they speak for a communicative purpose, but part of this communicative purpose is always to establish the relational conditions in which the meaning can be understood. Thus each utterance, even if just for a moment, structures a social relation (or participates in the structuring of repetitive relational patterns). As the utterance structures this relation, it sets up relative speaking rights, legitimates topics of conversation, and creates an immediate (albeit implicit) moral evaluation of possible meanings. Because each utterance in a conversation implies a set of choices of action, it may be said to establish a "moment by moment oughtness" (Linehan & McCarthy, 2000, p. 442) for each of the participants.

Repetition establishes these moments as social norms. Foucault's (1978, 1980) notion of disciplinary power established through the institution of social norms is built on the assumption that repetitive, patterned mosaics constitute a social discourse. In making utterances individuals respond to these patterns as well as to the immediate utterances of their conversation partners.

As they do so they seek to establish (usually favorable) relational positions for themselves, both in an immediate relation with an "other" and in relation to the many background exchanges that go to make up patterns of discursive exchange on a topic.

How Position Calls Function

At the same time as people in conversation are busy establishing a discursive position for themselves in making an utterance, they are also offering the person(s) addressed a position (or a range, usually narrow, of positions) from which to respond. If each utterance establishes a position in a social relation, then the other poles in that relation are necessarily implied in the utterance. We refer to this as *calling* the other into a position. For example, as a person offers an opinion on any matter, she may call another into a position of agreement or disagreement. Or she may call another person into an affiliation with a whole framework of meaning. The relational position one person calls another into constructs a platform from which to respond and invites him to stand on that platform in making a response.

Here is an example of how position calls work. One party in a mediation says:

Participant: Look, I'm just trying to be reasonable here.

In this utterance the speaker is seeking to establish a position of legitimacy for his claims in the dispute. If he is indeed being "reasonable," then the other party has fewer grounds for complaining about what he has said. To do so would appear churlish. So the position of being churlish is one of the available positions the addressee is being called into. Another possibility is that the addressee is being called into the opposing position: that of the "unreasonable" disputant. Without the speaker actually saying so, the addressee is by implication being referred to as too emotional, possibly even irrational and, therefore, slightly crazy. Any angry response or objection to such positioning would actually confirm the relational narrative thus established.

If we extend the analysis further, we can inquire into the worldview that needs to be in existence before the concept of *being reasonable* can make any kind of sense. Here the cultural valuing of what is reasonable comes into play. It is, of course, possible to define it in many ways. But the dominant idea that underscores this meaning is the long history of Western thought in which rationality has been defined, articulated, and practiced as a form of control over other ways of knowing, such as through emotionality. The concept of reasonableness draws upon the worldview in which rational control is valued over irrational expression. The speaker is implicitly calling on this long history and positioning himself favorably in relation to it. The addressee is implicitly positioned unfavorably in relation to the same history. The sense of oughtness constructed in this position call is that the addressee should acknowledge the first speaker's legitimacy by shifting to a position more in line with the dominant discourse of rationality.

The same process of positioning can take place through the use of a variety of other discourse usages. In the sentence, "Look, I am just trying to be reasonable here," the word "reasonable" can be easily replaced by other words, such as "open-minded" or "fair," each of which alters the locus of evaluation slightly, while accomplishing a similar purpose. A person can speak about herself primarily as the "victim" of the other person's cruelty and in so doing implicitly call the other person into the position of "villain." Or she can argue that her position is "justified" and implicitly call the other into position as having a view that is "unjustified."

Positioning in Multiple Conversations

As people speak, they position themselves not just in relation to the utterance(s) made by an immediate other person(s) in the conversation but also in relation to utterances made by others in many other conversations (Bakhtin, 1984, 1986). A person is never the first speaker on any particular subject. Every utterance is first a *rejoinder* (Shotter, 1993, p. 383) to some previous utterance(s). Thus any utterance must be understood as situated in a set of conversations on a topic and, to some extent, constituted by what has been spoken before. In order to be understood, people use words borrowed from other utterances. Bakhtin (1986) suggests, therefore, that any use of words carries with it an echo of other voices, down a "corridor of voices" (p. 121). Bakhtin most commonly used the term *heteroglossia* to define this phenomenon of each utterance containing within it many other echoes from other conversations. There are always many other voices speaking. The description of every utterance as *double-voiced* is another term for this phenomenon (Bakhtin, 1986; Gee, 1999).

Positioning in mediation can thus be multiply dimensioned, even in making a single utterance. As someone speaks to a mediator and describes his personal experience, he may be conscious of how his words may sound, not just to the mediator's ear but also to other significant addressees. For instance, an utterance in a mediation, as well as being a response to the mediator's question, may to some degree be a response to advice received from a friend, a legal adviser, a talk show host, or the author of a book the speaker has read. The concept of positioning therefore suggests a process of producing subjectivity that is intertextual (Bakhtin, 1986; Kristeva, 1986) and relational. Appreciating utterances as positioning both the speaker and the addressee locates them in their function within a dialogue or within a chain of communication exchanges. This emphasis is different from explaining an utterance with regard to primarily internal individual reference points, such as personal motivation or individual interests or basic biological drives.

This is potentially a theoretically radical idea. It proposes that mediators understand people's utterances not so much as originating in their individual psyches but as links in a chain of communication. Hence, if one person is to understand another, it becomes more important to trace the utterances (and the social world) to which the speaker is responding than to trace the original movement in the speaker's heart.

For example, in the course of a family mediation one woman says, "I just want to do what the judge said we should do." How is this speaker establishing a subjective position, and how is she calling the other party into position? She is speaking into one conversation but making reference to an utterance in another one. Through calling on the judge's utterance, she makes a claim of legitimacy for her own opinion by aligning it with an authoritative source. At the same time, she is calling the other into position as not doing what the judge said. While shoring up her own position, she is simultaneously undermining the other party's, or calling him into a position of failing to honor the judge's intentions.

Positioning and the Self

A particular view of the self is implicit in the theory of positioning. It lies in the suggestion that people are made up of a series of positions in a multitude of conversations and that they come to understand themselves through being positioned by many others and then through their choices of ways to respond. This is a constructionist (rather than a humanist) vision of selfhood. It envisions a self constructed out of discourse, rather than out of a set of inner forces that emerge in the context of social relations. Sometimes these inner forces are referred to in the humanist tradition as inner needs. We would argue that they are often better represented as a sense of *entitlement* to which a person becomes attached through her exposure to discourses in particular social worlds (see Winslade & Monk, 2000).

Positioning and Social Roles

A discursive position can also be distinguished from a social role (Davies & Harré, 1990). Roles are more static than positions. In the analysis of interactions in a mediation, the roles of *disputant* and *mediator* are not sharp enough instruments for an observer to use for making meaning out of the conversational moves in a conflict resolution process. Utterances have more variability than can be accounted for by these roles. If a mediation participant's utterances were to be understood from the perspective of, say, his role as a *father,* then they would be largely stable from one moment to the next. Positioning, in contrast, is more fluid. Although in one utterance this participant might seek to position himself in one way, in the next he might be positioned quite differently, depending on what discourse world he, or another speaker, is calling on. For example, in one moment he might position himself as a caring parent. In the next he might take up the position of a wronged and aggrieved partner who has withdrawn from contact with his children. The advantage of this fluidity is that it allows the analysis of subtle shifts and nuances in discourse that are not visible through the lens of role theory. When looked at through the lens of positioning theory, however, power in social relations does not appear fixed but always subject to the shifting emphases of meaning. This fluidity provides positioning theory's explanatory power because it makes possible representations of even subtly nuanced exchanges.

The possibility of nuanced and shifting discursive positions is critical to theorizing about the change that can occur during mediation. People make moves toward greater understanding and cooperation with other individuals through their experience of effective mediation practices, and these moves can be described in terms of shifts of positioning. They often revolve around the dropping of some aspects of conflict-saturated discourse expression in favor of more inclusive and respectful forms of expression. In the process the relational conditions can be forged in which movement forward out of the grip of a conflict is possible. Through discursive positioning people move themselves and others around in conversation.

Why You Can't Change a Discourse in One Conversation (But You Can Shift Discursive Positions)

By its nature a discourse is not owned by any one person. It is a product of thousands of conversations. Therefore it is not possible to change a discourse in one conversation. Discourse change happens through the accumulation of many smaller shifts over time. What may be possible in a single conversation, however, is that people may shift in their positioning in relation to a discourse. For example, it is not possible to excise racist discourse from the public arena through working with one or even two persons. But it is possible to facilitate a conversation in which one or two persons shift position in relation to racist discourse. In other words, mediation can be thought of as a context in which repositioning can take place. People can refuse the positions into which they are called and can establish their preferred positions in response.

In conflict the patterns of discourse positioning frequently become rigidly fixed in a narrow range of possibilities. Whereas in the normal course of conversation people move fluidly in and out of many discourse positions, in conflict-saturated situations their range of options becomes considerably narrower. For example, in the aftermath of a divorce, the parties will often look back at the marriage and tell a story about it that is constructed primarily in terms of the conflict within it. To do so they must exclude many other possible stories and therefore many other possible relational positions that do not fit with the story of conflict. Similarly, two people who have been friends or colleagues and then end up in a conflict quickly lose sight of the friendship or colleagueship and start to view each other solely from the purview of the dispute between them. In conflict, people frequently resort to totalizing accusations directed at each other. Accusatory discourse accords room for only denial or capitulation. It leaves little room for negotiation. Hence it might be productive for mediators to pay close attention to the ways in which conflict operates on people's exchanges. If it narrows the range of relational positions, one of the tasks of mediation might be to open up this range so that more positions are possible.

How Mediators Position Parties

Positioning theory can be useful not only to an understanding of the relations between parties to a dispute but also to an understanding of the relations between professionals and their clients. Mediators can examine their own utterances and ask questions about the relational positions into which they are inviting people. Differential positioning of participants in a mediation can lead to very different conversations. Let us look at some examples.

The mediation literature has paid close attention to mediators' initial statements about the mediation process. This has arisen in part out of a concern with appropriate protocol, which might to some degree be characterized in turn as a concern for how conversational exchanges in mediation fit into the wider domain of legal dispute resolution processes. In the process of introduction it is not uncommon for a mediator to say something like this:

Mediator: Our task today is to reach an agreement . . .

This statement positions those listening within a particular type of conversation. It invites them to join this conversation from the position of negotiating parties. Folger and Bush (1994) have characterized the discourse within which this type of conversation must take place as a *settlement orientation*. Within this discourse parties are encouraged to talk about certain things and discouraged from talking about other things. Hence positioning parties in this discourse shapes what can be talked about in the mediation. As Folger and Bush argue, a settlement orientation leads to talk about tangible things, which can be counted and over which deals can be done, such as money and time. It is less likely to privilege talk about the intangible aspects of relationship that Folger and Bush suggest also need a place in mediation conversation: for example, emotional expression and recognition. A further effect of this utterance from a settlement orientation is that it positions parties as "difficult" if they are not ready to settle. It sets mediators up for frustration, or an experience of "failure," if the parties to the dispute refuse to settle. To better understand the contrast, compare the previous introductory statement with this fuller one:

Mediator: Mediation is a process where two people meet in a safe place to talk about and look for joint solutions in a collaborative way. You get the opportunity to listen to each other's point of view, talk through differences, or if need be, brainstorm and negotiate solutions.

Notice how this statement can position the parties in one of several different possible conversations, depending on which one they choose to take up. The settlement orientation is still present but is presented as an option. The choice involved constitutes the participants as agents in the construction of the mediation conversation, rather than reserving this design function for the mediator. It therefore positions the mediator and the parties in a different conversation from the start.

Positioning and Expertise

Another aspect of mediator positioning refers to the discursive context of professional practice. Mediation is on the way to becoming an established new professional practice that is distinctive in its own right. Hence it is taking its place in a long line of more established professions. Since the Enlightenment, there has been a burgeoning of new professions, all based on the practical application of the knowledge generated in academic settings through the social and biological sciences. A result of this development is that far more than ever before, people are required to situate their personal and relational experience within terms derived from some area of scientific expertise. For every life challenge it seems that there is now an expert to tell people how to live. It is therefore not an uncommon experience for people to enter into relational exchanges in which the power to name and interpret experience is yielded up to some kind of expert. Expertise thus constitutes a form of authority over people's knowledge of themselves and of each other. It was one of Michel Foucault's (1980) concerns to analyze the role of knowledge in the construction of power relations in the modern world. Positioning theory takes this analysis and allows mediation researchers to ask just how professional relations are constituted in the moment as mediators position their clients.

For example, imagine that a mediator comes out with the following statement in the context of a family mediation.

Mediator: We know from studies about children of divorced
families that . . .

With this statement the mediator positions herself as a participant in the academic conversations in which knowledge about children from divorced families is generated. On the basis of the authority that accrues from this participation, the mediator is seeking a position of legitimacy for what she has to say to the participants in the mediation. It can scarcely be contested, because it has the force of scientific method behind it. The addressees of this utterance are therefore called into a position of submission to this authority. They are not offered much ground on which to stand if they wish to contest what the mediator says, at least not as much as they would have had if the mediator had merely offered a personal opinion. Even then, though, the voice of the mediator would have a degree of authority based on all the ways in which a professional relation is established. For example, the choice of the venue by the mediator can in itself position participants in a professional relation toward which they must adopt the position of submission.

In this next example a mediator is introducing the possibility of caucusing. Once again, let us examine the positioning established:

Mediator: During this mediation I would like the opportunity to meet for twenty minutes alone with each of you. In this way I will be better able to understand the positions of each of you and be better able to help you both find an agreeable resolution. Is that something that you would be comfortable with?

Here the mediator positions himself as the one who will do the understanding and as a major player in the production of a resolution. This statement might be questioned in terms of the position calls issued to the parties. They are not explicitly invited into a conversation in which they might come to greater understanding of each other. They are, however invited to comment on the mediator's positioning of them in this way. They are thus called into the position of participants in a dialogue and granted the editorial position of passing comment.

Positioning People in Different Conversations

Wendy Drewery (2005, p. 314) has cited a further example of two possible introductory statements that a mediator might make in a family mediation about a custody matter. In the first instance the mediator begins the conversation about the substantive issues by saying:

Mediator: Have you thought about who will look after the children after the separation?

This utterance calls the couple into position in a competing or oppositional relation, one in which claims of entitlement will be placed in contest with each other, such that the eventual outcome is likely to be some form of exclusion. It is hardly surprising that such positioning would occur, given that the dominant legal discourse of divorce leads people to assume an adversarial process. The very use of the word *custody* positions parents and children in a possessive competition. It carries overtones of the imprisonment of children in one parent's home. However, the question can also be asked in a way that calls the couple into a quite different position:

Mediator: Have you thought about how you will care for the children after the separation?

The position calls in this question are more inclusive and invite a cooperative involvement in the care of the children. The conversation that is assumed by this piece of positioning is much more likely to be one that features shared power and entitlement. Parenting is constructed here more in terms of the tasks of caring for children and less in the rights discourse of ownership. The positions a person may be called into in this discourse are shaped by this task of caring. A person may potentially be characterized as "caring" or "not caring" (and by implication as not a fit parent).

These examples illustrate the difference that the choice of discursive constructions can make. The choices involved in deciding on a phrasing are always affected by the dominant legal discourse, as are the choices that follow for the couple who are called into position in response. They are not, however, fixed by this discourse to the extent that other choices cannot be made, particularly when people are given opportunities to be reflexive and to decide which positions to take up or refuse. Hence Drewery argues that mediators should take care with how they use language to position people and that in this sense we all should "watch what we say" (p. 305).

Addressing the Problem of the First Speaker

A special case of positioning occurs in mediation through what Sara Cobb (1994) refers to as the "problem of the first speaker." Cobb was interested in studying how power is constructed in the process of conversational exchange. Her interest in this topic draws from a poststructuralist analysis of the role of discourse in power relations. Her research focused attention on how the first speaker to tell his story in mediation does more than take a speaking turn. He also establishes a degree of narrative control over the space from which the second speaker has to respond. In the terms that we have been using here, the second speaker is called into a position by the first speaker and must speak to some extent from that position, unless a substantial effort is made to reject that positioning. The first speaker, therefore, has privilege in the definition of what will be talked about and, therefore, what will be the basis of any resolution that emerges from the mediation. As he tells his story, the first speaker will lay out a map of relations around the conflict and slot the second speaker into position within those relations. To the extent to which the first speaker can relate a strong account that achieves a substantial proportion of what Cobb (1994) calls "narrative closure" (p. 54), the first speaker will have the opportunity to stabilize the story of what has happened. The second speaker, in order to tell a different story, will have more work to do, first of all to challenge the stability of the first speaker's story and then to establish a second story.

Sara Cobb (1994) has closely studied a number of mediation conversations and found that, in 75 percent of the cases, the first speaker's establishment of relational positions framed the eventual outcome of the mediation. The second speaker in her study was not without power. However, in only 25 percent of the cases did the second speaker frame the outcome of the mediation. These findings suggest that mediators should take special care with how they invite people to speak at the beginning of a mediation and especially with who is granted the right to tell his or her story first.

Our response to this problem is both theoretical and practical. Theoretically, we are persuaded by Mikhail Bakhtin to complicate this issue a little. Bakhtin (1981) argues that in any conversation the addressee of any utterance is not without influence. Each utterance, he suggests, is made with an eye to possible responses, and the listener (or the listener's expected response) exerts a powerful influence on what can be said. He put it like this:

> Every word is directed towards an answer and cannot escape
> the profound influence of the answering word that it anticipates
> [p. 280].

To some extent primacy belongs to the response, as the activating principle: it creates the ground for understanding, it prepares the ground for an active and engaged understanding. Understanding comes to fruition only in the response [p. 282].

This idea amounts to a challenge to the singularity of the author's voice (also challenged by Foucault, 1977). It privileges a more dialogical or relational view of communication processes and focuses attention on the reflexive aspects of speaking. The term Bakhtin coined for this aspect of any utterance was *addressivity*. It refers to the aspect of any utterance that anticipates a response from the *addressee* and seeks to shape that response in some way. The addressee's influence might be felt in the words chosen, in the style of communication, in the rhetorical strategies employed, and in the very content of the message. The speaker makes judgments in the moment of speaking about the addressee's "apperceptive background" and "degree of responsiveness" (Bakhtin, 1981, p. 346; also see Shotter, 1993).

Taking account of Bakhtin here opens a further topic of potential research study: the extent to which the second speaker is already exerting a pull on what the first speaker is saying when he speaks. How much does the first speaker seek to anticipate and rule out the story that the second speaker will tell?

Lessening the Effect of the First Speaker's Power

In practical terms we are also interested in the ways in which mediation conversations can be conducted in order to lessen the influence of the first speaker. We have several suggestions:

1. Mediators can hold separate meetings with each party before a joint meeting in order to give each a chance to tell her story to the mediator without the presence of the other party there to exert influence. This can give each person a chance to rehearse and develop the coherence of her own account, so as to make it less susceptible to being sidelined by the other party's story, should that person become the first speaker.
2. The mediator can pose a question to the first speaker and then deliberately pose the same question to the second speaker, rather than asking the second speaker to respond to what the first speaker has said.

3. The mediator can specifically ask the second speaker not to respond to the first speaker's account and to start from his own starting point. We have done this on some occasions and have received at least two comments later from participants that this was helpful.

4. The mediator can avoid conducting the mediation like a court case in which each party gets a substantial amount of time to tell her story. Instead, the early part of a mediation can be conducted as a series of briefer conversational exchanges, rather than as the telling of a lengthy story by each party of what has happened. The mediator achieves this by asking smaller questions rather than positioning people in the expectation that they should give a lengthy coherent account. Each question can be put first to the party who was not the first to answer the previous question, so that the position of being the first speaker is shared rather than monopolized.

5. The first speaker can be deliberately asked to respond to how he is being positioned by the second speaker's account, rather than leaving the burden of being positioned only with the second speaker.

We cannot be sure of the extent to which these practices can mitigate the power of the first speaker, but we would be hopeful that they can at least to some degree guard against the creation of excessive privilege through narrative control. The highlighting of this issue at the very least enables mediators to pay attention to the effects of this special case of positioning and therefore to exercise choices in how they position people through invitations to speak first or second.

An examination of the ways in which mediators' utterances position the parties in a mediation conversation poses a challenge to common notions of neutrality. If the reality is that a mediator's choice of words cannot help but establish a discursive relational world that is already imbued with value judgments, then the mediator needs to be understood as always establishing for himself or herself, and for the other parties, a position in a worldview. This position must always be to some extent a partial position in relation to some discourse or other.

How Positioning Theory Can Be Used in Mediation

Positioning theory has usefulness as an analytical or research tool. But we also want to argue for its usefulness as a practical tool in the process of mediation. Although it is not practicable to stop a conversation after every utterance and analyze the positioning that has taken place, there are some instances where introducing some questions about positioning can move a mediation forward. In particular, the brief and often speculative examination of a piece of positioning can lead to shifts in meaning between participants that make it possible to unlock impasses between them.

Let us illustrate the potential of positioning as a practice tool with an example from a mediation role play. In the scenario from which this exchange was drawn, Dennis had once been married to Marlene but they had separated after Dennis had recognized that he was gay and wanted to pursue a gay identity and lifestyle. He eventually formed a committed relationship with Mario, and after a while, they began to discuss raising a child together. Meanwhile he had remained good friends with Marlene, and she had entered into their discussions about raising a child. Marlene then agreed to carry a child for Dennis and Mario, which they would then care for and bring up. After the birth, however, Marlene decided she wanted to keep the child, and the conflict that led to mediation had ensued. Early in the mediation conversation, Dennis made this comment:

Dennis: Well . . . in the beginning we had a . . . a verbal agreement that she was going to be the catalyst to bringing Samuel into our lives . . . me and Mario's lives . . .

John was taking the part of the mediator for this role play, and as he heard this statement, his attention was taken by Dennis's use of the word *catalyst*. It sounded like a piece of discourse positioning that would have consequences for the parties' relationship and for the potential conversation that John and the parties might have in mediation. John was concerned that this usage would effectively call Marlene into a position that had little agency. She was objectified by being referred to as a catalyst, she was being spoken of only in terms of her usefulness to Dennis and Mario, and she was accorded little room for subjective speaking. John therefore chose to inquire into the effects of this example of positioning by highlighting it and asking Marlene to comment on it. By doing so, he was implicitly positioning her himself, this time as a subject rather than as an object. He was asking her to speak, to make an editorial comment or to take up a position herself.

John: Dennis used the word catalyst before . . . like he described the original understanding as being that you would be like a catalyst for them . . . for Dennis and Mario to have a child . . . how did that fit with your understanding of what the agreement was to start with . . . how does that word fit?

In response, Marlene did several things. She rejected the "catalyst" discourse. She explained how she had previously agreed to see herself in this position, and she worked to establish a new position for herself now.

Marlene: Now I just think it's horrible but at the time . . . I guess at the beginning I was wrapped up in my own career and I didn't even see a child in my future . . . so I didn't mind. . . . I wasn't in a relationship and I saw how committed him and Mario were so I . . . I didn't think there would be any harm in allowing, you know, two great men to raise a child, so I don't want to describe myself as a catalyst but as . . . the means to the end . . . if I was able to provide them what they needed that they couldn't provide for themselves, then at that time I didn't think it was a problem . . . however . . . it's all changed . . . I didn't think it was going to change.

John then turned to Dennis and invited him to respond. What John noticed in Dennis's response was that he dropped the original position call he had made and began to distance himself from it. In its place he sought to establish positions for himself and Marlene in a different discourse, one in which they are friends who trust each other:

Dennis: I used the term catalyst and it may sound cold but . . .
some time ago . . . I came to the realization that . . .
the relationship Marlene and I had together was not
working. . . . But I trusted her . . . we spent a lot of time
together . . . eventually I . . . I moved on . . . I'm very
happy in my relationship with Mario now . . . I . . . she
is right when she says that we did have a strong friendship . . . yes and I still value that friendship, that's why
I went to her instead of a person I didn't know. . . . I
went to a person I did know and did trust and did
believe in . . .

What is shown here is a small example of the negotiation of
power relations at the microscopic level. Dennis's use of objectifying language sets up a power relation. Marlene then contests
the position she is called into. Dennis then moves away from the
language in which he has positioned her as an object and invites
her into a discourse that affords her a more favorable position
with greater agency. In the process a small shift of power takes
place. Through a series of such exchanges a new relationship is
constructed between them.

The role of the mediator in this context is to open up the
possibilities for such repositioning to occur. It is achieved by hearing a piece of positioning and stopping to be curious about it. All
that is necessary to deconstruct the original positioning is to ask
Marlene a question about what a word meant to her. This inquiry
invites her to move out of a position of diminished agency and
to comment on the position call. Even in the act of making a
commentary on what the original expression meant to her, she is
repositioning herself. As she repositions herself, Dennis does so
as well. It does not always happen so smoothly. Often in conflict
situations, people have repeatedly rehearsed the positions they
are taking up, and they are more reluctant to negotiate shifts in
positioning. Still, mediators who are persistent in being curious
about people's relationship with discourse will frequently be able
to open up possibilities for making such shifts.

Discursive positioning often takes place just outside people's awareness. Its deployment of taken-for-granted aspects of
how things are means that it can happen right under people's
noses. In one instant, or in one word, people can find themselves

slotted into a narrow space and feeling uncomfortable, without quite knowing how they arrived there. It is in such moments that taking the time to stop and examine the positioning that has taken place, and the discourse that is being relied on to take a person there, can be useful. Using externalizing conversation in this inquiry can help the mediator and the disputants to avoid generating yet more anger and blame. Instead, a curious inquiry at this moment can yield a powerful deconstructive effect.

A Repositioning Exercise

To close this chapter we present an exercise that can be used to notice how an instance of positioning works and to offer a person an opportunity for repositioning. It is an exercise we have used in training contexts after introducing the concepts of positioning theory. We reproduce it here in order to show how a repositioning conversation can be structured. This exercise can be practiced by two people, one acting as the listener and the other as the speaker. In this format it might be used in a meeting with one party in a mediation, such as a caucus meeting. This same approach can also, however, be used in a joint meeting between two parties in conflict. The exercise consists of asking a set of standard questions, organized in five stages. The questions can of course be varied in response to the particulars of the story, and we are not prescribing these questions as a recipe. We also recognize that real conversations seldom follow such a linear pattern. But we have found it useful for mediators to practice this kind of structuring in order to develop a map in their own heads that shows how to build a narrative conversation for the purpose of repositioning.

Repositioning Conversation

Work in pairs: one interviewer, one interviewee.

Stage 1: Facilitating the Telling of the Story

SPEAKER

1. Think about a small example of someone offering you a position which felt uncomfortable for you in some way.

2. Tell the story of this example of how you were positioned. Explain the context in which it took place.

LISTENER

3. Facilitate the other person in telling this story, paraphrasing and asking questions along the way.

4. Ask: What position were you offered? In what relationship? In what kind of conversation? In what story or discourse?

5. Summarize, in a few sentences, the story as you have heard it.

Stage 2: Externalizing and Mapping the Effects of the Positioning

SPEAKER AND LISTENER

6. Between you, make up an externalized name for the position the speaker was called into. (It should describe a piece of language not a person.)

LISTENER ASKS THE SPEAKER

7. What were the effects at the time of this piece of positioning on you? On the relationship? On others? Were there any ongoing effects? Anything else? (Note: effects may be emotional, relational, physical, practical, financial, and so forth.)

Stage 3: Responding to the Piece of Positioning

LISTENER ASKS THE SPEAKER

8. How did you respond to this piece of positioning at the time? As you thought about it later? Now?

9. What do you think of your own responses?

10. Can you explain why?

Stage 4: Describing Preferred Positioning

LISTENER ASKS THE SPEAKER

11. How would you describe how you would prefer to be positioned? (In this discourse, in this story, or in this conversation.)

12. What is a name you could give to this position?

13. What different kind of relationship would this preferred position produce? How would you like the other person(s) to be affected?

14. What does your preferred position say about what is important to you?

15. How else have you sought to express this preference (in this context, conversation, relationship, or somewhere else)? How will you seek to express it in the future?

Debrief

Speaker and Listener Discuss Together

16. What was it like both asking the questions and answering them?

17. What emerged from the conversation that was interesting to you?

18. What might be the implications of this experience for your professional practice?

Chapter Three

Tracing Discursive Positioning Through a Conversation

In Chapter Two we introduced the idea of discursive positioning in mediation conversations. We also provided some examples of how we might use this concept as a tool for making sense of what happens in mediation. In this chapter we develop this work further through the use of an extended example. We engage with the transcribed text of a narrative mediation conversation and present an analysis of this conversation based on a set of questions that examine how people take up discursive positions in conversation and at the same time call each other into position.

This conversation does not represent a whole mediation process but rather a segment of a role-played joint meeting between a mediator and the two parties to a family mediation. The participants' interactions have been edited to focus on the relevant material and then interlaced with commentary that explains what is happening from a narrative perspective.

The commentary on the interaction details is based on a set of questions designed to serve as a tool for the analysis of the negotiated power relations in mediation interactions. They are based loosely on the research tradition known as *critical discourse analysis* (Billig, 1998; Burman & Parker, 1993; Chouliaraki & Fairclough, 1999; Fairclough, 1992; Parker, 1992), but with a particular focus on discursive positioning.

Positioning Questions

1. What position calls are being offered by the mediator and by the disputing parties in this dialogue? How are they taken up or refused?
2. What systems of meaning or discursive assumptions need to be present in order for what each participant says to have meaning?
3. What positions do participants seek to establish for themselves in this exchange?
4. What options are made available or are excluded from availability in the position calls issued?
5. To whom else (not in the room) might the participants be responding?
6. What sense of *oughtness* might be operating on participants in this conversation?
7. To what extent does the taking up of positions involve the assumption of or the compromise of possibilities for agency?
8. What alternative narratives are being opened up or closed off by the positions established in the storylines that are privileged in each person's account?
9. What kinds of power relations are being promoted within the position calls being offered and taken up?
10. How do the practices engaged in or referenced in this conversation stand in relation to conventional or normative practices?
11. What shifts in position are enabled in the course of this conversation?
12. What systems of knowledge are drawn upon or undermined in this conversation?

The Scenario

Genna and Alan had been married for six years when their relationship fell apart after Genna discovered that Alan had been having an affair for more than two years. Genna and Alan have one child, Rebecca (sometimes called Becca), who was three years old at the time of separation. Genna ended the relationship and went to live with her mother. Their divorce became final after two years. Alan's relationship with the other woman had ended soon after his separation from Genna, and he has not had a permanent or meaningful relationship since.

When Genna got a job in the area, Genna's mother, Theresa, looked after Rebecca while Genna was at work. Genna's father had died a few years before. This situation continued for four years, during which time Theresa spent more time with Rebecca than Genna did, as Genna enjoyed an active social life as well as a challenging career. The situation suited both women, as Genna enjoyed the relative freedom her singleness and work life afforded her and Theresa had become extremely attached to Rebecca.

When Rebecca was seven, Genna was killed in a car accident. It was a tragic situation for both Rebecca and Theresa, and they supported each other through a difficult time. On hearing of Genna's death, Rebecca's father, Alan, who had had virtually no contact with his daughter since his separation from Genna, decided that he should now have custody of Rebecca and stated his intentions to Theresa. Theresa was distraught and urged Alan to reconsider for everyone's sake. Alan was determined to file for custody of Rebecca but agreed with Theresa that they would seek mediation before lawyers became involved.

Mediation Conversation

As the mediation begins, Gerald, as the mediator, takes up the position of speaking first and asking the questions that drive the conversation. Theresa and Alan are in the responding position and must choose whether to take up Gerald's position calls or refuse them. Throughout, all three will have the range and type of their utterances shaped by the conventions of participation in a professional interview.

A mediator in Gerald's position carries the professional authority of his profession and, in this instance, the institutional authority of the family court into such a conversation. Although this authority may be diluted compared to a judge's authority, it is nevertheless present and will affect how his every utterance is incorporated into meaning by the parties. There is a sense in which a mediation meeting is a "preconstructed space" (Bourdieu, in a television interview cited by Chouliaraki & Fairclough, 1999, p. 99) in which the composition of the meeting and the positions the participants take up in relation to each other are constrained in advance of the particular individuals entering into the interaction. Mediators need to be aware of the power that accrues to them in this space.

Opening Exchanges

Gerald: Thank you both for being here. . . . I understand that the reason we're here is to discuss the primary caregiving arrangements for Rebecca . . . and Alan I understand that you began the proceedings to look at caregiving arrangements. . . . What I would like to do to begin is to get a fuller understanding of the circumstances that have led to this meeting to discuss the care of Rebecca and so I'd like each of you to take turns so we start with one of you, and the other, if you wouldn't mind, just being patient with me as we talk and then we will change and then I'll talk to the other person. . . . Who would like to begin?
[*Alan gestures toward Theresa to begin; she does the same in return . . .*]

Theresa: This was his idea so I think that he should begin.

Gerald: OK . . . OK, Alan? So can you give me a little background as to what has led to you wishing to have the meeting and your thinking about that.

The mediator's focus here is on process issues, such as who will speak and in what order, a fair and even turn-taking norm for interaction, both parties having a say in the process, a request for patience while the other person is talking, and a norm of conversation control through addressing comments to the mediator rather than toward each other.

Positioning in Relation to Legal Discourse

But this first conversation is not just a process conversation. The content of the conversation is already being shaped by the choice of words used. Gerald recognizes the overall legal context in which the conversation participants are positioned as part of some "proceedings," a word that carries traces of legal discursive practice. All three participants are no doubt aware of the significance of this legal discourse, through which the public power of the state can be exercised to shape the private world of the family. The public gaze (Foucault, 1980) on Alan's and Theresa's adequacy as child rearers can be expected to lie in the background of this whole mediation, and both parties can be expected to be constructing their responses in full awareness of how they are positioned by this gaze. They will be speaking as if under examination to some degree or other.

Gerald carefully chooses words to describe the subject matter of this conversation as "primary caregiving arrangements" and "the care of Rebecca." With this choice of words he establishes a position on the mediation content that is not neutral. He avoids directing the discursive traffic toward the traditional legal discourse, as the choice of a word like *custody* would do (with its potential for objectifying Rebecca as a legal chattel), and instead indicates a preference for the discourse of family relationship. This clear position on the substantive issues will shape the cues that he as a mediator attends to and selects for emphasis and the kind of outcomes he will favor. Moreover, it is a stance that places him in a position of perhaps mild antagonism to the hegemony of the legal rights discourse.

Positioning as the First Speaker

Theresa takes up the respondent position in the "proceedings." In the process she gives away the power of the first speaker (Cobb, 1993). However, in a sense she retains her position through reserving her comment and granting Alan the rights of first speaker from a position of something like benevolence. He is not just speaking first therefore. He is speaking first on her say-so. Therefore her action here is complex and should not be too hastily seen as, for example, deferring to male privilege. It can be read more as foreshadowing her voicing of a counterstatement later. She also establishes her position in relation to the whole issue through saying, "This was his idea . . ." This statement begins to position her as not wanting the current caregiving arrangements upset and calls Alan into position as the one making trouble, disrupting Rebecca's life.

Initial Statements

Alan: Well I talked to my attorney after I found out . . . that Genna had passed . . . and he suggested that the best

way to go through this with the court is to go through
this mediation . . . and so that's why we're doing this
I guess.

Gerald: What are your hopes for this meeting? . . . What would
you like to come out of it?

Alan: Well I'd like to see if there's a way that we could both
agree that I could play an important role in my daughter's life and . . . I don't wanna exclude her grandmother, I don't wanna exclude Theresa, but I just wanna
make sure I also can play a part.

Gerald: OK. Thank you. . . . Theresa . . . I'd like to hear your perspective. . . . What's happened up until this meeting with
regard to the issues around Rebecca's care?

Theresa: Well I was really surprised to hear that . . . Alan wanted
to get custody of Rebecca, simply because he hasn't
really been a major figure in her life for all these years
and . . . this has been a really difficult time for my granddaughter and I'm concerned that . . . any more changes
in her life are going to have a really very powerful and
negative impact on her . . . so I think that it's important
that we both recognize Rebecca and her life and what's
comfortable and familiar for her and that's living with
me. . . . We've been together for years and we're very
close and . . . I don't want to lose that.

Listening for Connections with a Wider Discursive Context

Alan begins by making a connection between this conversation
and the wider discursive context in which it sits. It is part of a context of conversations with attorneys, precipitated by the circumstances following the death of Rebecca's mother, Genna. Traces
(in Bakhtin's [1981] sense) of Alan's conversation with his attorney
might be expected to turn up in this conversation, as might traces
of conversations that have taken place around Genna's death, perhaps at the funeral. Alan and Theresa come into the conversation
as individuals subject to discursive influences from the significant
contexts that they inhabit. A mediator might be wise to be alert to
such influences and be ready to deconstruct them along the way.
Theresa may well bring traces of conversations with her daughter,
Genna, that have taken on particular salience since Genna's death.

Positioning the Parties in an Alternative Story of Hope

Gerald begins by asking the parties to speak about their hopes for the meeting, offering them both the same discursive position of having a voice in this conversation, and he also offers them from the start a position in an incipient alternative story. He is shaping the content of the mediation by directing their attention to positive intentions, in contrast to seeking their definitions of the problem.

Alan indicates his awareness of the discourse of exclusive legal ownership of children that lies in the background of a word like "custody," which Theresa has now used. He seeks to counter this discourse and to position his initiation of these proceedings in a generous and favorable light. He picks up on Gerald's position call to speak about "care of Rebecca," rather than custody of her, and speaks about wanting to "play an important role in my daughter's life." He invites Theresa into a relational position of agreement rather than contest, and he specifically rejects the idea of excluding Theresa. Theresa announces directly her own opposition to the discourse of legal custody and to any exclusion that might be offered to her within that discourse. She positions Alan as a proponent of that discourse, ignoring his disavowal of it, and as a potentially disruptive force in Rebecca's life. The position she establishes is of her greater entitlement owing to her knowledge of Rebecca and of Rebecca's lifestyle, her close relationship with Rebecca, and her demonstration of concern for Rebecca's well-being.

Developing the Conflict Story: Theresa's Perspective

Gerald: Alan, would it be OK with you if I spent a little time talking with Theresa about her relationship with Becca and the time they've had together so I understand that more . . . then I want to come back to you to understand more the contact you've had and what your hopes are about how that might look. . . . Would that be OK with you to do that?

Alan: Sure [*nods*].

Gerald: OK . . . well, Theresa, would you mind telling me your history with Becca over time and the nature of your relationship and how that's changed.

Theresa: Well, I'm . . . since my daughter died I've . . . my granddaughter and I have gotten even closer but we've always been very close because my daughter was just a very busy person . . . she worked hard and she played hard and she had a really active social life . . . so that Becca and I spent a lot of time together. . . . I mean I take her to dance lessons, gymnastics, we do after-school activities, she's a very active child, and I've been with her through all of that, we're really close . . . since my daughter died we've become even *closer* . . . we spend a lot of time together . . . we comfort each other . . . we understand each other . . . so it's been a really really close relationship . . . and it's helped her *and* me to get through this period . . . and I just . . . I . . . I don't want to lose that and I don't want her to lose that.

Gerald: Can you tell me some more about the amount of time that you spend with her now and how that has changed and what the current situation is. . . . I'm wanting to get a sense of the day-to-day experience that you have with Becca and where you see her.

Theresa: OK, well . . . I work full-time . . . so we get up in the morning and I make her a big breakfast, she likes big breakfasts, and I take her to school, I drop her off at school and then I go to work and after school she's enrolled in an after-school program, and then I pick her up when I get off work at five o'clock and I take her home and she does her homework at the dining room table while I'm cooking dinner . . . so we have dinner together, we go over her homework, and then usually we read together before she goes to bed . . . and then on the weekends I take her to different classes and lessons and . . . she's been taking gymnastics for a couple of years now. . . . When Genna was alive, we'd all spend Sundays together on family picnics.

Understanding Positioning and Mediator Authority

The previous segment begins with Gerald reflexively negotiating the process move of giving his attention to one party and asking the other to listen for a while. Gerald negotiates this move by asking permission, thus positioning Alan and Theresa as permission givers and therefore as having some authority in the direction the conversation will take. This move might be understood in contrast to the assumption in common professional discourse that such decisions are the prerogative of the mediator. Such a move is one of the methods with which narrative mediators seek to remain accountable to their clients and at the same time, in a small way, to disrupt the discursive assumptions through which *power/knowledge* (Foucault, 1980) operates to constitute professional privilege and authority.

Hearing Theresa's Claims of Entitlement

The conversation moves into a discussion of the history of Theresa's relationship with Rebecca. This discussion locates Theresa's entitlement claims (Winslade & Monk, 2000) in her role in Rebecca's life as it has been constituted over time. The bases of this entitlement are established in Theresa's responses as closeness (for example, "we're very close," "it's been a really really close relationship," "since my daughter died we've gotten even closer"), the amount of time they have "spent . . . together," and Theresa's knowledge of and participation in the child's daily routine. A note about ethnicity is necessary here too. The written scenario did not specify the ethnic background of the participants. But the ethnicity of the role-players themselves introduced an ethnic cultural locatedness into the conversation. Jackie, who played Theresa, is African American, and Craig, who played Alan, is Anglo American. It is therefore necessary to take account of the ethnic influences on what is being said.

Theresa's sense of entitlement, then, can also be understood within an African American cultural tradition that values *othermothering* (by grandparents, aunts, sisters, friends, or neighbors) alongside *bloodmothering*. Patricia Hill Collins (1991) argues that sharing the task of mothering among women has discursive support in both West African cultures and African American cultural traditions. However, Theresa's claims of entitlement, although legitimated within African American cultural discourse, may well be muted in their expression because of her knowledge that these claims do not carry much legitimate weight for her white former son-in-law and are unlikely to be recognized by the courts.

In the next set of exchanges Gerald engages with Theresa about the events surrounding the death of her daughter and how this has affected her and her grandchild. He seeks to learn about the impact of these events on Theresa's role in caring for Rebecca.

Gerald: And so, how involved have you been in relation to Becca's education and her health and well-being. What role have you played in that?

Theresa: Well, her mom and I kind of shared that, we'd both go to parents' meetings and conferences at the school . . . but Genna's life was very busy so when she wasn't available then I would attend those things myself . . . but there were times when we both went . . . and my daughter also enrolled her in the gymnastics classes . . . sometimes she took her but generally I took her . . . so I've been very much involved in all aspects of Becca's life.

Gerald: OK, what are you aware of in terms of Alan's contact with Rebecca . . . from your perspective . . . how have you seen that from the way you look at things?

Theresa: Alan hasn't had a lot of contact with her since he and my daughter separated. He does remember her birthday every year and he's called the house a couple of times and spoken to her . . . not very often but as far as actual physical contact, there hasn't really been a lot that.

Now the daily picture of Rebecca's life with Theresa is widened with reference to other contexts of her life. The conversation focuses mainly on her schooling. Theresa positions herself within the discourse of the *good parent*, pointing out her participation in parent-teacher conferences and taking the child to extracurricular activities like gymnastics, and she uses these examples to extend her entitlement claims. The basis for her entitlement claim is summarized as being "very much involved in all aspects of Becca's life." Theresa's discursive strategy is built around her contrasting of her involvement with Alan's lack of involvement. The more she positions herself as involved, the more she positions Alan as uninvolved. Gerald anticipates her move to some extent by asking for her "perspective" on Alan's "contact" (his synonym for involvement) with Rebecca.

The phrase "from your perspective" establishes the possibility of differences in perspective. It implies the limited truth value of any single perspective, and it sets up the opportunity for a comparison of perspectives as the conversation continues. Theresa, after making her own claims of entitlement very explicit, cedes a little legitimacy to Alan's entitlement to participate in Rebecca's life. But Theresa is not yet in a place where she can do that with comfort. She does not have enough information to counter the story of Alan's lack of involvement, the story that currently makes the most sense to her. Alan's lack of involvement is tempered with references to some exceptions to it (birthday cards and phone calls), but after referring to these exceptions she returns to stressing the story of Alan's uninvolvement.

Gerald's posture in this stage of the mediation is that of a highly curious, inquisitive interviewer or researcher. He is positioning Theresa (and later Alan) as key informants, with stories to tell that are of intrinsic interest to him. So he asks many questions to enrich these stories. Alan and Theresa are called to be tellers of stories or authors, each with her or his own interpretive slant.

Developing the Conflict Story: Alan's Perspective

Gerald now seeks to understand Alan's perspective on his involvement with Rebecca. Alan describes an intimate and close involvement with his daughter when she was a very young child and cites numerous examples of his prominent parenting role. He then turns to describing the difficulties and conflicts he experienced with Genna when they were married. He describes needing to leave Genna and the enormous conflict that unfolded between them. He also begins to explain why he then pulled away from his prominent parenting role with his daughter.

Gerald: OK . . . so now I'd like to catch up with Alan a little. . . .
Can you tell me a little about your involvement with your daughter since her birth?

Alan: Yeah, we were very close. . . . Since the beginning . . .
we had a real good physical bond and we would go out,
I remember merry-go-rounds a lot when she was really small . . . and she used to like to cuddle with me a lot . . .

and I used to read to her a lot . . . and we had a lot of good times. . . . Unfortunately it was complicated by my relationship with my ex.

Gerald: With Genna?

Alan: Yeah, Genna actually . . . she had a different lifestyle, a different way of wanting to spend her time. She would want to go out in the evening, maybe two, three, four times a week to a movie or to a play, she thought . . . it's boring just to stay at home. . . . I was happy just to have a family, to stay home with our daughter, but I tried to go out, more than I would have wanted to, but actually with my daughter, the two of us used to do a lot of father-daughter sorts of things, rough-and-tumble . . . and I really felt a good strong connection. Sometimes it was hard because Genna would get ticked off with me because . . . "What's wrong with going out? Why don't you wanna do that?" . . . but I would say to her, "Look, I'm fine with you just going out by yourself," because I actually enjoyed spending time just directly with Rebecca.

Gerald: So at that point when you were together you had a *lot* of involvement with Rebecca . . . and that changed, I understand, is that right, given what Theresa has described happening?

Alan: Well, yeah, it's a complicated thing because . . . [*exhales*] Genna and I . . . we didn't really get along and she wasn't really . . . that available . . . and I guess . . . she was always wanting to do things, do, do, do, and so she really wasn't very nice to be around and she was angry with me a lot and I wound up meeting somebody else and we kind of connected . . . and then everything sort of went downhill as far as my relationship with Rebecca from that point on . . . my heart was broken . . . but every time I tried to talk to Genna reasonably about me seeing Rebecca she would just give me so much grief . . . "Oh, so you think you have time for her when you have your . . . your lover" [*mocking tone*]. . . . She would just give me such grief that it just became impossible.

Gerald: So how did that affect your relationship with Rebecca . . . What happened in terms of your contact with her after that had happened?

Alan: Well, we were living apart obviously at that point and . . . [*exhales strongly*] I asked her to . . . I wanted to see Rebecca . . . and I started to come by and Genna just made all kinds of threats and she would yell and become hysterical and scream at me and . . . it just became too difficult. . . . My attorney advised that I didn't really have much legal recourse, as much as I thought . . . I should fight for this, but he said there's not . . .you're not going to be . . . there's nothing much you're gonna gain with this. . . .

Hearing Alan's Claims of Entitlement

In this piece of conversation the basis for Alan's claims of entitlement to expand his role in Rebecca's life is explored. Gerald uses the word "involvement," echoing Theresa's "very much involved," as he invites Alan to develop his own claim to care for Rebecca. Picking up from Gerald's cue and perhaps also from Theresa's claim, Alan makes his own pitch on the basis of emotional and physical closeness. He establishes a position in relation to Rebecca's early years before the separation between him and Genna. He uses the word "bond," which carries a possible trace of an essential psychological link between family members, as described in Bowlby's (1969–1980) widely popularized attachment theory. His physical contact with his daughter is cited as an expression of this bond in the words "cuddle with me a lot" and "rough-and-tumble" (an acceptable description for affectionate play that does not carry overtones of being too "effeminate" within the norms of male culture).

Alan's Positioning of Genna

Next Alan goes on to account for his subsequent lack of expression of the "bond" that he has just argued for. He uses the rhetorical strategy of positioning his recently deceased ex-wife Genna as an obstacle to the ongoing development of his bond with his daughter. This is risky in front of Theresa, who can be expected to still be tender in her grief for her dead daughter. He could anger Theresa through speaking ill of the dead. Note also, in passing, the use of the objectifying, depersonalizing shorthand "my ex" and Gerald's refusal of this term in his immediate referral to Genna by name. But Alan is also aware of the possibility of alienating Theresa and adopts a number of discursive tactics to deflect this danger. He refers to Genna a little euphemistically as having a "different lifestyle." This description matches Theresa's earlier one in its softening of Genna's agency. Saying that Genna "had a different lifestyle" is a weaker statement about behavior than saying that she "chose a different lifestyle," for example, and it suggests that any ill effects on Rebecca from this lifestyle are scarcely Genna's responsibility. Alan goes on to say that Genna was not "nice to be around." He positions her as a something of a *bad mother*, one who wanted to go out all the time rather than adopt a norm of domesticity and personal sacrifice, and himself as the *good father*, one who, in contrast, was willing to do so and even "enjoyed" spending time with his young daughter. However, he does this without appearing to express a direct judgment of Genna. Then he slowly builds a picture of Genna as often unreasonably angry. At first she is described mildly as "ticked off" with him. This intensifies into a slightly euphemistic "we didn't really get along," followed by a more direct "she was angry with me a lot." She is portrayed as using bitter sarcasm, ("Oh, so you think you have time for her when you have your . . . your lover") and finally as one who "just made all kinds of threats" and who "would yell and become hysterical and scream at me." The ground for these strong statements has been carefully prepared with the earlier, more neutral descriptions. But in the end, Alan does deploy the common gendered strategy of rendering a woman's concerns illegitimate through referring to them as "hysterical."

In the process, Alan drops into the conversation the information about his own affair with another woman. This is constructed as the most natural thing in the world in the context of his and Genna's not getting along and her not being "available." He "wound up meeting somebody else" suggests a sequence of events over which he has little control, and "we kind of connected" also sounds positive, natural, and innocent of any hurtful intent or, indeed, deliberate planning. After that "everything sort of went downhill," as he describes it, a little vaguely. There is nothing in this description that recognizes his own actions as disqualifying his entitlements as a father, a discursive stance that Genna obviously took. He reverses the usual discursive position of the cuckolded wife as brokenhearted by claiming for himself that his "heart was broken." His use of the expression "she would just give me such grief" is interesting too. The image produced is of him as sad in response to anger. It perhaps amounts to claiming the morally superior position of being sad and long-suffering in the face of unreasonable anger.

Then Alan speaks about his desire to see his daughter after his separation from Genna. He says, "I started to come by," positioning himself as taking action and Genna as responding. There is no mention of an agreement for him to see his daughter. Did he just "come by" unannounced and take Genna by surprise, giving her little dialogical space? Or was she unwilling to negotiate and therefore leaving him without dialogical options? It is not completely clear. He continues by saying:

Alan: Well listen . . . it would really have been not in Rebecca's interest for me to try and force myself into the situation. Genna could really just fly off the handle and . . . she was really crazy and I didn't want my daughter to be subjected to all that. . . . I've heard . . . I've read books and I've seen talk shows where they talk about how you shouldn't argue in front of your daughter and . . . Genna didn't mind but, if I was trying to force the issue to see her, it really would have screwed up Rebecca big time.

Here, some popular psychological discourse enters into the conversation. Alan is responding, in both his actions and his account of his actions, to many conversations he has heard about how a good parent should take responsibility for the psychological health of children. He wants to avoid creating a traumatic childhood experience for Rebecca and so shapes his own decisions in response to injunctions such as "you shouldn't argue in front of your daughter" because you will screw her up. He references television "talk shows" as a recent development in the technologies of disciplinary power (Foucault, 1978) that serve the purpose of constituting normal parental behavior and family relations. Such shows subject some volunteers to a public gaze as a spectacle to inform the general public discourse. They often use psychological experts to pronounce on the norms of how people should behave. Such pronouncements are clearly in the background of Alan's comments here.

Alan moves quickly back to his own agenda of portraying Genna as a serious obstacle to his relationship with his daughter. He positions himself as the reasonable parent, concerned to avoid conflict, and constructs Genna as the active agent who is interfering and blocking. He constructs himself as the victim of her actions and implicitly calls for sympathy for his past victim position and for his appeal for justice in the present. Nevertheless, plot elements in a conflict story can become resources to be deployed in the emergence of an alternative story. Alan's and Theresa's different understandings of the conflict and what each should do in the face of it can be explored. In the following discussion, the mediator helps to open up opportunities for a new story to develop in the midst of the dialogue of the conflict story.

Opening Space for an Alternative Story

Gerald: Theresa, I'd like to come back to you. From your perspective, what's your relationship and connection with Alan? How's that unfolded and changed and how is it today?

Theresa: I feel like Alan just tends to take the easy way out . . . maybe he just doesn't want to engage in conflict . . . he's saying he didn't want to have conflict in front of Becca but I think that if he loved his daughter then he would have fought to see her. [*Alan shakes his head in disagreement.*] He knows that when he called the house . . . whenever *I* answered the phone I would let him talk to her and I think if he had asked me to make arrangements to bring her to a park or something so he could have seen her I would have done that. I'm just angry because he *didn't* do that, because he *didn't* try and see her and because he *hasn't* been a part of her life. Now all of a sudden he wants to take her and I just don't think it's fair.

Here, for the first time, Gerald invites direct comment from one party about the entitlement claims of the other. Theresa is invited to respond to what Alan has been saying. She does so by reacting strongly and directly to his words. She dismisses his reasons for not pursuing contact with Rebecca over Genna's objections as taking "the easy way out." She almost implies that he is a wimp, a gendered term for a man who lacks courage in a fight and is therefore worthy of some degree of contempt. Her logic for this criticism is interesting. She says that "if he loved his daughter he would have fought to see her." What are the discursive origins of this logic? Perhaps she is drawing from a Romantic discourse of the male hero walking over hot coals for his beloved (even if the beloved is a child). Perhaps she is thinking more in terms of a female image of the lioness fighting for her cubs, an image often called up approvingly to account for a woman's fierceness in defense of her children. It is one of the situations where women are not only allowed but expected to show aggression. To do so marks a female as a "true" woman. Such discourse sets a standard by which a woman's behavior might be assessed. But here she would be using it to assess a man's behavior. She thus positions Alan's parenting instincts as inferior to her instinctual response as a woman. Men are usually expected to show courage and aggression in different arenas and to be willing to sacrifice their devotion to their children for some wider public cause. However, Alan has made his claim to be entitled to be part of Rebecca's life on the basis of emotional intimacy and on the basis of being more maternal in his instincts than Rebecca's mother was. So he is being judged here on criteria normally reserved for women.

In the end, after expressing anger on this basis, Theresa reiterates her argument that Alan's entitlement claims are not legitimate because he has not been part of Rebecca's life. His desire to be part of it now is characterized as "all of a sudden," suggesting that he is not consistent and trustworthy. Finally, Theresa claims that despite Alan's assurances to the contrary, "he wants to take" Rebecca, raising once again the discourse of legal ownership of children as chattels.

Engaging in Double Listening

However, despite the strength and anger of these statements there is another voice in the midst of Theresa's utterance. It is a less polarizing voice and one that opens up a possibility that her anger is not necessarily her final position and that options other than an adversarial battle are still possible. In an earlier exchange she referred to her willingness to allow Alan to speak on the phone with Rebecca and to arrange a meeting between them both in a park. A narrative mediator needs to be on the alert for such gaps in a conflict story and ready to examine their possible significance. Gerald begins to do this in this next exchange.

Gerald: Can you think of a time where the connection with Alan was under easier circumstances . . . at an earlier point?

Theresa: Oh sure . . . when he and Genna were together . . . I babysat for them when they went out and I think things were fine . . . and he was close to his daughter when she was young . . . but . . . I think that I've got more distant from him because he's distanced himself from his daughter . . . and that angers me. [*She looks directly at Alan.*]

Gerald is seeking the inclusion of some different discursive positions in the relationship history of Theresa and Alan. Such positions have the potential to become the basis for a way forward in this conflict. However, the conflict story is still powerful enough and the alternative positions are not yet strong enough for a new story to get off the ground. Theresa acknowledges the story of difference and then quickly reasserts the story of conflict.

Gerald: And your perspective on conflict was that you saw it was important for Alan to fight and challenge and engage in the conflict with Genna . . . to declare his ongoing love for Becca. [*Alan shakes his head in disagreement.*]

Theresa: Exactly.

Gerald: So your idea of conflict is of meeting it and working through it to declare your passion.

Theresa: I think so . . . because I think the message he gave to his daughter was that she wasn't worth fighting for. [*Alan is shaking his head throughout Theresa's utterance.*]

Gerald: Uh huh . . . and yet for you, Alan, it's very clear that fighting and . . . I sense a very painful set of

> entanglements and conflict that you experienced
> with Genna had felt far too distressing to put you and
> Rebecca in, and when you weighed everything up, you
> made a decision to step back . . . is that accurate?

Alan: Yeah, I mean at the end it was like a war zone . . . and
there's no point when two people are just right in each
other's faces . . . there's nothing you can do.

Gerald: Right . . . so one important piece in this conversation is
about your different views around conflict and what can
be done with that.

Positioning in Relation to the Discourses of Conflict Itself

It has become apparent to Gerald that the two parties are positioned differently within a discourse about conflict itself. In this
exchange with both parties, he engages in a brief deconstructive
inquiry into the meanings of conflict that each is operating from.
They are drawing on military metaphors or perhaps the metaphors of street fights. Alan even compares conflict with Genna to
a "war zone." There are codes of behavior that go with any context of conflict. What is the honorable way to behave in a conflict? Is it to make a stand on principle and fight with "passion,"
(a word Gerald used and Theresa agreed with)? Or is it to avoid
the collateral damage of battle and to withdraw (Alan's preferred
strategy)? With different discursive norms in place, Theresa's and
Alan's constructions of their own and of each other's positions
result in very different moral interpretations, especially of Alan's
actions. This piece of deconstructive inquiry might be said to
contribute to the overall purpose of mediation by loosening the
grip of these discursive positions. Once they have been acknowledged to be "different views around conflict," they can no longer do their divisive work behind the scenes. They may still be
influential, but their influence is at least more open to scrutiny
than it was. Gerald is careful to respectfully construct both viewpoints as conscious and agentic choices rather than as reactions
to others' actions. Theresa is described as actively "meeting" conflict, "working through it," and "declaring [her] passion." Alan is
described as having "weighed everything up" and having "made
a decision to step back." Implicitly, Gerald is externalizing the

conflict and inviting each of the parties to name and then negotiate his or her own style of relationship with it. This move positions them in a conversation different from one in which each
may focus on the other as the source of the conflict.

Positioning in a Story of Cooperation: Theresa's Response

Gerald: What I'm wanting to know is where you're at right at
this moment in terms of how much room each of you
see you should have as caregivers in Rebecca's life. I
hear you [*looks at Theresa*] saying earlier that you would,
if Alan was talking to you directly on the telephone, you
would definitely not hang up, in fact on the contrary
you would make efforts for Becca to be able to meet
with Alan in the park and have time with him, and there
have been periods of time when you have been very
supportive of that contact . . . and I hear you [*turning
to Alan*] say that grandmothers are very important in
children's lives [*Alan nods*]. This could be an important
relationship to foster for Rebecca. Is that accurate?

Alan: That's right.

Gerald: I just want to know right now . . . acknowledging that
things can change . . . what ideas you have about one
another having involvement with Rebecca?

Theresa: Well, I'm totally against him having custody of
Rebecca . . . It's just too drastic a change for a child to
go through . . . and I don't think he's equipped to deal
with a child . . . I don't think he has a clue what it's like
to raise a little girl. . . . What's he going to do with her
hair? I mean this is a child with bushy African hair, this
is a white man . . . what's he going to do with that? Do
you [*to Alan*] know what her favorite color is? Or what
toys she takes to bed with her at night? These are things
that are part of our everyday life and he has no clue
about. . . . So I don't mind him having contact with her
but I think it should be just a few hours every couple of
weeks or something [*Alan shakes his head*] because I don't
think Rebecca deserves to have her whole world turned
upside down cause suddenly he's decided to be a father.

In this segment Gerald continues his pursuit of some relational basis for cooperation and agreement between Theresa and Alan. Having not found a strong enough story of this in their relational history, he moves to the future. He attempts to move past the mouthing of polarizing slogans by addressing his question to the complexities of daily life. In support of this strategy he cites two examples from what Theresa and Alan each have said that suggest more inclusive positioning of the other. These are unique outcomes (White & Epston, 1990; White, 2007; Winslade & Monk, 2000) in relation to the conflict story.

However, even though Alan offers brief agreement with the idea that Gerald is developing, Theresa has not yet finished arguing her claim to be entitled to have the major role in Rebecca's life. So she refuses the conciliatory position Gerald offers her and instead goes back on the offensive by throwing up the word "custody" again and establishing her position in reaction to it. Then she goes on to elaborate some of the details that Gerald was asking for, not in support of a shared story but in support of her own entitlement claim. Moreover, she introduces some new elements to this claim. For the first time, she raises an argument based on racial and cultural grounds (she is African American and her granddaughter is a biracial child). She also extends her earlier statements of entitlement based on her intimate knowledge of the details of Rebecca's life. In the end she does offer a glimpse of the kind of vision that Gerald was asking for. She speaks about a role for Alan in Rebecca's life, but uses the term "contact," which positions him more in the role of occasional visitor than in the role of responsible caregiver. Alan's moves to seek greater involvement in his daughter's life are seen as resulting in Rebecca's "whole world [being] turned upside down" and are characterized as a sudden, whimsical decision. The positions offered to Alan in these descriptions are those of a parent who cannot be relied upon and who casually and insensitively disrupts his daughter's life.

Positioning in a Story of Cooperation: Alan's Response

Gerald: Alan, what's your perspective on the kind of involvement that each of you would have in Rebecca's life right now?

Alan: Oh, I'd like to see something more half and half really. What [Theresa] said about [Becca's] African American roots is true and the hair and those kinds of things, but there are also things I can offer her as a father that no grandmother can offer and I know how much she loves me and that it's really important for a little girl to have a father. No one else can take the place of that and, sure, it will take a while for us to get back to where we were but I'm confident that we can. The love is there, the bond is there, and it will happen.

Gerald: So what would having more involvement look like?

Alan: Well, I think it would be nice to have the three of us do things together . . . go to the beach, and then I could learn from some of the things that we do together about how Theresa is with her granddaughter. I can learn about some of her up-to-the-minute interests. I'm pretty good at picking up on things . . . so I think to ease into it, it would be good to do some things together.

Gerald: What would you imagine in terms of the hours that would be involved?

Alan: Well . . . maybe to start with I could meet with her for a few hours a few times a week.

Here, Gerald pursues with Alan the same kind of question he asked Theresa earlier. But Alan does not stay with answering Gerald's question for long. The conflict story still exerts a powerful pull on him and he begins to respond more to Theresa's previous utterance than to Gerald's question. There is a concessionary acknowledgment of Theresa's entitlements on the basis of race, which is then countered with a reference to the special entitlements based on biological fatherhood, backed up with more assertions of emotional closeness. The discursive argument that male role models are essential for children is produced to support Alan's claims. There is a popular psychological knowledge to this effect, often based on an uncritical acceptance of gendered social roles and sometimes used to render inadequate the work done by mothers (Silverstein & Rashbaum, 1995).

Gerald ignores the reignition of the conflict story and the inflammatory rhetoric that has gone before and pursues the development of a story of inclusion. He does this by bypassing the claims of entitlement as a basis for a tug-of-war over Rebecca's life and asks about the possible future Alan is constructing on the basis of these entitlements. He seeks details (hours, activities, purposes) about the kind of contact with Rebecca that Alan would prefer. Such details serve the purpose of developing greater coherence (Cobb, 1994) in the story of Alan's involvement with Rebecca. In the process Gerald constructs with Alan a story of the gradual development of relationship, expressed in a modest-sounding way.

The meaning of what Alan is seeking from this conversation begins to shift at this point, and it is likely that Theresa also begins to experience a shift. He gets to hear himself detail a story of future possibility that now starts to include some of Theresa's expressed concerns (such as not to introduce large, sudden changes into Rebecca's life). She gets to hear a story of future possibility that does not resemble the ones she feared on Rebecca's behalf (for example, the sudden, disruptive uprooting of a child from what is familiar to her).

Constructing a Joint Story Around the New Opening

Gerald now moves back to Theresa to explore the possibility of developing a joint story around what is now an opening to some relational repositioning between Alan and Theresa.

Gerald: There's something occurring to me as I'm hearing both of you talk. I've been involved for a number of years as a mediator working with disputes between people about caregiving arrangements for children . . . and I'm just struck by each of you. Despite all you've gone through, there's some appreciation of the other and their role in Becca's life but more than that . . . you, Alan, were saying that you felt comfortable spending time with Theresa for periods of time in the weekend to start to slowly connect with her [*Alan nods*] and to learn to be in Rebecca's life again and an openness to engaging with Theresa in a fuller way than you have in the past. And I hear you [*turning to Theresa*] also say that despite everything that happened with your daughter and I'm sure the conflicts that you witnessed firsthand [*Theresa nods*] and the affair and so on . . . despite all of that you still felt like you could open your heart enough to Alan for him to telephone Becca and that *you* were prepared to make space and time for him to be with Becca and I'm really struck by that recognition of the importance of each of you in Becca's life. I'm just wondering how come it's like that because oftentimes the kind of conflicts and the pain that you're experiencing now destroys those kind of connections. Would you mind telling me a little bit how that hasn't been just written off completely?

Positioning Through Summarizing

At this point Gerald makes a little speech. It is a summary made with the purpose in mind of helping develop a joint narrative about the emerging conversation. He wants to capitalize on the unique outcome that has happened—the move that both parties have made into a story that positions them more as cooperative with each other. Treating this move as an event on the landscape of action (Bruner, 1986; White, 1992; Winslade & Monk, 2000), he seeks to develop meaning around it on the landscape of consciousness. He wants to develop its significance in a way that will encourage the parties to take more notice of it. The moves here are worth close attention.

First, Gerald uses a nominalization to downplay a presentation of himself as an expert interpreter. He says, somewhat vaguely, there is "something occurring to him," as if he were slowly catching up from behind, rather than directly saying, "I think this is what you are both saying . . ." Theresa and Alan are thus positioned as informing him rather than the other way round. Then a story of appreciation and respect is plucked out of the numerous other stories that have been spoken about during the conversation so far. This is constructed in Gerald's utterance as the central story by its placement in a clause in the foreground of the grammatical construction. The conflict story that has dominated both parties' communications so far is relegated (three times) to a clause in the background headed by the word "despite." In the foreground in the third instance is placed the agentive statement, "you still felt like you could open your heart enough." The background aspects introduced by the word "despite" are framed as annoying and unfortunate restraints on the emergence of a more heroic story of courage and strength of purpose in the interests of cooperation. Gerald offers both Alan and Theresa different positions in relation to the conflict itself (that is, different from how they have positioned each other) and in relation to the substantive issues. Alan and Theresa are constructed as holding onto some positive things in the face of adversity, rather than as polarized around a problem to be solved. In this utterance the problem recedes rather than looms larger.

Positioning the Parties as Agents

Having developed briefly a plausible story in this regard, Gerald asks a question that presupposes the story that he has just told. He asks Theresa and Alan to theorize about and explain how they have managed to do this. Thus they are positioned as agents in the construction of this alternative story and as editorial commentators on a selected aspect of their own experience. Gerald has been offering some editorial comment himself, and he asks them to join him in this. Alan and Theresa are also positioned in this summary as exceptional people in comparison to some unnamed others who would not be able to do this, who would have had their best intentions swamped by the events that Theresa and Alan have been through.

Persisting with the Story of Cooperation

The question now becomes whether Alan and Theresa will take up the positions Gerald is inviting them into or whether the conflict story will pull them back into its orbit. Gerald is persistent though in following up on the story of possible cooperation.

Gerald: So despite the fact that you're really clear about what Becca's needs are right now in terms of stability and routine and familiarity you still have some openness to Alan being present in some way . . . is that accurate?

Theresa: Yeah.

Gerald: What's your sense of what Alan might add to Becca's life?

Theresa: Well she's a biracial child and so I think it's important for her to know her heritage on both sides . . . so that's something that he can provide in her life . . . and I think the child needs a male role model . . . and so I'm sure he's able to do that or I think he is . . . and I think it will give her a certain amount of balance to have a loving parent now that Genna's gone . . . I think those are the important things.

Gerald: Do you see Alan as a loving parent?

Theresa: That's my hope. I'm not sure; he's going to have to demonstrate that . . .

This time Theresa takes up the position that Gerald offers her. Gerald seeks to build on it by asking a further question directed toward expanding the story of Alan's possible inclusion in her relationship with Rebecca. She responds with reference to a discourse about the psychological importance of knowing one's cultural heritage. Then she cites the same discourse that Alan has already alluded to about the necessity of positive male role models for healthy psychological development. And Alan is described as being able to "provide" something in Rebecca's life, an expression that is faintly evocative of the conventional male role in the patriarchal family—that of *provider.*

Seizing on an Opening

At this point Theresa drops into her utterance a comment about Alan as a "loving parent." The moment is significant and Gerald does not let it pass. He asks more about the significance of this expression. In so doing he invites Theresa to perform meaning around it, to step further into a commitment to these words and to extend the story of cooperation and mutual respect another pace forward.

Gerald: A lot of parents . . . or grandparents in a circumstance like you have . . . could easily close their hearts right off and close that connection right off and I'm wondering what is it that Alan's done over the years, despite the fact that he's had very little contact with her, that's kept alive in you the idea that he has the potential to be a loving parent—a good father to Becca. Are there things that you've seen in Alan or things he's done despite the little contact?

Theresa: Well, I think his relationship with her when she was
younger . . . they were very close and I think the potential
is there for them to do that again. He hasn't actively
done anything to harm her. He's just been not active in
her life. So I see he's trying to correct that at this point.

Gerald: Is that a desirable move from your perspective?

Theresa: It's *late* . . . it's late . . . it's just really late . . .

Gerald: But not *too* late . . . given all the other things that you've
said.

Theresa: I think that the timing of it limits just how close he's
gonna be able to get. . . . I think he's missed a *really*
important part of her life . . . and that pisses me off . . .
that she's missed that time with him . . . but no, you're
right, it's not *too* late for him to have some kind of a
relationship with her. There are limits to how much,
how close it can be just because he's messed up.

Inviting an Answer from a Position Within the New Story

Gerald goes on to ask Theresa to speculate about Alan's qualities as a parent and to relate these qualities to events she has
witnessed. He is doing double listening here in order to bring
forward a story that otherwise would remain somewhat masked
behind the story of relationship loss. Gerald positions Theresa
carefully in the story of cooperation that she has been referencing and asks her to respond from there. His question asks her to
generate new meanings, rather than simply to report on what has
happened. It also positions Theresa in a place of respect. First,
Gerald speaks of her as an exception to his knowledge of other
parents because she could "easily close her heart" yet she has
not. The inference is that Gerald sees her as openhearted. He
offers her this new identity construction, one that she can step
into simply by answering the question, and he does it by contrasting this position with what can safely be expected to be an unat-
tractive position (someone who is coldhearted and quickly closes
off connections with others). Second, he corrects his reference to
"parents" to include "grandparents," such as Theresa. This is an
effort to ensure that his language does not inadvertently create a
position of exclusion for her.

Moreover, let us look more closely at the step that she is being invited to take. It is to do what she has done previously, "kept alive . . . the idea" that Alan has the "potential" to be a "loving parent" and a "good father," and then to search through her memory for experiences that would corroborate this description. This is such a small step that it is hard to refuse. To do so could appear churlish and carries the risk that she could be called cold-hearted. Theresa does not refuse the invitation. She steps into the position of constructing Alan as a potential parent, referencing his relationship with Rebecca when she was young and adding that Alan has not done Rebecca any harm.

The dominant conflict story asserts itself still in her reference to Alan's lack of presence in his daughter's life, indicating a degree of ambivalence in her responses. She is being tugged by two competing stories of Alan. The moment is a delicate one for the future direction of this conversation. However, she swings back to the story of potential cooperation and assigns a motive to Alan as currently trying to correct his past failures. There is even a hint of a more positive interpretation of Alan's distance from Rebecca. It has at least prevented harm. Gerald picks up on Theresa's concession and invites her to evaluate it, to take a position in relation to it. Is it desirable or not? This is another invitation to take a step forward into a relational position that will include Alan in the future in a positive fashion. Theresa teeters on the edge of responding to this invitation. It is "late," she equivocates. Gerald agrees but then suggests it is "not too late," which keeps the ambivalence alive. In the end Theresa opts for the idea that she can envisage Alan having a positive relationship with his daughter. Her statement to this effect includes some comments that refer to the dominant story but also clearly and decisively opens up space for a negotiation of how this can happen. She has stepped into a position in a new story at this point. The rest of the conversation will amount to an effort to elaborate this story.

Fashioning a Narrative of Joint Care for Rebecca

In the next stage of the mediation the narrative of Alan's and Theresa's joint care for Rebecca is being slowly fashioned. Gerald is pursuing the story construction by asking questions that press for details about small developmental increments. In each question Theresa is invited further into supporting the story of Alan's involvement. And on each occasion she does take up this position, albeit with some caution and careful thought about the consequences. She still has a genuine sense of dilemma, and she continues to be protective of Rebecca.

Gerald continues by asking Theresa about whether she is willing to speak to Rebecca about how Alan wants to become more involved in her life and to ask Rebecca if she is willing to allow this. Theresa is willing and Gerald asks further whether when she does so she will speak with encouragement in her voice or discouragement. Theresa makes it clear that she would not be discouraging. Gerald then turns to Alan.

Gerald: Alan, what are you making of the conversation we're having right now.

Alan: I really liked that you asked that because that's exactly the fear that I had—that she would be discouraging. . . . She could stack the cards really easily if she chose to. . . . If she asks that in a positive way and tells [Becca] how much I really love her and want to see her . . . I think that at least it's a fair chance for her to answer.

Gerald: What have you heard about what Theresa has said about you being in Becca's life?

Alan: That she doesn't want to upset the applecart really quickly and disrupt Rebecca's world and I can understand that. That's why I suggested that we start by doing things together.

Gerald: Did you hear her seeing the value of you being involved in Rebecca's life as a father?

Alan: I heard some of that.

Gerald: What was it like to hear that from Theresa?

Alan: Well, I would have enjoyed hearing a little bit more [*smiles*] but what I did hear was nice.

Moving from the Subjunctive to the Indicative

In an effort to knit the story of cooperation together further, Gerald asks Alan a series of questions that invite him to make meaning out of Theresa's preceding utterances. In this way the story that described a future possibility can be woven into the present reality. It is noticeable that the mood is not subjunctive now but indicative. What was talked about first in the tentative language of possibility is now being discussed in the language of material reality. Talk of what could possibly be realized, through its very utterance as a discursive event, now can be talked about as having happened. This does not yet mean that the imagined conversation between Theresa and Rebecca has taken place (become a reality), but the likelihood that it will is increased through discussion of the meanings that not only would ensue if it did take place but that are already ensuing just through its being envisaged.

However, the old story of conflict and distrust can still reappear. Alan attributes Theresa's cautious, protective comments on Rebecca's behalf to an underlying concern, supporting this with reference to his own "fear." One consequence here is that the old story blinds Alan to a possible interpretation of Theresa as a practicing caregiver, appropriately protecting her granddaughter in a time of fragility. The interpretation he is persuaded by constructs her more as acting selfishly out of her own emotional disposition than as acting altruistically out of her assessment of what is important for Rebecca. This construction threatens the delicate new story, and Gerald is deliberate and persistent in steering the conversation back to a basis on which the new story can continue to develop. He asks a specific question about whether Alan has heard Theresa's (cautious) support of Alan's inclusion in Rebecca's life. He has. So Gerald asks about the significance of this to Alan. This time Alan is positioned as editorial commentator.

Arranging for Further Discussion

Gerald: So what are the next steps?

Theresa: [*To Alan*] I guess . . . looking at our schedules and setting a tentative time . . . assuming that Becca goes along with it, and then for me to talk to her and make arrangements when you'll call . . . after I've talked to her.

Alan: [*To Theresa*] Sounds good. We could go to the beach. It's supposed to be really nice this weekend. I can get some boogie boards and get there early to get a nice space and everything.

Theresa: [*To Alan*] OK, we'd have to do that on Sunday because she has gymnastics on Saturday.

Alan: [*To Theresa*] That's fine.

Gerald: I hear you both starting to talk with one another about planning this meeting and I'm also aware that when we began this meeting what was on the table was more around the primary caregiving arrangements and I'm wondering whether the two of you, in the spirit that you've presented today, will look at the situation one step at a time and look at the chance of having a weekend experience for a couple of hours, and that we meet together again to talk through the nature of an ongoing caregiving relationship. I just want to recognize your willingness to take a step in a very gradual and careful way. . . . What are your thoughts about deciding to have another meeting . . . to talk more about the nature of ongoing arrangements?

Alan: You know it's been four years since I really had the opportunity to see her and so a few weeks or months transition is not gonna be that big a deal and so I'm fine with going slow. . . . [*To Theresa*] I don't wanna cause disruption for Rebecca and I realize that you have a lot of history together . . . and I frankly, from what you've said today, I could learn from what you've done with her . . .

Theresa: Yeah . . . in the back of my mind though I still have the concern that eventually you're going to try and take her away from me . . . I still have that.

Alan: I have no desire to take her away from you. . . . I guess I would hope that in the coming weeks and months you'll see what kind of provider I can actually be and that I'm not out to push you aside . . . maybe I could prove that to you . . . that would be my hope.

Theresa: We'll see.

Gerald: We'll see . . . so can we make another appointment to . . . discuss the caregiving plan for Becca and . . . we'll schedule that for our next meeting.

Alan: Sounds good.

Theresa: OK.

In this final segment of the conversation the details of time and place for the agreed-upon reconnection meeting are beginning to be sorted out. Because the relational narrative context for these details has been carefully established, it does not appear to be difficult to achieve agreement. The larger picture of caregiving for Rebecca, however, is still not settled. This needs to be acknowledged. Gerald seeks to contextualize this particular conversation in relation to this bigger picture and invites Alan and Theresa to join him in this meaning. He uses phrases like "one step at a time," "take a step," "very gradual and careful way," and "talk more" to emphasize the partial nature of the current conversation and to appeal for time for the progress made to be embedded. It amounts to an appeal not to finalize the conversation but to keep it open.

He avoids finalizing language, like "custody," and speaks in language that suggests ongoing dialogue about the care of Rebecca: for example, "ongoing caregiving relationship," "the nature of ongoing arrangements," and "the caregiving plan." The number of present continuous tense verbs and of verbal nouns (gerunds) that he uses is striking in this utterance. The discursive message seems to amount to this: "Get used to the idea that this is going to be a continuing conversation."

Summary of the Movement of Discursive Positioning

In the course of this conversation both parties to the mediation seek to establish positions for themselves, particularly in relation to legal, family, and gender discourses. They also call each other into position in the discourses that wash their way across the landscape of this conversation. Looking at the discursive positions that the parties take up and offer each other early in the conversation will set the stage for an analysis of the way these positions changed as the conversation developed.

Entitlement

In conflict situations people are concerned to establish for themselves positions of entitlement and, frequently, to discredit the entitlements of the other party. Theresa positions herself as Rebecca's current and most appropriate caregiver. She establishes a history for this function, founded on her intimate knowledge of Rebecca's daily life, her consistent availability for her granddaughter, her link to her granddaughter through her deceased daughter, her cultural knowledge, and her relationship with Rebecca, which features emotional closeness. She says that Alan "hasn't really been a major figure in [Becca's] life" and implies that she has been. She offers Alan a position of something close to exclusion on the basis of his record of having "distanced himself from his daughter," his failure to fight harder for his daughter against Genna's restrictions, and his being the one who had the affair. She establishes herself as the representative of stability, familiarity, and continuity in Rebecca's life, and positions Alan as disruptive. His disruptions, moreover, are on the basis of sudden, unpredictable, and therefore untrustworthy moves. They are overdue and "late" and therefore not legitimate.

Alan begins by adopting a position of reasonableness. The position from which he seeks to claim entitlement is that of concerned, reasonable parent. The flip side is an implicit position call for Theresa. If she objects to his claims too strongly, she will be positioned as unreasonable. Alan does not stand on a rights discourse very much, despite occasional comments that indicate his awareness of the potential of this legal discourse. Throughout the whole conversation, he does not make a claim for custody of Rebecca and generally avoids speaking in a legal discourse. With these choices he avoids positioning Theresa as an adversary in a legal battle, although the background institutional power of the courts can still be felt.

In relation to Rebecca, Alan stakes a claim based on emotional closeness in the past. He positions himself as somewhat aggrieved, because he has been kept away from his daughter by Genna. In his story, Genna is placed in the position of persecutor and he is the victim. This is a risky strategy, which could provoke Theresa to come her dead daughter's defense, but he tries to manage this possibility by acknowledging Theresa in various ways as not getting in the way of his relationship with Rebecca, as a good caregiver for Rebecca, as a possible co-parent, and as having important cultural knowledge that he does not have. He does not want to come across as pressuring. He explicitly says at the outset that he does not want to "exclude" Theresa, or to shock Rebecca and cause a stir. The main critique Alan has of Theresa (in a conversation segment not included previously) is that she is keeping Rebecca tied to her apron strings, and he is concerned that she will use her influence with Rebecca to undermine the possibility of his relationship with Rebecca.

Shifts in Position

By the end of the conversation, some subtle shifts in position have opened up. Theresa has become willing to involve Alan in joint activities with Rebecca, with a view to an ongoing relationship. Alan has conceded that his custody move is not really in Rebecca's best interests, and he is willing to take things slowly and work with Theresa to build relationship with his daughter. Both have stepped back from opposition to each other's entitlement claims. Theresa has dropped the positioning of Alan as not deserving contact with Rebecca because of his failure to fight to see Rebecca after the separation and his lack of regular contact with her. She acknowledges that Alan has things to offer his daughter from his racial and cultural perspective, which is different from hers. She acknowledges him as a father who loves his daughter and makes desirable moves to correct the distance in his relationship with her, and she states her willingness to encourage Rebecca to respond to this. Alan has dropped his accusation that Theresa keeps Rebecca tied to her apron strings and his concern that Theresa might undermine his relationship with Rebecca has eased. He expresses a willingness to learn from Theresa.

What has opened up for Alan and Theresa is a cautious mutual positioning as partners in a joint enterprise. At the moment this enterprise is limited to setting up a weekend outing, but the promise is that this will build into an ongoing sharing of Rebecca's care. They begin to speak directly to each other, rather than through the mediator. An enriched dialogue begins to take shape in which they negotiate details about how to organize the outing. Each positions the other as a dialogical partner with something worthwhile to say.

Taking Up Positions of Agency in Relation to Dominant Discourse

In relation to the dominant discourses of legal process, family, and gender, how then do the two parties take up positions of agency? Clearly, they have withstood the pressure from legal discourse of subjecting each other to notions of ownership of children. They have not even discussed "custody" and yet they have begun to form some important agreements for a shared arrangement for the care of Rebecca. To do so they have had to consciously stand apart from the dominant story of family. The positions they are offering each other in the latter part of the interview do not seem to fit with suggestions of *interfering grandmother* or *unfit father*.

With regard to gender, by the end of the interview Alan has recognized a greater degree of legitimacy for Theresa's position than he did for Genna's at the start. He has learned something from Theresa; he is not simply assimilating her wishes into a compromise arrangement. The arrangements discussed recognize both parties' relational claims for participation in Rebecca's life, but entitlement claims based on legal discourses of ownership have not been privileged, either by the mediator or by the disputing parties, despite the existence of these discourses in their available repertoires. Nor has anyone used the discourse of race to make exclusive claims either. Theresa has used it to claim specific knowledge that will be of advantage to Rebecca, but she has clearly also recognized that Alan too has special knowledge that will be of use to his daughter.

In this chapter we have analyzed a mediation conversation through the lens of positioning theory. We believe this analysis is sensitive to the subtleties and nuances of moment-by-moment interaction and that it locates these subtleties and nuances in the context of wider societal discourse. The conversation participants are active in the establishment of relational positions for themselves and for each other. They seek mediator support for the legitimacy of their entitlement claims. They struggle with ambivalence as they find themselves located in competing stories. And they make repositioning shifts into relational stories that were not obvious at the start of the conversation. Finally, this analysis shows how a mediator can work with positioning and position calls to open up alternative stories and alternative relational positions in which conflict need not dominate.

Chapter Four

Working with Cultural Narratives in Mediation

This chapter considers the nuanced and detailed effects of the cultural narratives that are at play in most conflict situations. In recent decades many domains of social practice have begun to take more account of the cultural forces at play in the production of life. Mediation is no different. The previous dominance of assumptions that all people share certain traits, that there is a common *human nature*, has been gradually giving way to a greater valuing of each person's and group's profoundly *cultural nature*. Notions of cultural melting pots and requirements to integrate into a singular national culture have given way to an appreciation of and a revaluing of diversity. The current policy emphasis in the United States and in many other countries favors some version of multiculturalism or cultural pluralism rather than a requirement for everyone to give up his or her cultural roots to become part of a new master culture. And yet the idea of the melting pot still finds expression in many places.

These developments are important to how a mediator might approach the process of narrative mediation. Narratives are, of course, known to be cultural artifacts. Therefore a narrative approach to mediation necessarily requires an emphasis on the cultural contexts that people draw from in the construction of their personal stories of conflict and of cooperation. The concept of culture is not, however, a simple concept free from debate and contestation. There are problems involved in deciding how mediators might think of culture. We have some positions that we want to argue for in these debates, and in this chapter we briefly outline and speak to these positions. The role of discourses and position calls (described in Chapters Two and Three) in the cultural world, which all individuals occupy, is a factor in these positions. The concepts of discourse and positioning are tools with which to think about how cultural influences work and therefore about how mediators might work with these influences.

In order to outline our perspective on cultural influences in mediation, we first contrast a liberal-humanist vision of culture with a constructionist vision, and then we show, by way of example, how cultural narratives are intimately involved in conflict situations. We also discuss how this constructionist conceptualization of conflict provides mediators with resources that can be used to respectfully untangle cultural narratives in mediation conversations, narratives that otherwise would narrow the mediator's and the parties' vision of what is possible.

The Liberal-Humanist Vision

The mediation community, like the mental health community, in North America is dominated to a large extent by the liberal-humanist discourse that grants the individual pride of place in the social world. From a liberal-humanist perspective individuals are regarded as prime movers in their own worlds. Within this discourse persons are rational, independent, unitary beings who act in their own interests and are individually morally responsible for their decisions. The individual is understood largely as separate and distinct from the social and historical world around him. Erica Burman (1994) suggests that in this discourse, everyone tends to think of persons as being like chocolate-coated ice-cream bars. The ice cream in the center is human nature, and culture is the chocolate coating around the outside. In the academic world, psychology is granted the central ice-cream part to study, and sociology and anthropology are allowed the chocolate coating as their domain of study. The emphasis in much of modern thinking founded on this liberal-humanist discourse is on universal characteristics of human beings and the commonality that persons share with one another. The major schools of psychology have followed this discursive emphasis, and their primary focus has been on understanding the core functions of the universal human condition. This orientation, up until recently, has downplayed the role that historical and sociocultural influences might have in determining human volition and action. Resolving conflict, from the liberal-humanist perspective, is primarily focused on individuals' choices and their ability to draw on their personal power.

The Primacy of the Individual

Historically, an emphasis on individualism, as opposed to a primarily cultural perspective, has not been the premise that has driven most people's understanding of the human condition. As anthropologist Clifford Geertz (1983) puts it, for example: "The Western conception of the person as a bounded, unique, more or less integrated motivational and cognitive universe, a dynamic centre of awareness, emotion, judgment, and action, organized into a distinctive whole and set contrastively against other such wholes and against a social and natural background is, however incorrigible it may seem to us, a rather peculiar idea within the context of the world's cultures" (p. 59).

The emphasis on the primacy of this individual cognitive universe is, in terms of world history, of relatively recent origin, but it has dominated the cultural landscape of the Western world during a critical period, with the result that this movement has not only shaped the major social science disciplines as they developed over the twentieth century but has had a strong influence on shaping the cultural norms of the West. Successful individuals are understood to be those who have achieved through hard work, strength of character, self-determination, individual mastery, and material achievement. The psychological concepts that accompany this success include what is generally embraced by the lay community as self-esteem, self-actualization, creativity, competence, and autonomy, characteristics that are all based on an understanding of human nature as individualistic. In the mediation literature, discussions of individual *interests* have represented this perspective.

Conflict, from this standpoint, is thought to result from the thwarting of people's natural human drive to fulfill their needs, and so the task of the mediator becomes to help disputants remove obstacles to need satisfaction through the creation of win-win solutions. Interest-based mediation is based on the liberal-humanist vision. Closely associated with this theory is the idea that the mediator has human needs similar to those of the parties and thus is, in most respects, like the parties. Because the reference point for empathy and understanding is the universal human condition, mediators using a humanist approach are likely to believe that everyone has the capacity to "walk in another's shoes."

Cultural Essentialism

The liberal-humanist tradition does offer a view of culture. But it is usually an essentialist view of culture. Culture is conceived as something that each individual has. An essentialist view of culture assigns individuals to social categories (Native American, lesbian, Asian), as if these categories were natural givens. It then pursues the counting of the individual people who occupy these categories, on the assumption that the language categories used to describe them in the first place are reliable dividers. In this view, to be a member of one culture means that you can be clearly distinguished from members of another culture because each cultural group is discrete and separate from all other groups. The discourse influences on the perspective of the person looking at or studying a culture are not considered terribly important because she can rely on cultures to exist in their own right and thus to be available to be understood. What she can do therefore is to discover another cultural worldview, learn about it, and develop sensitivity to all those who belong to this culture. She might, for example, seek out the key features of a culture (perhaps by some statistical measures of central tendency or perhaps through ethnographic study) and assume that these are definitive of the people who belong to the culture. Essentialist views of culture, then, promote close identification of individuals with cultural norms and with a kind of timeless cultural stability. Geertz (1995) has summarized this perspective as the "cookie cutter" (p. 43) view of culture and has shown that it is still the dominant view of culture in the social sciences.

In the last twenty years there has been a strong emphasis in social practice on identifying the unique cultural characteristics of diverse groups in order to better cater for their needs through a variety of social services—social work, counseling, mediation, and so on. This focus has been particularly prominent in mental health and medical fields. Although this endeavor has contributed a great deal to understanding the diverse needs of citizens in a community, it has also tended to artificially homogenize collections of people who in fact have diverse cultural distinctions. A problem occurs when people in the social sciences think they can understand the cultural worldview of Hispanics, for example, and then think they can simply offer their services in ways that are culturally sensitive. The problem with this approach lies not so much in the effort to be more sensitive as in the underlying concepts on which it is founded.

A Constructionist Vision

In contrast to the liberal-humanist approach, a narrative or constructionist approach emphasizes the cultural context rather than a universal analysis in understanding the individual and family experience. French psychoanalyst Jacques Lacan (1977) raised serious questions about the "question of knowing whether I am the same as that of which I speak" (p. 165). Lacan's position is summarized by Allen Ivey (1986) as, "I do not speak. Rather, I am spoken" (p. 329). This statement illustrates the constructionist concept that the sociohistorical context each person inhabits is so fundamental to the creation of his identity that his thoughts are not simply his own but rather are, in very substantial ways, the product of his forebears and his ancestral history. From this perspective, individuals are not unitary creations who speak only for themselves. Rather, they are bearers of and reproducers of the cultural patterns that are given to them from their cultural world. Their very language and patterns of thinking are given to them. Paul Tillich (1987) suggests that "we are thrown into the world" (pp. 141–142). This *thrownness* is produced by the cultural fabric that has shaped the conduct and behavior of each person's immediate family, his community, and the world in which he lives. From this perspective, culture is not just the chocolate coating around a person's individual nature. It is as fundamental as biology to every aspect of who each person is and how each person responds to others.

Culture and Complexity

As a result of philosophical shifts introduced in the postmodern and constructionist worldview, culture is beginning to be understood in more complex terms. Culture is becoming more about the process by which people actively give meaning to things and less about a discrete set of ready-made assumptions about a specific group of people. In practice it is difficult to categorize people as belonging to a discrete cultural group and to proceed on that basis. When mediating conflicts between individuals of different ethnicities, genders, classes, religions, and sexual orientations, for example, it is difficult to pinpoint the specific cultural membership to give priority to. Cultural identity groups also turn out to be slippery. Consider all the arguments about who is a true Native American, who is acting white rather than black, who is a legitimate feminist, whose experience of disability confers the right to speak for disability groups, and so on. It is not always possible to determine who is a valid member of a group and who is not, as members of each group often hold conflicting views about how to define a valid member. The view that there is a one-to-one correspondence between a so-called cultural group and the cultural practices each member observes or the stimuli to which each member responds is erroneous. Think of how difficult it might be to plan a conflict resolution intervention with African American or white people given the diverse backgrounds, lifestyles, beliefs, and experiences embraced by different members of each group.

The *reductionist* version of cultural membership produces a rather simple and unidimensional view of the cultural landscape and yet, at the same time, produces immediate contradictions for many of the apparent members of each broadly defined culture. It also fails to provide much useful information about how a particular mediator should proceed with the participants involved in a particular conflict. The reality is that individuals' background cultural narratives are enormously complex and contradictory and sometimes overlapping; nevertheless, that does not mean that mediators have to resort to individualistic notions for understanding human functioning.

Culture as Narrative

What is emerging in the recent literature from a variety of sources is a new understanding of culture. The narrative metaphor is increasingly being invoked to anchor this perspective. Rather than thinking of culture in terms of discrete wholes, various thinkers are arguing for an emphasis on the cultural narratives that course through people's lives (see, for example, Appiah, 2005; Benhabib, 2002; Bruner, 1990; Rosaldo, 1993; 1994; Said, 1994). The metaphor used by Renato Rosaldo (1994) appeals to us. Rosaldo describes life as containing multiple cultural intersections through which are running multiple and often contradictory narratives. This metaphor suggests that rather than thinking of persons as belonging simply to one culture it is more relevant to think of them as *exposed to a variety of cultural influences,* and different influences will be dominant for each person and will also vary as that person changes contexts. The emphasis is on multiplicity, rather than on essentialist or reductionist singularity.

Not only do individuals' identities change in response to particular contexts, they also change over time. Amin Maalouf (2000) writes of a man who proudly stands up as a Yugoslavian in 1980. A number of years later, as the war in Bosnia is waged, this man denies his identity as a Yugoslavian. Instead, he proudly identifies as a Muslim. Today, he may be Bosnian first and Muslim second. Who knows what identity he will be in another twenty years! It can be argued that every individual possesses multiple identities. One needs only to ask a few questions to uncover a person's forgotten divergences and unsuspected allegiances. And yet it is not uncommon to hear individuals express sweeping judgments about a whole people in a single breath. As Maalouf (2000) suggests, to be born black is a different matter according to where in the world you come from, whether it be New York, São Paulo, or Addis Ababa. In Nigeria, people are not labeled black or white but are recognized as Yoruba or Hausa.

Multiple Identity Narratives

At the local level of identity construction, identity can take a number of forms, and the context is enormously influential in shaping one's way of understanding oneself and of relating to the world. In our trainings we ask participants to consider the profound role that context plays in understanding cultural identity by presenting them with a series of questions about who they are at particular cultural intersections. For example:

- Who were you when you watched the planes hit the World Trade Center towers?
- Who are you when you visit a gay bar?
- What identity are you conscious of when you see a Muslim praying?
- What cultural identity are you aware of when you walk through a wealthy neighborhood?
- What cultural identity do you belong to when you are asked to milk a cow?
- What identity are you when you sit next to a man and woman kissing on a bench?
- Who are you when you are crossing the Mexican-American border?

These questions direct our attention to the context in which people make sense of their identities. This kind of analysis loosens some of the rigid descriptions that pigeonhole people into narrow and inflexible categories. Acknowledging that cultural categories are constantly fluid, contradictory, and complex can open doorways to forward movement in disputes frozen by a unitary analysis of cultural differences.

Border Identities

Tight definitions of cultural characteristics have the effect of marginalizing those who live on the *borders* of any particular grouping. Far more people occupy ambiguous border positions than is commonly assumed. When such individuals are asked about their ethnic identity for example, they are forced to make a choice between cultural influences from different parts of their family heritage. This happens whenever they are asked to fill in a form or answer a survey. Sara Chavez, for example, discusses the oppressive effects of a community that seeks to define her into fixed categories. She says it is difficult to be proud to call herself multiracial. Throughout her life she has felt pressured to choose one of her ethnicities or the other. She tells the following story (personal communication, 2007):

> From as early as grade school, I remember cultural heritage day and not knowing what I should dress up as. I remember choosing to dress as a Mariachi singer, because I did not know much about my mother's white culture at the time. I felt guilty at ten years old because I was not representing my mother. Later on in my life, I also remember not knowing which box to fill out for the SAT exams when I was asked about ethnicity, because the stigma of "other" was not an option for me. My cousins have made comments throughout my life about how thin my hair is, because I'm not Mexican enough, but my white friends at school would call me their token "Mexican" in our group of friends. I constantly feel that I am torn between my white and my Mexican ethnicities, and it is still difficult to this day to find a place where I know what to call myself.
>
> This oppression has affected me emotionally and I struggle to be completely comfortable with myself, because I often question my identity and the way that I think about myself. Only recently have I been exposed to the idea of being biracial or multiracial. Since I have felt like I have a split identity for the majority of my life, I am only recently starting to reconcile with the fact that it is possible to be multiracial but I am still not comfortable associating that way.
>
> I have been negatively affected by society's judgments that I should belong to one ethnic group or the other. For example, people from my Mexican heritage may judge me because I do not look like them. I do not speak Spanish, and I do not know much about my Mexican family's heritage. I feel ashamed to call myself Mexican in front of them, so I choose to not become very close with them. On the other hand, I have been reluctant to learn Spanish because I have been nervous about how my white friends will view me. Upon reflection, I now realize that I actually receive more support from my white friends to "act more Mexican" than I do from my Hispanic friends and family. I feel like this because they want to learn more about my culture and get to know me better, but for some reason I am still very much hindered in learning the

language of my grandparents. Depending on the ethnicity of the majority of the people I'm with, I choose to change the ethnicity that I identify with to fit the situation. When surrounded by white people I identify as Mexican because I do not fit completely in with their culture. When I am with people that are full-blooded Mexican, I identify as white because I am anxious about being asked if I speak Spanish or asked where my family comes from. I am still wrestling with whether or not it is cognitively healthy for me to identify with my white cultural background at times and my Mexican culture at others. I am wrestling with these issues even to this very day.

From the perspective of dominant discourse about culture, Sara might be pitied, if not criticized, for being torn between cultures. Some might suggest that she make a choice and stick with it. From a constructionist perspective, however, Sara might take reassurance from the fact that her experience is more common and more normal than most people admit. The discomfort she feels comes, perhaps, not so much from her dual heritage as from the dominant assumptions built into the governing of populations (Foucault, 2000) through the collection of demographic statistics.

A constructionist vision of culture challenges the boundaries of cultural membership and how they are policed. Cultural norms and traditions are not viewed as natural or stable but as decisions made by particular people in specific places at specific time. For these reasons they are understandably often changing or shifting. Take the category called Hispanic. One can discuss for a while whether people prefer to be called Mexican, Latino or Latina, or Chicano or Chicana. But even if the word *Hispanic* is accepted, it needs to be remembered that this is a demographic category that exists nowhere else in the world except for the United States. And it was invented to respond to particular historical conditions that are fairly recent. Up until the 1970s, Hispanic people did not exist as an official, statistically recognized group. Before that time, the same people might be called, depending on the reason for the categorizing, white or native.

Race

Racial categories are even more dubious than ethnic ones. The terms used to describe races have never been stable, have always been constructed from a white perspective, and have been closely tied to a history of racism and colonization since the seventeenth century (see Monk, Winslade, & Sinclair, 2008, for a full account of these issues). The term *race,* as it is used today, did not exist before the era of European colonization. The development of critical race theory (see, for example, Delgado & Stefancic, 2000) has raised all sorts of questions about the common assumption that people simply know who is black and who is white.

Categorizing people into fixed groups can invite people into polarizing positions and into judging others' worthiness to belong to a category of persons or into determining whether others' claimed level of oppression is legitimate or not. In the constructionist vision, culture does not lie with some essential birthright through which cultural practices are prescribed and defined. Rather, it is something that one designs and crafts, much like a work of art. It is less about who one is and more about what one does. In this way culture is performative rather than static. The constructionist view of culture also challenges the idea that culture is an add-on to the essence of the individual and thus challenges the individualist assumptions on which mainstream psychology rests.

Understandings of Power in Conflict

If mediators are to understand the complexities of conflict and its resolution, they also need to have an analysis of the nature of power and how it works in conflict interactions. Understanding the influences of power in conflict is enormously helpful in identifying how conflict should be analyzed and made sense of in the first place. It also allows mediators to take account of people's positions in networks of cultural relations, rather than building assumptions on the basis of people's identification with discrete cultural groups. Different views of power arise from different views of the world and lead to markedly different orientations to social practice and therefore to different kinds of conflict resolution interventions.

The Liberal-Humanist View of Power

Perhaps the most familiar and commonly understood analysis of power comes from the liberal-humanist perspective discussed previously. The humanist view of power is central to understanding the world's democratic systems of government. The Constitution of the United States and the Universal Declaration of Human Rights adopted by the United Nations are both constructed on a humanist understanding, where the individual is viewed as the prime actor in the social world. Advocates of this perspective therefore concentrate on how power is attached to individuals (through education, wealth, charisma, social status, or office). Most conflict resolution models are built on these philosophical underpinnings. Interest-based conflict resolution models, for example, seek to understand individual interests in order to identify common underlying human interests between people in conflict. This approach honors the notion that individuals have personal power and can use it to negotiate with each other.

The Structuralist View of Power

Another analysis of the workings of power serves as a helpful contrast to both the constructionist and humanist perspectives. The structuralist view of power understands conflict as resulting from the effects of an underlying social structure, rather than from the effects of an accumulation of personal decisions of individuals. This structuralist approach can be seen to inform the social analysis of Karl Marx. This view of power has had an enormous influence on social thinking in many fields of academic study, such as politics, economics, history, and sociology. A structuralist analysis has, moreover, spurred a series of social movements that seek to address structural inequities, and hence it has been influential in the development of a variety of forms of social practice. Businesses and government departments that restructure themselves also draw on a structuralist analysis. Some restorative justice models use a structuralist analysis of positions to address conflict in a community between somebody who is viewed as a perpetrator and somebody who is a victim.

The Constructionist View of Power

The constructionist view of power is based on the still emerging poststructuralist philosophical perspective, which has brought challenges to both the liberal-humanist and the structuralist perspectives. The work of Michel Foucault (1980, 2000) has made a major contribution to the development of this analysis of power. We believe he offers mediators some revolutionary tools with which to think about power relations and how they affect conflict analysis and conflict resolution processes. Therefore in this section we briefly explain his conceptualizations of power relations and explore their implications for mediation practice.

In the constructionist analysis, power relations in the modern world are based largely on people's use of discourse. Foucault (1978) argues that "discourse transmits and produces power, reinforces it, but also undermines and exposes it, renders it fragile and makes it possible to thwart it" (p. 100). From this perspective, power is not a commodity to be owned but a property of a relation. If it is constituted in discourse, it is vulnerable to shifts in discourse. Hence it is dependent on the context in which discourse is used, rather than essentially tied to a person or to a group of persons. It is likely to cut across individual lives in ways that can entail privilege and oppression for the same person in different respects. Such fluidity, however, does not preclude the possibility of systematic and patterned applications of discursive power so that some individuals are more consistently disadvantaged than others.

For example, discourses of family and of gender relations underlie many of the decisions and actions of men and women on a daily basis. Family mediation, for instance, will therefore always involve arguments over the legitimacy of discourses or over the fairness of the discursive positions set up by these discourses. These discourses equip people with a matrix of assumptions that they reproduce and use for their own purposes each time they open their mouths. Although they are certainly agents (rather than puppets), acting to express themselves and to influence others, individuals can be agents only by making use of the discourses that they are familiar with and that dominate their thinking. Where a discourse favors and privileges life opportunities for men and provides diminished opportunities for women, the repetition of this discourse in people's speech patterns can blind them to the way that things could be different. Because discourse is everywhere, power too is everywhere and pervades the social world. Foucault (1980) refers to the capillary action of power, a metaphor that references the tiny blood vessels that carry life to the all corners of the body. Power is not simply held by some groups and unavailable to others. All people exercise it to some degree, and therefore it makes no sense to describe any participant in mediation as powerless. Foucault's argument is that power is not as centralized as structuralists believe. However, it is still true that there are places where power becomes concentrated. And there are places on the margins where it is less easily available. Some people can gain easy access to the authority to shape the lives of others, and others face many obstacles if they are to do so.

Governmentality

From a constructionist perspective, authority to govern the lives of others develops in many places in the modern world. It is not organized just around race, gender, and class, as structuralist analyses have often emphasized. Nor is all such authority centrally controlled by the government, or the state. Authority from many other sources is exercised over people's lives. For example, banks and credit agencies exercise government over people's financial lives. Teachers and counselors govern children's school lives. Fashion magazines govern people's clothing tastes. Advertising governs people's appetites to consume. Airline personnel govern people's travel behavior. Employers exercise government over the lives of employees.

It is important to see mediators as governing, to some degree, the lives of those they work with. Mediators exercise power in people's lives as they sit with disputing parties, ask them personal questions, shape their communications, and fashion agreements about their futures. Foucault uses the word *govern* in the sense of producing desired forms of behavior in a population of people. In his formulation the world is usually not neatly divided into two groups of people, one dominant and one oppressed. Things are not so fixed. Instead, there is always a degree of indeterminacy in the midst of ongoing contests of power. The discourses that individuals draw on produce patterns of privilege, but people also make many efforts to assert themselves and to govern their own lives, individually and in groups. Hence, mediators need to pay careful attention to the microdynamics of power and to the effects of these dynamics in order to make the most of opportunities for change. According to Foucault's analysis of power, power relations are constantly fluid in their expression. Whenever one attempts to govern the conduct of others, one must engage in a struggle, and there is always the possibility that the others may resist. Power relations are always reciprocal in this sense.

Such struggles are always cultural, simply because they take place in discourse. Hence we believe that any understanding of the cultural world of disputants who come to mediation needs to include a focus on how they are positioned within a series of struggles over cultural issues. These struggles may be represented in the polarization of the two parties to a dispute. Or the parties may be positioned in different places by some wider struggles over power in the world around them. What we are envisaging for the mediator is a dynamic focus on culture and cultural relations. We believe this focus goes far beyond making simple identifications of individuals as members of cultural groups and then trying to be sensitive to the customary practices of each group.

The Mediator's Stance from a Constructionist Perspective

A mediator using a constructionist understanding of conflict embraces ambiguity and indeterminacy in an escalating conflict and nurtures a spirit of informed curiosity about what is unfolding. From this perspective there are no universal, truth-based approaches to rely on as guides for the mediator's actions. This ambiguity provokes a moral dilemma for the mediator. Like the disputing parties, the mediator cannot avoid being positioned discursively in the conflict, even as he is mediating it. There is no privileged position outside of discourse from which one can speak. Each time mediators open their mouths and choose certain expressions over others, they choose one set of positions and not others. In this sense mediators are never neutral, as conventional mediation theory requires. So the important question is not so much whether the mediator is neutral with regard to the content of the dispute, but from which discursive position the mediator will work. What moral stance will inform the mediator's work. And how transparent will that stance be?

Power and Professional Knowledge

The challenge for mediators is to remain curious and open-minded within their own discursive and moral location (which is always a cultural location). From a constructionist perspective, professional knowledge is produced from a cultural vantage point and therefore is always provisional, temporary, limited, and tentative. Constructionism is always suspicious about the grand narratives of theory (Lyotard, 1984), even when they are buttressed with empirical data. This perspective invites practitioners to hold their professional knowledge lightly and to be prepared to revise their efforts as a result of their encounters with conflicted parties. Perhaps in some instances they might reexamine and then change previously held assumptions about some aspect of their clients' viewpoints. Mediation, from a constructionist framework, involves practitioners' demonstrating willingness to review, critique, and if necessary change their stance in the face of new information. It requires them to act from an ethical position or moral standpoint rather than from a place of neutrality. From this standpoint the mediator is fully prepared to acknowledge that her ethical, moral, and professional stance will shape and influence the way in which the conflict will be addressed. She is mindful that each move she makes in the session emerges from a discursive position that will influence the questions asked and the way the responses will be acknowledged. This analysis of the role of the mediator contrasts with the liberal-humanist notion that the mediator can serve a neutral and impartial function. The reality is that the mediator is constantly influenced by the social forces discussed previously. Nevertheless, the mediator must manage these social processes so that the parties are treated in an evenhanded and respectful manner.

A constructionist perspective emphasizes cultural variability and implies that there are domains of human experience that may not be understandable to or translatable by all those involved in the mediation. This perspective contradicts the liberal-humanist claim of universality. It says that discourses may position one party in ways that may not be known, shared, or understood by the other party to the conflict or by the mediator. For example, it would be a challenge for a mediator who has spent much of his life positioned in places of privilege by discourses that are predominantly racist, classist, or sexist to be understanding of parties who have been directly targeted by those very discourses.

What mediators need to actively develop is discursive empathy. This involves reviewing constantly the dominant cultural discourses that are shaping the conflict they are working with and noticing how these discourses are positioning the parties in relation to each other. In this way, mediators do not presume to understand their clients' experiences; rather, they spend time *unpacking* the cultural knapsack that each client carries. This process of unpacking is called deconstruction.

Deconstruction

Deconstruction refers to the practice of exploring the assumptions taken for granted in the discourses that underpin a dialogue, a behavior, or an emotional expression (Derrida, 1976; White, 1992). The mediator using a deconstructive approach to conflict constantly interrogates the possible prejudices, dogmatisms, biases, and certainties that could shut down avenues of exploration and inquiry with disputing parties. In mediation a deconstructive approach means asking oneself, "What interactions am I having that demonstrate I am jumping to conclusions or too easily accepting prior assumptions about the nature of the issues?" and, "What limitations are produced by my own positioning in cultural relations, and how is this position influencing my understanding of the cultural contexts acting on the parties and on their difficulties?"

Deconstruction invites a tentative, curious, and deliberately naïve posture. For example, it asks of any mediator action, "What was left out? What was covered over? What was paid attention to and what was not?" (Monk, Winslade, Crocket, & Epston, 1997). Deconstruction practices are especially helpful in addressing some of the more subtle effects of a dominant discourse on the mediator, "because dominant discourses are so familiar, they are taken-for-granted and even recede from view" (Hare-Mustin, 1994, p. 20).

Narrative mediation focuses on the contextual staging of problems to assist professionals in keeping things moving. It is less preoccupied than traditional mediation is with seeking definitive and objective answers that omit the larger background of the lives of the mediator and the conflicted parties. Deconstruction challenges the ways in which background cultural narratives can thwart alternative possibilities and maintain the status quo. When deconstruction is applied successfully, the mediator questions his or her own preoccupations and preferred points of reference, familiar habits, social practices, beliefs, and judgments, things that when left unexamined are often regarded as common sense. Deconstruction is, therefore, about the regular production of moments of surprise.

Although some mediators may see deconstruction and the unpacking of discourse as an overly intellectual pursuit, we see it as intensely practical. Those who develop a facility for thinking deconstructively (which might begin as an intellectual activity) can become adept at seeing the work of discourse in every utterance in every conversation. Discourses are not just abstractions but are embodied in everyone's life and are implicit in each person's emotional responses and in his or her actions. The social constructionist metaphor does not separate language and thinking from behavior and feeling. Thus "every utterance to some degree constructs the world in accordance with the cultural world being referenced in the linguistic constructions used. Speaking is thus considered a social action with material consequences" (Winslade, 2003, p. 7).

A discursive approach to mediation therefore reflects human meaning-making processes through all language use, thought, feeling, and behavior. The concept of discourse allows mediators to understand every word, every feeling, and every action as a cultural product and as projected into the cultural worlds people inhabit.

Furthermore, the practice of deconstruction helps mediators appreciate how people can be seduced by the imperatives built into cultural narratives to behave in certain ways. When individuals are unaware of the particular discursive influences affecting them, they are limited and constrained in the range of responses available to them. Deconstructive analysis of particular discourse usages opens up choice and a wider range of positions that can be taken up. In this way it encourages greater agency and alters the balance in cultural power relations.

Here is an example of the use to which deconstruction can be put in the practice of mediation. In this example, deconstruction opens up for examination the cultural imperatives that may be shaping the conflict George and Maria have been experiencing.

George and Maria are divorcing and are conflicted about financial and caregiving arrangements for their two children. One of the dominant cultural narratives that positions George in this divorce is the idea that men are the heads of their households. As primary income earners, they should have the most say about how money is distributed after the divorce. A deconstructive move by their mediator could be to pose a question such as this:

Mediator: You have had the role of being the breadwinner and your wife has been the primary caregiver of the children. How does this history affect your views about the transitions that will be necessary after the divorce?

This question is an effort to expose the patriarchal narratives affecting George that are escalating the conflict. This question might be followed up by asking this:

Mediator: In the twenty-first century the law in California requires that matrimonial assets should be split fifty-fifty. How wedded are you to the idea that "men should be the decision makers" when this conflict is going to escalate and go to trial if you don't entertain some kind of sharing of matrimonial assets?

Meanwhile, the discourse that assumes "children belong with their mother and women are best equipped to address their needs" creates a position for Maria that requires that she fight for exclusive custody of the two children and offer only minimal caregiving opportunities to the children's father, George. A deconstructive question to Maria might go like this:

Mediator: It seems like you have been brought up with strong ideas about the role of wife as primary caregiver. With the divorce there will be major changes in your roles. What ideas about caregiving arrangements for your children are affecting your decision to exclude George from having time with the children?

Again, this question seeks to expose the background narratives so they can at least be overtly addressed in the divorce mediation.

The logic of externalizing conversations is noticeable here. "Ideas about caregiving arrangements" are spoken about as if these ideas are not essential to Maria but are externalized discourse fragments that are influencing her thinking. Such deconstructive questions have the potential to open spaces where the couple can interact with less blame and judgment because these inquiries invite a reexamination of the discursive positions that helped shape the conflict.

Discourse and Mediation

Liberal-humanist understandings of culture provide limited and awkward responses to cultural diversity because of their built-in essentialist assumptions. The concept of discourse, in contrast, allows mediators to work more with the complexity of the situations in which people live. It provides mediators with thinking tools with which to make sense of the ways people are pulled in contradictory directions, ways that can never be adequately described from within the assumptions of singular cultural identity. Discourse theory accommodates a process of identity construction that is always complex. Identities are constructed out of the positions available from among a swathe of competing discourses, established through large-scale historical movements but having a unique impact on each person at every moment of his or her life.

This concept of discourse, influenced chiefly by constructionist and poststructuralist theory, is based on the work of Michel Foucault (1972), who described discourse as a *social practice* disseminated through cultural space that exerts a dominating effect on what can be thought or spoken. All people speak from discourse, feel from discourse, and behave from discourse. In its simplest terms, a discourse may be thought of as a cultural idea. You can get a sense of a discourse by listening to any statement that someone makes and asking yourself, "What are the background assumptions on which that statement rests?"

We shall draw on conflicts we have worked with in health care settings (see Chapter Nine) for examples to illustrate the points we are making here about cultural assumptions. On many occasions, patients and their families in hospital settings become caught up in difficult and intense conflicts with health care providers.

Their distress is typically produced out of a cluster of dominating discourses circulating in hospital contexts. Here are some of dominating discourses that affect patients and their families:

- The nurse and the doctor can be trusted and people should deliver themselves into these professionals' care and become good patients.
- Doctors and nurses are dedicated professionals who will work tirelessly for a cure.
- Medicine today can work miracles.
- Family members are important in the patient's treatment and care.
- My family member who is sick is in the best place here in hospital.
- Patients have a right to have their complaints heard when their needs are not being met by hospital staff.
- Lifestyle is irrelevant to the diagnosis or condition.
- Patient autonomy should always be honored.
- Patients and their families are entitled to financial compensation when health care professionals make mistakes or offer substandard care.

Many explicit practices get built upon the foundations laid by these assumptions. They are not always said out loud, but everybody within the cultural world that the speaker comes from knows these assumptions and thinks of them as just normal, everyday truths. When these cultural narratives or discourses are not complied with or are contravened by health care professionals, people often feel intensely outraged. The norms that they have come to rely on are disturbed, and they may be propelled into a conflictual encounter. Tensions may escalate and significant misunderstandings may grow.

At the same time, there are other discourses that lie in the background for health care professionals and that shape the positions from which they respond to complaints. Some of these dominating discourses follow:

- Patients should appreciate everything done to serve them.
- Health care professionals make mistakes all the time.
- The focus is on healing the patient. The family is secondary.

- Patients, not their family members, need to be responsible for their well-being.
- The ideal medical focus should be on preventive health care, healthy lifestyles, and fitness.
- Efficiency and effectiveness are more important than performance of social and cultural niceties.
- Patients and their families should apply self-discipline over emotional expressiveness.
- Patients and their families should be future focused rather than present focused.

Thinking in terms of discourse always makes the social and cultural aspects of the conflicts that people bring to mediators more visible. The metaphor of discourse illuminates how people's understandings of what is normal, acceptable, right, real, or possible are constructed. In contrast, thinking in terms of, for example, biological metaphors can render the social and cultural world invisible or irrelevant. We believe it is in the interest of the mediation field, specifically, to reexamine from a cultural and discursive perspective how conflicts are thought of and how they are resolved. We think the concept of discourse provides a new language with which to name the background social processes operating on parties in conflict. It also provides a way forward in practice without resorting to blaming talk.

Summary of Constructionist Principles

At this juncture let us consider some of the conceptual tools we have discussed and summarize the key points conveyed. Then we will turn these conceptual tools into resources to guide the mediator in working with background cultural narratives in relation to a specific scenario.

- It is more useful to think of people as shaped by cultural narratives than as belonging to categories of persons or as members of a supposedly discrete culture.
- People can take up contradictory positions in response to multiple cultural narratives, making it difficult to place any individual into a neatly categorized cultural box.

- Culture, as opposed to inner forces and individual needs, shapes and constructs people's positions and interests.
- Conflicts are produced out of the background cultural narratives that position people in particular ways.
- Dominant cultural stories shape people's attitudes, beliefs, and identities.
- Conflicted parties' cultural identities exist in the context of cultural power relations that are constantly shifting and changing.
- Discourses have both a restraining and a compelling role in shaping parties' experiences of conflict.
- Deconstructive questioning can help the mediator expose the cultural narratives that are unexpressed and unnamed.
- Discourse theory provides a language with which to address dominant and subjugated cultural influences at work in conflict situations.

Practice Example

We can now show you the work these conceptual tools can do to inform the practice of mediation. Some of the most challenging situations that present themselves to mediators are conflicts within families over the care of elderly parents. This conflict issue can serve as a lens for looking into the role that cultural narratives play in shaping what family members deem vital. Moreover, family conflicts over elderly parent care are likely to intensify in the near future because of the increasing numbers of elderly people in the general population as the baby boomer generation ages while the number of younger family members available to provide that care diminishes owing to dropping birth rates. Consider this scenario:

> Diane Jamieson seeks mediation services to help her manage the intense conflict that has arisen between her and her two siblings because the greatest burden of advocating for and caring for their elderly parents seems to have fallen on her shoulders. Diane is highly stressed because her adult siblings seem to have assumed that she and her husband, Scott, because they live close by the elderly parents (Helena and Jon), are responsible for monitoring the

parents' day-to-day care. Diane's sister, Martine, lives two hours' drive away and infrequently visits her parents to see how they are getting along. A third sibling, Michael, lives one hour's flying time away and has not been home to see his parents for a year and a half. The stress has compounded because two months ago Helena suffered a small stroke and lost her short-term memory. She is semiparalyzed on her right side and cannot easily move around the house. Jon is frail and is distressed about how he will care for his wife. Although a nursing service visits the house every third day, Diane, the sibling who understands best what is happening to her parents, is deeply worried that this service cannot provide an adequate level of attention for her mother and father.

Diane and her husband, on the one hand, are angry and resentful toward Martine and Michael and describe them as derelict in their responsibilities as adult children and preoccupied with their own selfish pursuits. Martine and Michael, on the other hand, complain that Diane is always attacking them and showing no understanding about the huge stresses they are under in managing their own day-to-day affairs. Like many other families, the adult members of this family are experiencing serious conflict over the care of ill parents.

How might a mediator and conflict resolver think about these issues? How the mediator thinks will have real effects on the strategies he or she employs when working with the conflicted parties. Moreover, how the conflicted parties explain to themselves why they are experiencing conflict will influence how they will respond to the actions of the mediator.

Through a Liberal-Humanist Lens

Using the liberal-humanist lens the mediator might understand the conflict as generated by competing, selfish personal agendas, individual hedonistic pursuits, perhaps even character flaws and personality disorders. An analysis of conflict focused on the internal processes of individuals will invite the mediator to pursue a conflict resolution approach embedded in an individualist orientation. When proceeding on the assumption that the parties are responsible for their individual feelings and actions and are pursuing their own paths of self-interest, a successful mediation must offer disputing family members the chance to have their individual needs meet. It may be taken for granted that the identification of an individual's needs and the fulfillment of his or her interests are the central purposes of a community. From an interest-based perspective, the mediator's main goal will be to identify the underlying interests each family member has in relation to the care and well-being of the parents and work from that assumption.

Through a Constructionist Lens

When seen through a constructionist lens, the sibling conflict is understood from within the wider cultural narratives that position the siblings so as to create conflict. One dominating cultural narrative is the story that family members are responsible for taking care of each other when they are sick, in trouble, or incapacitated in some way. In some communities, children grow up with strong messages about being responsible for the care of elderly parents. Children learn that it is their duty to provide this care in repayment for the parents' care for them when they were vulnerable and dependent. This cultural narrative has been most prominent in communities that do not have a long history of social services based on communal and collective practices. The discourse of families caring for their own is still dominant in North American society. However, in the middle and upper socioeconomic groupings the primary care for incapacitated and seriously sick family members has been passed on to private health care providers. These private providers often have the necessary training, experience, and resources to cater for the physical care of the elderly, and often for their emotional and social needs as well. In families without the financial resources to afford expensive facilities, the conflict issues are compounded. In some instances families and adult siblings who are isolated or disengaged from one another, or overwhelmed by personal problems, may not be able to care for an elderly parent in need of daily care. In these instances the care of an elderly person may fall to the state. In most Western countries the state or a voluntary agency provides at least some rudimentary level of care rather than allowing people to die on the street. Yet serious conflicts ensue, between community and government services, professionals offering care for the elderly, and the family members of an elderly person, about who is really responsible for providing good quality care.

Background Cultural Narratives

This conflict is fed by strong cultural narratives that affirm individuality and consumerism. Dominating Western discourses are in harmony with the liberal-humanist agenda that we have already described as promoting self-determination, individual mastery, and material achievement ahead of collective responsibility. In this discourse, collective responsibility is assumed to weaken the individual's motivation to strive for a better life. All around the globe economic neoliberalism is constantly promoting cultural narratives that position family members as needing to actively pursue individual achievements and material success. These family members do not invent this discourse on their own. It shapes and produces their motives and actions, and they must make choices about the meaning of family relationships in relation to it. More and more there are discursive clashes in our communities between the responsibility to offer family and communal care on the one hand and the drive for individual mastery and self-achievement on the other. The more the neoliberal discourse has gained control, the more politically charged issues such as health care and education have become because both represent domains of life where individuals are comparatively more vulnerable and less able to be responsible for themselves.

Although this neoliberal discourse is globally pervasive, it can be overlaid with the narratives of the meaning of family that are found in many ethnic traditions. In some such traditions special responsibility is assigned to the eldest child, for example. There are also gender narratives that can come into play. The patriarchal norm is for caretaking roles that pertain to children and the aged to devolve upon women. However, women have developed some strong voices of resistance to the idea that this assumption should be automatic, and there has been a strong revaluation, at least in middle-class contexts, of the importance of women's careers. Each of these discourses might also be at work in the production of a family's experience of conflict.

The Jamieson family is being subjected to the pulls of these background narratives, which are expressed in each member's intimate experience of the situation. The background narratives produce feelings of frustration or anger that quickly generate difficult and painful family conflict. The specifics of the conflict arise from the different position each family member occupies in relation to the issue of family care. Diane and her husband, Scott, are positioned more strongly in the ethic of care arising from the discourse of family responsibility. They choose to emphasize this ethic of care for others over individual self-care in shaping their personal priorities. Martine and Michael feel judged and disrespected by their sister, who expects them to play a more prominent role in the care of their mother and father. Diane and her husband feel taken advantage of and disrespected because there is an absence of mutuality and sharing in the care of Diane's parents.

Given all these background discursive forces at work, we do not find it useful to characterize this conflict as fueled primarily by unique internal or intrapsychic processes. Focusing on the wider cultural discourses that position family members in different ways opens up more possibilities for shifts in the conflict. Let's review how the identification of and the naming of these cultural narratives might be helpful to the mediator in assisting the family.

As we have been emphasizing throughout, the mediator is not separate and above the influence of cultural narratives of this kind. The mediator has been raised in a family and community permeated by ideas and beliefs about how families should function and how people should treat the elderly. To believe the mediator will be indifferent to the effects of these conflicting cultural ideas and behave in a neutral and unaffected way is not realistic. The mediator's challenge is to acknowledge the pull of the background narratives and at the same time to engage with the parties in as evenhanded a manner as possible, so that they feel they are treated equitably and respectfully.

Deconstructing Background Cultural Narratives

The mediator can also use the narrative skills of deconstruction to explore the impact of the diverse discourses affecting the Jamieson family. In a joint session with Scott and Diane, the mediator asks what it means to them to be responsible for taking care of Diane's mother and father. The mediator has an open and curious posture and asks these deconstructive questions.

- Tell us about what it means to you both to be a constant presence in the lives of your parents, or parents-in-law, at this stage in their lives?
- Where did you learn to be so committed, dedicated, and personally sacrificing to care for your parents in the way that you do?
- How have you been able to prioritize the quality of care offered to your parents over the demands of daily life?
- Because there are very diverse ideas about how families function, what ideas have influenced you to take the stand you have about the care of your parents?
- Do you have any conflict between taking care of your day-to-day needs and the pressures to be available to your parents?

These kinds of questions begin to elicit responses from Scott and Diane that show why they feel so strongly about providing care for Diane's parents. When these cultural narratives are explicitly named, the focus falls on the matrix of Scott and Diane's culturally shaped beliefs, rather than on possible psychological deficits in the siblings who are less involved in caring for their parents. This mediator intervention is an effort to externalize the problem, rather than to locate it inside Martine and Michael. The mediator now turns to Martine and Michael and asks deconstructive questions that help to expose the cultural narratives operating in their lives, without shaming or blaming them for the positions they have taken up with regard to the care of their parents. Here are some examples:

- What do you find are the most demanding pressures on you in your day-to-day lives that lead you to prioritize the time the way you both do?
- How do you balance the demands of caring for family alongside the intense demands of work and making a livelihood?
- If you were to be judged about why you are choosing your current priorities in life, what would you say in response? Which judgments do you find yourself most vulnerable to?

- How have you been able to be available for this meeting, despite other pressures that could have made it difficult to be here?

These questions give Martine and Michael an opportunity to discuss in full the events going on in their day-to-day lives that provide the context for their prioritizing.

Externalizing the cultural narratives gives the mediator and the parties an opportunity to talk explicitly about themes such as sacrifice, responsibility, commitment, stress, survival, and the meaning of family. This move can loosen the grip of the version of the conflict story that locates it in the personhood of the parties. More usefully, the conflict is now located in the diverse cultural narratives about the nature of family and caring for the elderly.

In this conflict the Jamieson family did not move easily toward some kind of resolution. The fact that Martine and Michael participated in the mediation process suggested that they had not abandoned the possibility that things could be different. This was not completely lost on Diane and Scott either. It became apparent, after a marathon mediation session, that Martine and Michael had felt guilty about their inability to provide the kind of care for their parents that Diane had shown. When the mediator externalized feelings of guilt and blame, it became apparent that these discourse effects had pushed Martine and Michael further away from addressing the situation and from facing Diane's concerns about fairness in providing care. All the members of the family had been pressured by many day-to-day demands that accompanied holding down demanding and stressful jobs. Diane responded by explaining how the situation had also made her feel guilty and blameworthy that she was not doing more, and she acknowledged that she was projecting a lot of her own frustration and feelings of inadequacy onto her siblings. It was also true that the costs of travel and the constraints of time and distance were an important factor. Michael spoke of his own relational difficulties and his own struggle to be available to his parents in the way he wanted. Martine spoke of the strains she experienced when interacting with her mother. She felt as though her mother judged her as less capable than her sister, and she had for a long time felt second best.

The mediation provided an opportunity for all family members to speak about the toll taken on all of them over the last eighteen months when stress, judgment, and distance had kept the siblings separated from one another. Michael and Martine said that they could do very little to be physically helpful to their mother and father. However, each decided to sacrifice some income to increase the amount of time that a private health care provider could spend in the home with their elderly parents. Understandings were reached and decisions made about how to go forward, with an agreement to meet again in three months to monitor progress. In this situation the greatest leverage in the mediation came from focusing on how cultural ideas have material effects, how they help construct problems, and how they often permit only a narrow range of solutions.

In this chapter we have emphasized the centrality of the cultural narratives at work in the production of all human conflict. What is unique about the practice of narrative mediation is its prominent interest in the relation between the microcosm of individuals' conflictual events and the macrocosm of discursive clashes. In the remaining chapters we turn to specific examples of the application of narrative mediation in large cultural systems that are fertile sites for this practice.

Chapter Five

Divorce Mediation and Collaborative Practice

Written with Chip Rose

By now you are familiar with the concepts of discourse and the explanations of the ways in which the pervasive cultural narratives circulating in any community have an intimate shaping influence on people's private experience. We have shown how these culturally produced private and personal experiences become central to the conflict narratives that play out between any parties when they perceive that their expectations and beliefs are being contravened. In this chapter we begin by briefly examining the power of the cultural narratives that shape people's experience of the transition from marriage to divorce. We review the practices of the legal system and how it often actively participates in reinforcing the problem-saturated stories of divorce. We compare a court-dominated practice with some of the new mediation and collaborative models that assist people with this important life event. As we describe these relatively new conflict resolution methodologies we show how a narrative approach can enrich divorce mediation and collaborative divorce models.

The Dominant Discourses of Marriage and Divorce

For most couples, divorce is an ugly event. It is ugly because many couples experience it as a transgression against the societal imperative to remain married to the same person for the whole of one's adult life. Lifelong marriage is assumed to be necessary for a normal, happy, and healthy life in which family, children, and community flourish. The act of marrying for eternity is introduced through childhood fairy tales of princes and princesses marrying and living happy ever after and is continually reinforced and secured by books, television shows, and movies. Young children enact these rituals of courtship and marriage in their play. Most young girls and women grow up with the notion that one day they will receive a proposal for marriage, a culmination of that childhood dream. Heterosexual media images showing the man on bended knee offering the engagement ring to his bride to be, followed soon after by a walk down the aisle with his bride in a white wedding gown, dominate the cultural landscape. People who have been married for even a decade or two are often publicly applauded for their commitment to the institution of marriage and family. The favored status of married couples is evident in both cultural and legal settings and is so pervasive that gay and homosexual couples are now seeking out what heterosexual couples have had available to them for centuries.

Divorce as a Violation of Culturally Sanctioned Narratives

To become separated and divorced is therefore often experienced by one or both parties not just as a cancellation of a contract but as a violation of childhood dreams, aspirations, and fantasies of lifelong commitment. Even during today's wedding ceremonies, people may consent to be with their partners "in sickness and in health," "for richer or poorer," "from this day forth until death do us part." Separation can be viewed as an experience of deep betrayal of the cultural norms of marriage as a sanctuary of love, safety, security, success, and permanence. Sometimes the prince or the princess of the courtship becomes viewed in divorce as the evil villain or the wicked witch.

Because divorce is still viewed as a cultural transgression, many people experience a complex array of emotions, ranging from guilt and shame for the failure of the marriage to betrayal, humiliation, and even frightening feelings of murderous rage and revenge. The divorcing couple's immediate families are deeply affected and often pulled willingly or not into the maelstrom of confusion and pain. Grandparents, parents, relatives, friends, and most of all, children struggle to manage the intensity of this life disruption. Some family members and friends have gone through their own divorces and have numerous opinions to offer about what their loved one should do to protect and defend themselves against the immoral and violating behaviors of the ex-spouse.

Divorce has existed in some form in most cultures through-out history (Coontz, 2005), but its frequency has increased in recent decades. However, the fact that divorce occurs in most Western countries among about half of the married population has done little to diminish the demonizing responses expressed to the person perceived as responsible for a divorce. Mediators, attorneys, psychologists, therapists, and judges learn very quickly the potency of the feelings and emotions, behaviors, and atti-tudes that are activated within a couple when their marriage ends. *No-fault divorce* has been accepted in many contexts, but it is still a relatively new legal discourse that is not always echoed in the way people speak.

The Legal System

Given that separation and divorce have become normal events, it is surprising that twenty-first-century communities are so poorly equipped to assist divorcing couples. In North America the court system continues to be the overarching institution that shapes and influences what happens between divorcing couples. Even though only approximately 5 percent of couples end up physi-cally in the courtroom, many divorce attorneys are compelled to practice as though their clients will have to settle the divorce in court.

If people were asked what they wanted as they transition out of their marriage to being single again, they might say that they want to keep their dignity intact and be respectful and support-ive toward themselves, their children, and their family members. Some might even profess a desire to conduct themselves in a dignified and respectful manner toward their ex-spouse, who is often the other parent of their children. Many people ultimately want to look back on their marriage and salvage from it at least some positive memories. They certainly want to diminish their pain and distress and move on. In narrative mediation these aspirations are gently nurtured. An effort is made at every turn to help divorcing couples keep alive their aspirations to maintain dignity and mutual respect.

The Court System and Conflict Escalation

The court system is set up to create the opposite outcome. In many ways the legal system perfectly serves the emotional impulse of spouses to blame one another for what went wrong in the marriage. Naïvely, some divorcing couples believe the legal system will provide a context for justice, resolution, and even healing. Although these outcomes might sometimes be achieved, the typical outcome is an escalation in the strength of problem-saturated narratives held by each spouse about the other. The demonization of the soon-to-be ex-spouse and the ratcheting up of negative behaviors and emotions is a regular consequence of the traditional court divorce.

Despite all the divorce court reality shows on television, many lay people have little idea of the anguish that awaits them as they enter the court system. Often divorcing couples are poorly advised by family members who do not know any viable alternatives to taking the husband or wife to court. Most people are familiar with the theory of the court process. The court is supposed to be where one's attorney will argue as strongly as possible to discredit and defeat one's opponent—in this case one's spouse. Many believe that after the judge has heard their lawyer's compelling arguments, he will figure out who is telling the truth and reach a just decision, probably in their favor. Few realize that as long as they are engaged in this court process, they will increasingly lose control of the chance to shape the possible outcomes in their favor. The consequences may have profoundly negative results for the rest of their and their children's lives. In contrast, narrative mediation works at keeping parents focused on the idea that a hopeful future is based upon their taking charge of their decisions and being responsible for creating a positive and desirable outcome for their and their children's futures.

In legal conversations the complex issues arising from any relationship can be explored only within a very limited and narrow range. The granting of temporary orders by the judge typically entrenches any position before the parties begin the process of divorce. Both parties are tempted to take a more extreme position than they originally intended in order to leverage more bargaining power. The focus is on making legal arguments, defending positions, and managing the counterarguments that will occur. The legal system does not have a framework for addressing emotions such as shame, humiliation, betrayal, and sadness. Instead, such emotions are often intensified.

Few judges have advanced training in family systems knowledge, mental health issues, culturally appropriate and effective parenting styles, and attachment theories. Sometimes a gross distortion of what is really going on is produced in the heated atmosphere of a divorce trial. From a narrative perspective no one should be surprised by this. Courtrooms are places where stories are constructed and contested rather than sites where the truth is unearthed (Bruner, 2002). A final decree by a judge may be unsatisfying to everybody because it rarely attends to the nuanced and complex issues that must be worked through by the divorcing couple. It is very unusual for both spouses to walk out of the courtroom feeling satisfied with the process. As Tesler and Thompson (2006) suggest, a family court can "shoot the survivors" (p. 3).

The wider cultural narratives that influence judges and shape their decisions hardly render them neutral agents. Like all professionals in the divorce process, judges come from varied religious or nonreligious backgrounds and have varied histories in relation to money, politics, and family life. Her particular history and experience will influence what a judge thinks is just and fair. Even when a judge relies on legal precedent, she will still be relying on the expression of dominant discourse to the extent that this discourse is expressed as legal consensus. The concept of the courtroom as a place where truth is shared and a fair and just outcome attained is not borne out in most courts. Instead, the court process can magnify the conflict. Normally responsible people are invited to engage in the worst possible behavior. The likelihood of holding on to one's dignity and maintaining mutual respect can be seriously diminished by what happens in the courtroom.

The court process is, nevertheless, probably still the best approach when specific and extreme issues need addressing. Roderic Duncan (2007), a family court judge, identifies five instances where a court intervention may be desirable:

- When a party continually fails to make spousal or child support payments at all or fails to pay them on time.
- When a party will not sign a deed transferring funds to an ex-spouse after a house has been sold.
- When people do not follow visitation plans.
- When there is a need to deal quickly with issues involving serious financial loss.
- When physical or psychological violence occurs.

But there are many divorces that do not involve any of these specific elements.

The Culture of Attorneys

Because the divorce courts operate by the same procedural rules as courts that deal with such grievous tragedies as murder, rape, and violent assault, lawyers representing each of the divorcing parties can employ the same strategies they would if they were defending or attempting to convict a serial murderer. A lawyer's traditional training is aimed at defeating an adversary at trial by all legal means available. Lawyers are groomed to compete. Much of the curriculum at law school focuses on the winning and losing of cases. Rather than guiding their clients, lawyers have been historically taught to take charge of their clients. They are trained to make positional arguments even when such arguments do not lend themselves to completing the divorce process. Attorneys are not trained to find out from their clients the knowledge, resources, and insights that would facilitate understanding between divorcing parties. Neither are they invited to help a client appreciate the negative psychological impact of certain conduct on an ex-spouse. They are not taught to understand how such psychological impacts might ultimately undermine the emotional well-being of the family. Rather than helping a divorcing client take responsibility for containing and managing the desire for justice and revenge, attorneys often nurture the client's feelings of self-righteousness and distorted sense of entitlement on the journey to court.

Thus traditional attorney training can feed into the animosities and resentments produced over the course of a marriage breakdown. Attorneys have scant training in paying attention to the emotional costs and suffering of the parties embroiled in the legal process. They focus instead on rights and obligations under the law, on damages and negligence, on breaches of contract, and on rules and procedures. Nancy Cameron (2003) identifies the kind of education lawyers receive as one that prepares them to fight and compete and that trains them in the "ethics of rights and justice" rather than the "ethics of care" (p. 47). Rarely is attention paid to the personal well-being of the attorney or the client. The emphasis is on the pragmatic characteristics of being a lawyer, such as attending to professional norms and one's image, income, performance, and caseload. The focus is on legal analysis and intellectual rigor and on the promotion of the personal adversarial norm in a professional climate that expects one to "attack and defend."

Lawyers are also trained to practice defensively and not to build relationships of trust, even with colleagues. They are trained primarily as courtroom advocates, not as conflict resolvers. Although law schools are shifting toward offering more training in mediation and conflict resolution, the emphasis remains on winning the case. This training can make it difficult for lawyers to move into a collaborative, problem-solving role. In fact, not only is much of the traditional training in law school unhelpful in assisting lawyers to work in mediation or in a collaborative model but it also sometimes actively works against helping couples to negotiate their differences.

In North America, when things go bad for those who have considerable financial resources, the mantra is "get yourself a good lawyer." A good lawyer is normally defined as somebody who is tough and aggressive—somebody who is expert at fighting fire with fire. Such lawyers come with nicknames like the "hired gun" or the "gladiator," "barracuda," "bomber" lawyer, or "high-priced star." Such caricatures are often featured in the legal dramas seen in popular television shows and movies. When people hire a lawyer they are often hoping for a charismatic heavy hitter who will beat up the opposition, vindicate their version of the truth, and produce desired outcomes. It is not surprising then that divorcing people also want this kind of lawyer to help them obtain the vengeance they feel is appropriate, given the suffering they have experienced at the hands of their spouse. The match between a vengeful spouse and a hired gun fits perfectly into the court system. There are always enough problem events accumulated in an unhappy marriage to serve as central plot elements in a rousing story of wrongdoing. As a client and an attorney work to rigidify and intensify this conflict-ridden account, the inevitable consequences are the production of exorbitant financial costs, the magnification of pain, the destruction of relationships, and sometimes the permanent psychological scarring of the children and adults involved. As Ronald Ousky and Stuart Webb (2006) comment, "Hiring an aggressive attorney is like hiring a contractor to build your house based upon his or her reputation as a demolition expert" (p. 6).

Experienced family attorneys have seen this destructive scenario played out hundreds of times. To their credit, many are troubled by it. Many attorneys, mental health professionals, financial specialists, and expert witnesses make significant financial gains from the escalation of conflict and the intensification of desires for vengeance. Increasingly, however, many of these professionals get to the point where the personal toll from being embroiled in these repetitive and unnecessary human tragedies becomes too much. Perhaps they assist a client to win but realize that the result for the client is financial ruin. Or perhaps they learn about the deep psychological scars now borne by many family members. It is this growing personal and professional dissatisfaction, especially among attorneys who have worked for years in the divorce court system, that is turning them away from their former training and toward more humane forms of assistance for divorcing couples.

Changes in the Practice of Family Law

In recent years many attorneys and judges have been actively distancing themselves from the court system. Some judges retire early to establish themselves in practices that aim to help couples address rather than worsen complex family issues. Many young professionals graduating from law school want to create practices that resolve conflict rather than escalate it. They do not want to enter a profession that involves them in slogging through months or years of testimonials and courtroom battles to expose the deficits, dishonesties, and immoralities of a client's ex-partner while protecting their own client from the predictable counterattack. A groundswell of change is occurring in North America, away from court procedures and toward more creative methods of addressing divorce.

For example, the development and expansion of divorce mediation, collaborative law, and collaborative divorce is giving hope to experienced attorneys that their profession can help families actually heal relationships during a divorce. Thousands of attorneys in the United States are abandoning the professional security and familiarity of the court system as they turn to the practice of mediation, collaborative law, and other collaborative methods. These new professional practices require skills such as narrative strategies, which are completely different from the ones drilled into young law students a few decades ago.

These relatively new methodologies of divorce mediation, collaborative law, and collaborative divorce are also inviting mental health and law professionals to forge stronger working relationships than they formerly entertained. This is a positive development, given the relatively recent history of distance and even estrangement between them. Not too long ago, mediation professionals in North America, especially in mediation areas requiring advanced relational skills, such as assisting couples to divorce, were unlikely to be lawyers. Over the last fifteen or so years, however, the mediation field has become almost completely populated by lawyers. With the promotion of collaborative divorce practices, mental health professionals and attorneys are now developing renewed respect for the unique contributions that each can make to assisting divorcing couples.

In the remainder of this chapter we will apply these new methodologies to assisting divorcing couples. In particular, we review some of the cutting-edge divorce mediation and collaborative divorce practices currently being applied and explore how these practices are enhanced by a narrative perspective.

Divorce Mediation

Mediators, including some attorneys and mental health professionals, have been conducting divorce mediations for decades. There are, however, huge variations in what mediators do in their practice. Readers will be familiar with the definition of mediation as a practice that requires a third party, or a *neutral,* to assist two or more parties in seeking resolution to a conflict. What is less well known is the significant degree of variation in the types of mediation practiced as well as in the styles adopted by mediators.

Many attorneys and judges who are comfortable in the controlled and rule-bound setting of the courtroom gravitate in their mediator roles toward an evaluative and directive model of mediation. In this model the mediator controls both process and content. This control is achieved primarily through the use of a caucus process. The mediation typically begins with the disputing parties gathered in the same room to hear an explanation of this process. After that the parties are placed in separate rooms, and the mediator participates in shuttle mediation. The major focus is to engineer a settlement, and scant attention is given to relationship dimensions. This form of mediation can be dominated by the presentation of legal argument and by a push to settle. Parties are frequently reminded of the likely consequences of a courtroom battle if they fail to settle. Although it is unusual to use the evaluative and directive model for divorce mediation, habitual and ingrained practices among many attorneys and judges can lead to tight control over divorcing parties and an emphasis on substantive issues rather than relational ones.

It will already be clear to the reader that narrative mediation, unlike the mediation approach just described, has a strong facilitative orientation. In this approach the mediator shapes the process and the parties are responsible for shaping content issues. The mediator is responsible for managing the decision-making processes and for managing the relational and emotional climate of the mediation itself. On the one hand this is a challenging shift for many attorney mediators, who are used to being in charge of their clients. On the other hand it is exciting to meet the many highly skilled attorneys who have transformed their practice by adopting a facilitative model in which they view their clients as having valuable expertise to be drawn upon in the search for solutions. Facilitative mediators use persistent curiosity in their questioning to identify client resources that can be used in solving conflicts and building understanding. They are skilled listeners and intentional practitioners who help keep their clients' aspirations and goals clearly to the fore in the mediated exchanges.

We have invited Chip Rose, a highly experienced facilitative mediator and trainer, to contribute to this chapter some of the concepts, techniques, and procedures that he uses in his mediation practice. In the following section Chip reveals the common threads in his orientation and in narrative mediation.

A Facilitative Orientation

Many professionals who work with relationship conflict come from a place of control. This is particularly true of legal professionals given the training that John and Gerald have described earlier. Nor are mental health professionals immune from the seductive pull of evaluative and directive interventions. Mental health professionals can fall into the same ethos as many lawyers do as a result of the education and workplace conditioning they have been exposed to. They too can seek to establish professional power through taking up expert positions from which they control their clients in ways that invite client passivity.

Leading from Behind

There is a wonderful Zen concept known as *leading from behind*. This is a concept that resides at the heart of narrative mediation. It underlies the practice of ensuring throughout all stages of the conflict resolution process that it is the client who is making his or her own decisions. It is also a perfect point of departure for getting away from the leading-from-the-front role of the attorney in litigation. In facilitative and particularly in narrative mediation, empowering the client is at the same time elegantly simple and challengingly complex. As with any learned skill, it takes a great deal of practice to shed the encumbering layers of the professional as expert knower. Real-world experience can easily blind the mediator to the benefits of working with a client-focused agenda.

A facilitative or narrative orientation requires the mediator to refrain from assuming that professional expertise is the answer to the clients' problems. On the contrary, the solutions that will be the most meaningful to clients are those that the clients have identified. These solutions will be generated through deconstructive effort and careful questioning.

I was doing a collaborative practice training in London, Ontario, in May 2000 when I happened upon a curling match on television. As I watched with interest a sport that is not much seen in California, a metaphor formed in my mind: the game of bowling is to litigation as the sport of curling is to mediation. Consider these characteristics of each sport. In bowling, the bowler firmly grips the weighted ball by the holes and forcefully powers it down the alley. The greater the amount of damage to the standing pins, the higher the score achieved. The most critical action occurs as a result of the force, direction, and rotational pressure applied by the player to the ball.

Curling, in contrast, begins with a smooth granite stone, or rock, being set in motion on the ice by one of the curlers. The most critical action, however, takes place in front of the moving stone where the sweepers use brooms to eliminate the impediments that would prevent the stone from achieving its highest score. The parallels with the two different approaches to resolving interpersonal relationship disputes seem wonderfully obvious. In the former (bowling/litigation), each lawyer uses the power of the law and its procedures to create an outcome for the case based on terms most favorable to his own client. In the latter (curling/mediation), the mediator seeks to remove the psychological, emotional, relational, and educational impediments that prevent clients from obtaining the most mutually beneficial resolution. This metaphor also fits perfectly well with narrative practice. Narrative mediators are focused on identifying and deconstructing the restraints of cultural discourse, thereby freeing clients to embrace some of their heartfelt objectives, plans, and dreams.

The professional who relies on the power of the legal system to get to resolution is generally engaged in a competitive, zero-sum negotiation strategy and is generally not concerned with maximizing the value of the settlement to the other party. In a facilitative or narrative mediation process, the professional focuses on clearing the path of impediments so that both clients can determine if and when they have reached the most mutually beneficial resolution. Without this shift in responsibility for the outcome of the process from the professionals to the clients, the resulting settlement can never be described as maximized. The clients are the only ones who have the capacity to assess the personal value of any settlement. Experience has shown time and again that the most satisfying settlements are those that incorporate many more exchanges of value between the clients than those that are recognized in the law. These types of exchanges will emerge only from a safe, structured, and strategic collaboration in which the clients play an active role and embrace their responsibility for the quality of the outcome.

One of the essential principles I have shared with the people I have trained over the years is the importance of making clients aware that mediation is not a single process that they are sharing but rather many processes. For example, each client comes into the mediation with his or her own set of perspectives, beliefs, and problem-saturated stories. Although there may be overlapping points of connection between divorcing clients, these clients should not forget that they have different visions and goals for what they want in the future, and must also grapple with the fact that there are no magic powers to make one spouse come to share the other's perspectives. If the divorcing spouses had that ability, they would already have used it and would likely not be sitting in mediation.

Differences as Circumstances

I invite the parties to consider their differences as circumstances. This is similar to the narrative practice of using externalizing language. From a narrative perspective the couple would be asked to consider how "differing circumstances" have affected their situation, rather than each falling into the temptation to pathologize the other as "difficult" or "belligerent." Because neither party, nor the mediator, has the capacity to unilaterally change the mind of one party to meet the expectations of the other, the only pragmatic conclusion for each of the parties is to commit to working with, and respecting, the differing perspectives, beliefs, and stories of the other.

This is not necessarily an easy task to accomplish. It can be challenging for new mediators to invite the parties to sit in one another's presence and listen to opinions and outcome objectives in diametric opposition to their own. In this context the simple act of listening might at first seem counterintuitive. Because it does not fit with the demands of the conflict story, couples can initially conceive this action to be threatening to their own viewpoint. However, the parties quickly realize that if they offer an attentive ear, even when they may not agree, their ex-spouse can honor them in return by listening to their own plans and ideas. In narrative mediation, rather than having the mediator take an evaluative role, the parties must evaluate their preferences and decide whether to give continued credence to the conflict story or to invest commitment in an alternative story. They must decide either to work independently and in opposition to one another or to commit to collaborating in a mediated process and to doing their most important work in the presence of one another. In this approach, choices need to be viewed in the context of their consequences.

When clients choose to work in the isolated environment of litigation, they elect to work in a process that has, as one of its most critical implicit assumptions, the idea that there are a limited number of favorable outcomes. In the face of that assumption, it follows that the one who captures the most prevails. It is competition in a zero-sum game. In facilitative and narrative mediation the explicit assumption is that the number of desirable outcomes has been exponentially increased and the only way that one party can achieve a maximized benefit in the settlement is for the other party to do so as well. This is the unique potential of a collaborative endeavor. Parties can achieve a result that truly maximizes their potential only if that outcome is achieved by each of them.

A Strategic Metaphor

Such outcomes will not occur serendipitously. To achieve the goals of the parties, strategic design, structure, and implementation are process prerequisites. It is more than a little ironic that each participant, feeling threatened by the goals of the other, discovers that now he or she must tolerate, respect, and engage with the individual process needs of the other. This reality leads to an important design function for the process. For years I have used the following metaphor to help explain the purpose behind this design to skeptical clients.

Mediator: Recognizing the futility of trying to change each other's minds, consider approaching the process this way. Imagine that the two of you share backyards, separated only by a four-foot fence. Each of you can see everything that is going on in the other's backyard. Everything you need to know about how to negotiate with the other person will be displayed in front of you. There is a price to pay for this tremendous privilege. Do not assume that you have permission to talk over the fence.

If you want to know something about the other person, or his or her perspectives, interests, or goals, ask a respectful question that seeks information and does not try to make an editorial comment about the other. If you fail to treat the other person with respect, he or she will likely go inside and leave you alone in your backyard. Each of you has autonomy over what goes on in your backyard. You are free to ask any question, explore any perspective, pursue any interest, tell any story, so long as it does not invade the turf of the other. Act with the same civilities and courtesies as you would offer to a new neighbor who had just moved in next door to you. As this works effectively in a social context, it will work as well in these negotiations.

At a first glance, the mediator is doing nothing more than restoring necessary boundaries that provide protection for each party from the invasive and counterproductive engagements of the other. However, this stage setting is a powerful yet subtle invitation to the parties to consider how they are inextricably bound in a mutual cause-and-effect relationship. The irony of this metaphor is that clients universally experience it as providing them with protection from the other, and neither sees himself or herself as the one from whom protection is needed.

Asking clients if they are interested in being informed when they are unintentionally invading the autonomy of the other will almost always result in an affirmative answer. The simple reason for this is their lack of awareness of the extent to which each is poised at the fence ready to jump into the backyard of the other. As a result they will readily agree to being reminded to respect the autonomy of the other, as it reinforces their desire for protection.

As part of an introduction to the mediation process, I ask clients if they are interested in the mediation being effective. Almost without exception they concur that "being effective" is a good goal for the process. I follow that question with a request, inquiring whether they will give me permission to let them know when they are not acting effectively. I have never had anyone respond negatively to that question. With those two safe and simple questions, I have helped them become aware of the value of aspiring to a standard of behavior that was not on their radar screens when they came into the process. This is an artful way of inviting clients to listen to one another and to maintain respectful behavior throughout the course of mediation. I also model respectful inquiry and gain their permission to intervene to remind them when they forget.

Mutual Self-Interest

Self-interest can contribute to the attainment of a mutually beneficial and maximized outcome for the parties when it is used properly in a collaborative negotiation. Two important considerations must be observed. First, self-interest needs to be distinguished from self-centeredness. The latter is a form of self-absorption, whereas the former explores the relationship dynamic. Second, the flip side of self-interest is mutuality. In a relationship negotiation, one can maximize the fulfillment of self-interest only if it is achieved bilaterally, on each side of the negotiation. In my experience nearly all parties are motivated out of self-interest. The story of the *needs of the self* is powerfully persuasive for most people. I can join quickly with my clients when using the metaphor of self-interest. Paradoxically, it opens the door for clients to strive for mutuality as the most productive pathway to the realization of self-interest.

The most valuable aspects of an agreement come from the outcome possibilities put on the table by the parties. Before clients will contribute valuable settlement possibilities, each needs to believe that it fits with his or her story of self-interest to do so. If it does not, clients will withhold much of what might otherwise be helpful resources for building understanding and ultimately reaching agreement.

The skilled mediator will remain mindful, however, that clients frequently mask important intentions by selectively highlighting others in order to appear cooperative. In divorce mediation these other agendas might include demonstrating concern for the spouse, identifying personal commitment to the children, avoiding confrontation or conflict, assuaging a sense of guilt, or seeking to establish the moral framework within which an agreement will be reached.

If a mediator is to facilitate the parties in reaching agreement, it is important to encourage the parties to be as open as possible about their interests, goals, values, and objectives. One approach to this task is to directly address the issue of self-interest. A sample introduction of the role of self-interest might sound like this:

Mediator: I want to let you know that as we begin this mediation process, it is entirely appropriate that each of you should feel free to act out of your own self-interest. In reality you will probably do that whether I give you permission to do so or not. You are each beginning the journey of taking control over the next part of your life and there is no reason that you should abandon a what's-in-it-for-me mind-set. However, there is something very important to understand about the flip side of self-interest, and that is the element of mutuality. As you consider what is, or is not, in your self-interest, be aware that your self-interest cannot be maximized without the other person achieving the same. The two of you are the only ones who can add options to the settlement possibilities and expand the opportunities for ultimate agreement. While this might sound counterintuitive, the success of this approach has been demonstrated over and over.

I invite clients to see the value of the accruing benefits when acting out of a story of *mutual* self-interest. I also acknowledge that each of them will have different nonnegotiable visions and plans for the future. Together these can become motivating factors that draw them into the mediation process. These interventions are not imposed upon the clients. Rather, their thoughts, feelings, and concerns are probed to see if the mediator's ideas resonate for them.

Collaborative Law

In the last decade, attorneys have increasingly embraced collaborative law as an alternative to the court hearing in helping couples divorce. In collaborative law proceedings, divorcing spouses typically have their own attorney to represent them. However, this representation does not under any circumstances occur in a courtroom. In the early 1990s, Stuart Webb, a lawyer in Minneapolis, Minnesota, introduced the collaborative law approach, in which lawyers and their clients sign a participation agreement that excludes them from taking their case to court and requires the clients to provide full and complete financial disclosure. This simple yet profound difference has driven a wedge between, on the one hand, the court-conditioned impulse of lawyers to "win the case" at whatever brutal emotional and financial cost and, on the other hand, the vengeful desires of wounded spouses to see "justice" administered to their ex-partners in the courtroom. The attorneys practicing collaborative law are committed to no longer fueling the fire of spousal conflict. In fact, the participation agreement requires them to focus only on resolving their client's divorce *outside* the court system. This requirement has begun to transform the entire foundation of some divorce lawyers' practice. Given the recent success of collaborative law in the context of divorce, civil attorneys are now using the same procedures in addressing civil cases.

The participation agreement to collaborate and avoid court procedures sits in stark contrast to the serving of a summons and the filing of petitions. Because attorneys are obliged by this agreement to remove themselves from the process if their clients insist on a courtroom resolution, the lawyer's sole focus becomes resolving the conflict through a mediated process. Instead of being advocates who drive home their own clients' agendas without attention to the spouse's needs, attorneys are invited to become solvers of the problems between the divorcing persons. The collaborative lawyer must develop constructive negotiation skills rather than theatrical courtroom performance skills.

The collaborative lawyer's role is to educate and guide his client through a process of adjustment following the dissolution of a marriage, rather than to conquer his client's opponent, who in many cases still shares in the parenting of the children of the marriage. Instead of eliciting data to gain a strategic edge, the collaborative lawyer accesses his client's resources for conflict resolution in order to foster a climate of cooperation and negotiation. These changes in practice align very well with the narrative orientation to mediation. As a result, many collaborative attorneys have expressed strong interest in a narrative orientation to conflict resolution. It is estimated that about 20 percent of the challenge in helping couples divorce relates purely to legal matters. The other 80 percent is about managing the emotional reactions of the divorcing parties.

Narrative approaches to conflict resolution encourage openness among the conflicted parties. Attorneys aim to create an atmosphere of transparency around all the important issues. The narrative metaphor assists attorneys to deal with emotional and value-laden issues that in a court proceeding would be sealed off from examination. Collaborative lawyers are now trained in client-centered listening skills and use the techniques of the narrative externalizing metaphor and mapping the effects to work with strong negative emotions such as vengeful desires, feelings of shame and humiliation, mistrust, and betrayal. Rather than emphasizing only the legal dimensions of the case, attorneys learn to prioritize clients' needs and concerns and to steer their clients toward areas of consensus building. Out of the alternative stories of cooperation, productive agreements and constructive future plans can be drawn.

One of the biggest challenges for a collaborative attorney is to resist the pull to take center stage and drive the entire process of the divorce while the client sits passively in the passenger seat having the legal landscape pointed out to him. A collaborative process requires the lawyer to let go of some of the power and prestige of her traditional role and the status accrued in the hierarchical structure of the court. The attorney's expertise is instead directed toward identifying the client's priorities, goals, and personal resources. The attorney's job is now to elicit and work with her client's knowledge of his children's and family's strengths that can be called on throughout this difficult life event. A narrative method also positions the attorneys of the two parties in a collaborative effort to pool the resources of both spouses in order to build understandings and negotiate agreements. To work in this way lawyers must drop the knee-jerk reaction of warning their clients against making more than minimal concessions, the traditional practice of risk avoidance.

In most cases the collaborative model works well. Attorneys focus the couple on the needs of the children and work at a pace that is helpful for families. In rare instances the couple may abandon the participatory agreement. Once they do so, they must seek new representation and start the whole process over. What tends to threaten the collaborative law model most is the situation where the parties' emotional states cannot be contained by their legal counsel. When client rage and desire for vengeance cannot be contained by the attorneys and wild emotional swings fueled by feelings of betrayal and mistrust remain unchecked, the process is seriously threatened. These issues are best addressed in the full collaborative divorce model.

Collaborative Divorce

A model that has become highly successful in the turn toward collaborative practices is the development of a collaborative divorce team. This model was first instituted in San Francisco by Peggy Thompson and her colleagues.

The collaborative divorce model establishes a collaborative divorce team that will work with the divorcing couple through the divorce. In addition to a collaborative attorney, a divorce coach is retained by each of the divorcing spouses. These coaches are mental health professionals whose task it is to contain, manage, and channel the emotional and relational dimensions of the divorce. They do this in the same way as a mediator (a neutral third person) would, but each coach is working with a specific party in the divorce rather than being neutral. Their role is to help diffuse conflict and keep clients focused on their end goal rather than being diverted into problem-saturated stories of the past. They can help to co-create a safe, productive environment for sound decision making and reduce the level of fear and intimidation that their clients may feel. They also play a role in regulating the pacing and speed of dealing with thorny issues and addressing emotionally laden subjects. Sometimes coaches have to quiet low-level accusations and threats to go to court and help their clients to feel heard. They can guide their clients to separate emotionally volatile subjects from the legal matters that have to be decided. (This role is analyzed further in our discussion of the one-coach or one-mediator model later in this chapter.)

In addition to coaches the full collaborative divorce model uses child specialists who also have a mental health background. The task of these child specialists is to help the parents hear and understand the needs and wishes of the children. The child specialist becomes the children's mouthpiece in the negotiation of a comprehensive caregiving plan for the children. Another third party in the collaborative divorce model is the financial specialist. This person can provide advice to each party about matters to do with determining net worth, asset management, tax laws, budgeting, and cash flow. Because financial specialists do not represent any one part of the family system, they can play a key role in guiding the family through the whole process.

A Collaborative Divorce Team Metaphor

Peter Roussos (2006) has developed a helpful descriptive metaphor to capture the complex relationships that need to be addressed in working in a collaborative team. He describes the collaborative divorce model as a "Charter Airplane Service." The airplane is co-owned by the flight crew (that is, the collaborative divorce team), whose unique areas of expertise are necessary to fly the plane (that is, manage the process toward a successful divorce). The clients are passengers. The passengers are traveling to a destination that the team must agree to support. The divorcing couple must be willing to enter a collaboration agreement and sincerely address their various challenges in an open and honest fashion and ultimately plan to resolve their difficulties in a mutually respectful manner. However, as Roussos describes, there are destinations the team will not travel to and the team may suggest that the passengers will have to find other services if they wish to go there. For example, one of the parties may be hiding matrimonial assets. It may also be that one of the parties has an unaddressed, serious mental health issue or is participating in an ongoing, undisclosed affair. There may be a history of spousal violence, sexual or physical abuse of the children, or serious verbal or emotional abuse. In some instances the couple may not be prepared to observe the agreement not to litigate their case in court. On other occasions clients cannot afford the services of the collaborative team. According to the collaborative divorce model, all these couples are assumed to be heading for a destination the team cannot support and are deemed not suitable for a collaborative process.

Continuing the metaphor, the passengers select their own flight crew. They select their own collaborative team to work with them. Unlike the passengers on a commercial airliner, these passengers have a great deal of input into the flight plan. The flight plan is in the end negotiated between the couple and the team. There must be consensus on the operating guidelines, the stipulations about how this process will work. If the divorcing spouses do not adhere to the flight plan, they will have to fly with somebody else. Although the clients participate in defining the goals and objectives they wish to reach, the collaborative team is responsible for managing the process, in the same way that a mediator is responsible for facilitating understandings and agreements between disputants. The flight crew, which also owns the airplane, must be at the controls in order to maintain the "structural integrity" of the process. Roussos suggests that in flying the plane, each of the professionals should take turns at the controls to guide the plane safely toward its destination. He points out that it takes constant coordinated effort between the members of the collaborative team to assist a divorcing couple to achieve a healthy and constructive divorce.

Team Mechanics

The collaborative divorce process involves a complex negotiation of relationships between collaborative divorce team members and the divorcing couple. Peter Roussos and the San Diego Family Law Group, for example, begin the process by gathering the professional team together for a meeting before meeting with the parties. The team members can share initial impressions of client issues at this early stage and identify client strengths as well as challenges. They can also discuss their expectations about how they will work together, the kind of communication they will employ, (including the use and confidentiality of e-mail), case management responsibilities, fees, and billing procedures. Team members also use this opportunity to schedule meeting dates for eight-way meetings, which involve the two divorcing spouses, the two attorneys, a financial specialist, the two coaches, and a child specialist. In the first eight-way meeting the clients are invited to reflect on their hopes and aspirations about what will come from the collaborative process. The team will consistently refer to these hopes and goals when the clients encounter obstacles along the way. At this first meeting all formal documents outlining the principles and procedures that will guide future deliberations are signed. These documents include stipulations relating to the retention of the professional team. Signing these documents in the presence of the full team has symbolic value as it commits all players to a shared approach to addressing the challenges to be faced and overcome during the divorce process.

Each of the professional team members explains his or her role and responsibilities and the related responsibilities and duties of the parties. For example, the financial specialist explains the process of settling the divorcing spouses' financial affairs. He discusses the specific financial documentation that each client will be responsible for generating, deadlines for the submission of financial documents, and other specific financial matters such as business evaluations, unusual tax circumstances, urgent financial decisions, and the like. The child specialist discusses the logistics of meeting with the children and with the parents and the production of a report. The scheduling of meetings with the different team members is often determined by the pace of the financial specialist's activities. *Milestone* meeting dates are scheduled to keep the process moving. Among the meeting configurations are attorney, coach, and client three-way meetings; full-team telephone conferences; and specialist meetings between particular professional team members and their client or clients.

The One-Coach or One-Mediator Model

Many divorce mediators who work with the divorcing parties and the lawyers who represent them are attorneys or mental health professionals themselves. This is commonly the case in Canada and in other countries where mental health professionals and attorneys have worked together to mediate between divorcing spouses. Several years ago a hybrid model developed in the collaborative movement that is a more elaborate intervention than one that has only the disputing parties and a mediator present. It differs too from a model in which the disputing parties and two lawyers, each representing one of the parties, are present. The hybrid model adds to these basic configurations, a coach or mental health professional who facilitates the joint meetings of the professional team. Her coach or mediator role requires this practitioner to oversee the mental health aspects of the divorce. Another way to view this model is as a scaled-down version of the full collaborative divorce team, a team that has only one rather than two coaches. Linda Solomon, a counselor, therapist, and mediator in the Dallas–Fort Worth area, along with her colleagues developed this *neutral coach model,* as she calls it. Lawyers who had worked with her previously in the collaborative law model, with only the clients and their respective attorneys meetings, were often reporting that each client would "shut down" when the other client's lawyer spoke. Some were also reporting discomfort with the emotional intensity of the divorce process. This request for help with the emotional content of the process motivated the design of the neutral coach model with a single coach.

In essence this model uses an experienced mental health professional in a mediator-like, third-party role, but this professional is not confined to traditional mediator functions. She has a multifaceted role coaching and managing couple dynamics as well as managing the professional team members who support the couple. In this model the professionals on the team always include the third-party mental health professional and the two lawyers. A neutral financial professional and child specialist may join in as and when needed. The third-party mental health professional is involved with the case from the beginning, and may be the one who brings the couple into the collaborative process. A licensed and experience mental health professional has the skills to screen, assess, counsel, case manage, intervene in a crisis, make appropriate referrals, facilitate group dynamics, use family systems knowledge, problem solve and model healthy communication skills. In some instances this coach or mediator will develop a parenting plan and educate clients about healthy coparenting and communication skills. Sometimes she will hold caucus, or separate, meetings with the parties to assist them.

As with the full collaborative divorce model, the practice of narrative mediation is ideally suited to this one-coach or one-mediator model. It requires the mental health professional to work with the multiple background stories of the parties and with the parties' legal representation at the same time. Narrative mediation fosters awareness of how discursive influences in the conflict affect the parties and the attorneys in different ways. For example, attorneys can be affected by the discourses of their traditional training and can become strident legal advocates. Such cultural influences can compromise the process and must be managed. The parties can be affected by problematic traditional gender discourses that constrain their decision making around such issues as child-care plans and money. Externalizing the problem can be helpful when there are multiple professionals producing multiple agendas. Skillful externalizing can marshal the efforts of the clients and professionals into joint action against the externalized problems rather than against one another.

As Linda Solomon has found, for coaches to be effective in the neutral one-coach model it is crucial that they meet with the clients at the beginning of the process, even before meeting with the professional team (personal communication, December 12, 2007). The purpose of these client meetings is to listen to problem-saturated narratives, to identify potential resources to call on later, and to understand clients' vulnerabilities and challenges. These efforts build client's trust toward one another and toward the process. In the last section of this chapter we identify specific narrative approaches that contribute to the potency and effectiveness of divorce mediation, the coach or mediator model, and the full collaborative divorce team approach.

Narrative Strategies for Establishing Client Goals and a Vision

One of the first narrative moves of the coach is to inquire into the hopes and aspirations that the clients have for a successful divorce process. It is helpful to begin with the end in mind. To do so brings the alternative story into view from the start. Here are a variety of questions that a coach can ask clients at the first mediation or collaborative meeting.

- Imagine that this divorce process were conducted in a way that left your children feeling cared for, respected and understood. What would you be striving to attain during this very difficult period?
- When you are on the other side of this process of getting divorced, tell us the kind of family relationships that would be desirable to you?
- What would you like to be proud of having accomplished through this difficult time?
- What would a successful and healing collaborative divorce [or mediation] look like to you?
- What part could you play to keep dignity and integrity present throughout this divorce?

Each of these questions invites clients to engage with the plot elements or themes of an alternative story, a story likely to be in stark contrast to the conflict-saturated story that they are already familiar with. There is great value in asking each divorcing spouse to write down his or her own needs, priorities, hopes, and goals and to articulate in behavioral terms what success might look like. For example, success might mean talking to the children every second day during the course of the week. The members of the professional team can also carefully record the aspirations of the divorcing couple with regard to caring for the children's needs, promoting their own emotional well-being, building trust, maintaining integrity and dignity, and ensuring safety. This information can be regularly called upon if the couple begin to stray away from their stated intentions.

Preparing the Couple and the Team for Adversity in the Process

Being in close proximity to a spouse during a divorce process can be stressful. When people encounter intense adversity, their bodies have a hardwired physiological response that tells them to fight or take flight. Under the duress of painful emotional conflict, individuals can revert to behavioral patterns that were modeled and rehearsed for them in their family of origin. Physiological responses are innate but how these responses are manifested depends on the cultural training in a person's upbringing. Some people psychologically withdraw or shut down because of emotional overload. This is the flight response. They retreat in ways similar to the ways they behaved when their parents or caregivers were in crisis. In this state they are unlikely to be direct, communicate openly, or face up to difficult issues. Instead, they become anxious, avoidant, and depressed. Whole families can practice psychological retreat in the face of intense psychological crises.

This is a difficult dynamic for professionals to deal with. However, it may not be as challenging as managing the fight response that some individuals revert to under stress. In these instances people can be explosive, antagonistic, hypervigilant, volatile, and unpredictable. Interactions can quickly turn into shouting matches and become verbally abusive. Even professionals can become psychologically overloaded and revert to the habits familiar to them from their own families. This can render professionals ineffective in addressing the escalation. We have found it helpful to discuss stress responses with team members and the divorcing spouses before the divorce mediation or collaborative divorce is underway. Here are some narrative questions that we might ask our clients to help them prepare for potential adversity in a constructive way. These questions may alert them to patterns of behaviors that they can recognize as unhelpful, and may help them to be proactive in taking action to manage these behaviors.

- In your family of origin or current family or both, what have you learned about what to do in the middle of a stressful and upsetting conflict? For example, do you fight, compete, withdraw, harbor resentment under the surface, address the problem and collaborate, or use some other strategy?
- What style of conflict resolution are you using in this present conflict with your spouse? Are you interested in changing your approach to an approach that is less costly to you and the family?

Other narrative questions can help family members connect with resources they can call on in times of adversity.

- What strategies do you find most helpful to calm yourself down when you find yourself getting activated?
- What is the best method you have used to take care of yourself and still be constructive when your hot buttons are pushed?
- What approach works best when you are starting to withdraw and you know you need to stay present and work difficult issues through?
- What are the signals in your body that alert you that you need to do something different to settle yourself down?

Professional team members can benefit from considering these same issues when their hot-button issues are activated by other team members. In a private team meeting, members could find benefit in asking one another these questions:

- How might this couple's conflict be activating in us old reactions from our own families? Do you want to try something different in responding to this situation?
- I am wondering whether we are reverting to old habits that get in the way of our working more productively together?

Through an open dialogue about behavioral patterns that make it difficult to maintain integrity and dignity, the professional team and the divorcing couple can manage difficult hot-button issues. Team members can better understand the conflictual challenges occurring, develop more empathy for others who have a different style of relating, become better equipped to change the conflict story, and become more intentional in their own practice.

Managing Cultural Projections

People's responses can also be activated by those who remind them of people in their past. They project on to particular others responses that do not belong to these others. This is not just the psychological dynamic known as transference or countertransference. We are referring to cultural projections of what people expect others to do on the basis of cultural background. For example, if people expect a mental health professional to be an excellent listener and highly empathetic and she does not behave that way, they can be activated in a negative way because their projections and the professional's behavior do not match. Projections activate stories of association with people from an individual's past. Negative associations can fuel negative reactions in ways that people are often not aware of. When projected cultural expectations are not met, feelings of having been let down and of anger and betrayal can occur.

Sometimes team members' responses are activated by one or another of the parties and hot buttons are pressed. Team members can help colleagues understand what is going on by asking, "Does this client remind you of somebody else who has had a negative effect on you?" or, "It seems like he really activates you. What do you think is going on?"

Negative projections can get a collaborative team into trouble as well. When a team member is negatively activated by another team member, addressing the issue is a delicate process. If the issue is not directly managed it will pay out in indirect and covert ways that sabotage the effectiveness of the team. Here are some questions to help team members engage in a more open and respectful way.

- This style of discussing these issues is getting difficult for me. It seems to me that rights issues are dominating the conversation, and I would like us to pay attention to the ethics of care and respect as well. Are you open to this?

- It feels to me like we are getting caught up in a win-lose story. Can we find the win-win elements in this situation right now?
- I know we need sound legal analysis and intellectual rigor in viewing this case. I think we also need to pay attention to the relational and emotional issues that are surfacing right now in this family. Are we willing to go there now?
- I am feeling like I am in that old story of "attack and defend." I would really like us to focus on building more collaboration. It feels like the conversation is escalating toward the old adversarial posture that we are all too familiar with. Am I coming out of left field, or are others concerned with how this conversation is going?
- It seems like professional defensiveness is taking over this discussion. I wonder if we can address these issues by laying them out so we can see what we are dealing with?

We have worked in collaborative divorce teams where team members became caught up in a blame analysis of other team members that paralleled the blaming responses that the divorcing couple were exhibiting toward each other. Team members may indirectly accuse one another of being ineffective by making suggestions like these: "My client's feelings and concerns are not being addressed by your client," "Your client is behaving in an abusive way and you need to teach her to communicate better," or, "My client seems to have a more sophisticated analysis of what is going on than your client. How about you bring him up to speed before we meet next?"

These low-level and indirect accusatory messages can be approached by asking a question such as this: "Can we work together as we challenge the relationship dynamics that are going on between the clients?" Attention is thus diverted back to the problematic relational dynamics between the clients. Here is an example of a response that works by naming the systemic cyclical connections being played out in relation to the divorcing couple: "I notice that when Mary criticizes Richard for his inability to communicate with their daughter he goes on the defensive and criticizes Mary's lack of ability to manage some of the financial matters in the home. It seems at that point the problem pulls us into the fray in different ways and then we feel like we have to defend our client against other members of the team. What do you notice?"

Openly naming and externalizing problematic patterns of exchange between the couple that can begin to ensnare team members can help the team members step back from the conflict story so they can see more clearly what is going on. Doing this in a tentative, curious way and inviting other team members to report on what they are noticing can significantly diminish the desire to blame other team members.

Using a Reflecting Team

Sometimes the collaborative divorce professional team and the couple get stuck and there does not seem much hope of a resolution. At these times the team members talk among themselves about things that could be done to help the couple move forward. Many of these ideas are not shared directly with the divorcing couple for fear that the ideas would be rejected or found inappropriate. Narrative practitioners sometimes have the professional team act as a reflecting team to play the part of outsider witnesses for the couple and to help unstick problem situations. In this process, the team members talk together about their reflections and responses; they do this in front of the couple but not directly to them. Team members discuss what they notice regarding trends in the interaction and speak about how they are personally affected. This conversation has the strategic purpose of exposing the couple to new perspectives through hearing the reflections of the professional team.

This conversation is delivered in a thoughtful and respectful way in order to help the couple gain a greater sense of understanding, awareness, knowledge, and motivation with which to address outstanding problems. Written statements expressing the children's responses to what is happening to them could be included in a reflecting team conversation.

One important ground rule must be followed to make the reflecting team effective. Under no circumstances should the team members interact in such a manner as to attempt to teach one or both divorcing parents some kind of moral lesson. The conversation conducted by the professional team should be tentative and exploratory rather than a forum for the delivery of expert analysis. It is not intended to be an opportunity for the professional team members to grandstand their opinions. The discussion should in no way overtly or covertly imply that some kind of deficiency, deficit, pathology, or dysfunction is inherent in an individual or in the couple. Team members are certainly permitted to make personal reflections on related issues that may serve to heighten the couple's awareness of new ideas for addressing problematic and challenging issues. The purpose of this conversation is to create for the divorcing couple, in the silence of listening, a chance to reflect on the impact of what has been said so far, and that process may open up space for new directions in the conversation. This is how the reflecting team process might be introduced to the couple:

Mediator: The collaborative team would like to begin a conversation together about the issues, concerns, and challenges that have been presented by you during the time we have worked together. You will initially find this discussion a little unusual because the team members will talk to one another but will not address you directly. Essentially, you will be spying on the conversation of the team. The conversation will be about their personal and professional responses to the issues you are wrestling with. You will have an opportunity to listen in to the team interacting for about ten to fifteen minutes. Then you can address the team and make comments and ask questions. We have found that new perspectives revealed during this exercise may often be helpful to you and the team. We would like to make this an open process. You will hear us speak respectfully, frankly, and thoughtfully about our personal reflections. However, we will only do this if we have your permission to talk as a team in this way. What are your thoughts about this?

One of the professional team members can facilitate the reflecting team discussion. The divorcing couple should be asked about the use of the reflecting team before the team meeting, rather than negotiating this issue with the coach in front of the reflecting team.

Rules for Reflecting Team Members

- Talk to one another about your experience of working with the issues presented without disclosing confidential material from previous clients.
- Reflect on any personal experiences that in some way link to some of the issues the divorcing couple are experiencing.
- Reflect on the successes and failures that previous clients have had and how this affected the children and team members. What did you notice in your previous experience that worked or did not work?
- Ask one another questions about the source of the reflections and experiences and why team members think and react this way.
- Most important, discuss what the divorcing couple are doing that is working and wonder out loud what might happen if these things were to continue and to expand.

This is how a reflecting team conversation can be introduced in front of the couple. The coach or mediator begins by speaking to the team members:

Mediator: I would like to give each of you an opportunity to reflect, in an open, honest, thoughtful, and respectful way, upon your experiences and responses that might in some way relate to the concerns being experienced in our work together with XXX and YYY [the divorcing couple]. I would like to ask each of you to speak as professionals and as individuals who are moved and affected by what has transpired. Don't hesitate to ask one another questions and make responses to what has been said. Keep in mind that during this ten- to fifteen-minute discussion you are not to address XXX and YYY, and they are not to address you. You all will have plenty of time to do that when the reflecting team finishes its conversation. Is everybody clear on what we

are to do? I don't mind starting, and then after everybody has spoken I would like to hear from each of you
[the divorcing couple].

The team facilitator must keep track of the time and bring
the reflecting team discussion to a conclusion in a timely manner.
Then the divorcing couple have a turn to present any reactions
and responses they have to what was said or to ask for clarifica-
tions from reflecting team members. Reflecting team members
respond to the couple's comments and questions. The team facilitator can then invite the couple to provide any final reflections
based on their listening in on the reflecting team's conversation
(that is, what did they find was most helpful?).

Hearing the Children's Voices in a Collaborative Divorce

Collaborative practitioners know that there is immense value in
bringing the divorcing couple's attention to the needs and well-
being of their children. Many couples get so distracted by their
own issues that it is easy for them to neglect the children's experience of the divorce. However, when information is elicited from
the children about what they are experiencing, most parents are
willing to attend to the children's well-being, even amid their
own turmoil. Here are some helpful narrative questions that children can be asked that will help the parents know about their
children's needs, concerns, and resources. These questions can
also be very useful for helping children to understand what is
going on. Some children's answers can be very helpful in moving
the family through a difficult transition.

- What effect does it have on you when angry feelings take over
  your mom and dad?
- What do you say to yourself or how do you comfort yourself
  when there are a lot of angry feelings around?
- I know a lot of kids wish they had special powers to bring their
  parents back together (even when parents can't be brought
  back together). If you had a wish that would make your parents into an ideal mom and dad who parent you from different houses, what would that wish be?

- Suppose that one night while you were asleep a "getting along" miracle had occurred and your dad and mom were parenting you in different houses but in a happy way. How would you know that the miracle had occurred? What would be different?
- What makes for an ideal mom and dad who parent from two houses? What do they do? What do they say? How do they talk to one another? What do they do to stop themselves talking to their children about parent things?
- What suggestions do you have for your parents to help them manage their upset feelings?
- Have you noticed any occasions recently where you have seen your dad and mom getting along even for a little while? What was that like to see?
- What's the best thing you have seen your dad and mom do that can be called getting along?
- Is there anything you have told me today that you definitely don't want your mom and dad to know about?

Using Narrative Letters

Finally in this chapter, we turn to another narrative technique that can be enormously helpful in assisting a divorcing couple when the situation appears stuck and the collaborative team are running out of ideas about how to get things moving again. There is a long tradition in narrative therapy and mediation of using letters (White & Epston, 1990; Winslade & Monk, 2000) that are sent to couples who are struggling with the dominating effects of the problem-saturated story and who are attempting to free themselves and move toward some kind of resolution. These narrative letters are used to capture the power of the problem-saturated story while at the same time honoring and acknowledging the couple's efforts, resources, and abilities to manage the intensity of their suffering. Any efforts at progress are acknowledged in the letters. The underlying message in the letters is that the divorcing couple are responsible for unlocking the stalemate rather than the team members. Here is an example of a narrative letter that captures the main themes and purposes of this strategy.

Dear Louise & Tom,

The collaborative team wanted to share some reflections with you about the very challenging experience you both have gone through over these many months. First, let us say that we admire the courage, strength, and generosity that you have both demonstrated in the process of this relationship transition. It appears to us that you both have suffered some of the most tortured and distressing periods that any human beings can go through in life. Somehow in the midst of the pain and struggle, each of you has not given up on finding some way of bringing this hurtful transition to a close. We understand that you do not want it to continue for another minute. We also were deeply concerned that the understandings and agreements that we all thought you had reached were not quite complete. You both made major strides in compromising and giving to one another and yet this last issue stands between you.

It strikes us that you are at a critical turning point right now. The team members have quite frankly run out of ideas on how to assist you over this last stumbling block. We feel that we have all worked hard to try to help you negotiate around many of the obstacles that have kept getting in your path. The last financial obstacle appears to us to be a different understanding you each have about the final monetary settlement. While the sum of money that is separating you from reaching that final settlement is very small (less than $1,000) in comparison to the enormous financial costs you have incurred, it strikes us that the obstacle is more symbolic than monetary. We understand that you each feel you have already sacrificed tremendously and perhaps you feel like you are not prepared to sacrifice another cent. That makes perfect sense to us and we understand your position if this is the case.

The decision about what to do is yours to make. We cannot make you do any more than we have already asked of you. We are all deeply concerned about what will happen to your family if this process is not settled soon. As you both know, not reaching a settlement is likely to cause further devastation, not just financially but to your mental and physical health. Even if you were not concerned about your own personal suffering as much as you were concerned about a fair and just outcome, we are, like you, concerned about the ongoing distress that all your children directly or indirectly will suffer if this large open wound is not allowed to begin to heal. Please let us know what you are going to do.

This kind of letter invites the couple to step back and evaluate their circumstances against the future likelihood that even worse things could await them. The purpose is to name in language as clear as possible the strengths and resources the couple possess, the suffering they and their children have already experienced, the tremendous emotional and financial costs that they might still suffer, and the reality that they are completely responsible for making the next move to loosen the grip of the conflict.

Reflections on Divorce Mediation and Collaborative Practice

In order for the strategies discussed in this chapter to be successful, practitioners need to grasp the central premise of narrative mediation that clients have unused and untapped resources and expertise that can be harnessed to diminish or release the intense hold that problem-saturated conflict stories have on their lives. Identifying a clear vision that honors the dignity and respect of all family members, helping clients understand the toll taken by problem-saturated stories, overtly stating clear preferences for change, and connecting with client resources and abilities are fundamental to narrative practice. These narrative strategies have been used with couples and their families over many years and have provided fresh and innovative strategies for experienced mediators, coaches, and collaborative divorce specialists to include in their practice.

Chapter Six

Outsider-Witness Practices in Organizational Disputes

Written with Allan Holmgren

In this chapter we focus on the mediation of conflicts that arise in the context of organizations. Among other things, we focus on the development of what have become known in narrative therapy as outsider-witness practices and their introduction into the field of narrative mediation. The examples of practice included in this chapter are drawn from the work of Allan Holmgren, who leads a professional training organization for psychologists and management consultants and consults to companies and organizations in Denmark, Norway, and Sweden.

We first outline some principles of using the narrative metaphor when working in organizations and some specific guidelines for using outsider-witness practices when dealing with conflicts in organizational contexts. We trace these practices back to concepts derived from the writings of anthropologist Barbara Myerhoff, especially in dealing with marginalization and the metaphor of definitional ceremony. Then we give a detailed example of these practices. The example focuses on a multiparty workshop held to deal with a severe conflict that had arisen in a surgery department at a big public hospital.

Principles of Narrative Mediation in Organizations

Like the life within families and communities, the life within organizations can be thought of as constituted by narratives. These stories may be rehearsed and told to visitors, customers, or clients; they may be held in the institutional memory of the organization's membership; they may be referenced in documents and texts produced in the organization; or they may guide and shape the conversations that take place between people in the organization. Also like families and communities, organizations are discourse communities. They incorporate discourses from the world around them, and they also generate their own subtly specific discourses that provide ready-made interpretations of events for the members of the organization. Discourse communities are always interpretive communities.

It is commonplace to think of organizations first of all as structures and to map out the hierarchies and communication systems within them. It is the logic of thinking in terms of structures as underlying essences that leads to the very common practice of seeking to bring about change by doing what has become widely known as *restructuring*. We resist this way of thinking about organizations, on the grounds that a narrative practice is built primarily on an effort to deploy poststructuralist understandings. From a poststructuralist perspective, structures and hierarchies are not primary and need not be thought of as essences. We do not understand people's actions and conflicts in the first instance with reference to their function in a system or as an expression of their structural positioning. Our concern is that such metaphors lead to explanations that rely on logic that is too rigid or essentialist. Such explanations do not account easily for the fluid and nuanced moves that take place in the exchanges of discourse that occur in organizations. We are not suggesting that systems or hierarchies do not exist or that analyzing them produces no truth value or even that restructuring cannot at times have useful effects. We are arguing, though, that structures and hierarchies and systems are held in place by discourses that sustain and support their existence through frequent repetition. As shifts in discourse happen, so the structures and the systems follow suit. We therefore believe it is more useful to work directly with the discourses and the narratives that constitute organizational life than to focus on restructuring.

Individuals' Identity Narratives Within Organizations

As they do in families and communities, the narratives that constitute life within organizations exert powerful influences on the identity stories of the persons who make up such organizations. People often spend significant parts of their lives and devote significant amounts of their available energies to the work of an organization. As a result, conflict in organizations often generates passionate commitment to the stories that govern people's interpretation of the meaning of their positions in the organization. Although mediation should never become synonymous with the work done in therapy to help people fashion identity stories, there will always be some crossover between therapy and mediation for this reason. And even though mediation is not therapy, it might often be experienced as therapeutic. The positions that people take up in relation to conflict-saturated stories in organizations frequently coalesce into or are connected with strong identity stories. "I am someone who likes details attended to and changes to be made only after a lot of thought," someone might say in explanation of how a conflict has affected them. This is a statement of the connection between events in an organization and the personal identity narrative that an individual holds dear. The identity narrative will be expressed in many relational acts that the person performs. Narrative mediators might find themselves becoming extremely curious about how this identity story has been formed (especially in relation to previous events in the organization). They might also be curious about how the identity story is currently working (for example, positively or negatively) and about how this story itself is affecting the current conflict.

Organizational Identity Narratives

Organizations also have identity stories, which are distinct from the identities of the individuals making up an organization. It is fashionable for organizations to try to capture the spirit of organizational identities in mission statements. The official state-ment of identity, however, may not capture all the elements of the organization's identity as it is practiced on the ground. For exam-ple, a school may have a mission statement that expresses lofty ideals about providing learning and development for all children, but in practice the school may perform as a second-class institu-tion that "knows" it is never going to compete with the scholas-tic and sporting achievements of the nearby school "up on the hill." A organization's identity will be expressed in what everyone "knows" about the organization, whether or not that story is rep-resented in mission statements or publicity material.

The new or alternative organizational stories developed in mediation conversations will need to be knitted into the orga-nization's stories about itself. They will also need to be knitted into the identity stories of the main protagonists in a conflict if these alternative stories are to survive. Outsider-witness practices are instrumental in this process of constructing new stories and cementing them in.

When there is a conflict it is almost always the case that the persons involved in the conflict have got stuck in the way they position themselves. They have narrowed the range of possi-ble story lines down to some kind of melodrama in which they see the others as the bad guys and themselves as the good guys. The bad guys are often understood in moral terms as wrong or misguided, and the good guys often see themselves as right, or even righteous, and justified. This perspective can be very lim-iting. It amounts to a story with few options for making a move in a preferred or new direction because it is unlikely that those considered bad guys can suddenly become good guys. All par-ties involved in a conflict tend to resort very easily to such an either-or discourse that is devoid of richly nuanced and complex stories and hence does not create many opportunities for move-ment. Bruner (1990) writes that "the viability of a culture inheres in its capacity for resolving conflicts, for explicating differences and renegotiating communal meanings" (p. 47). The task when working with conflicts is therefore to come up with and to invent procedures that make it possible for the involved persons both to tell stories and to be listened to in a way in which meanings are renegotiated and reestablished.

In organizations, the strength of a narrative must be considered in terms of its salience for many people, not just for, say, the two people in the center of a dispute. If sustainable changes are to be made to the conflict story, then a number of others around the main parties must be recruited into an alternative story, either as agents of change or as witnesses to the shifts that take place during mediation. This recruitment of witnesses to change will perhaps happen of its own accord, but it can also be intentionally constructed through a process of deliberate questioning by a mediator. That is the purpose of an outsider-witness practice. But the focus of this practice is primarily on relationship, rather than on individual reinvention. Hence it is relevant for the work of mediators.

Outsider-Witness Practices

The idea of the *outsider-witness practice* was developed by Australian family therapist Michael White (see White, 2007) and was inspired by the American anthropologist Barbara Myerhoff (1982, 1986). An *outsider-witness conversation* amounts to a "ritual" conversation (White, 2007, p. 165) and is founded on Barbara Myerhoff's notion of a "definitional ceremony" (Myerhoff, 1986; White, 2007, p. 165). A definitional ceremony, for the purposes of mediation in the organizational context, is an event in the life of an organization in which relationships are acknowledged and given value through the telling and retelling of a story of relationship. Each retelling must be honored with a process of listening. The process is *definitional* because it defines the contours of a relationship in ways that reverberate forward into the future. Multiple participants may be engaged in the process of listening to these retellings, ensuring the development of narrative richness and also ensuring the expansion of the story's significance into the capillaries of the organization's network of relationships. Through these retellings, people often experience their lives as "joined around shared and precious themes" (White, 2007, p. 166), and this experience makes stories of ongoing conflict less sustainable.

The repeated retelling of a story by a number of participants involves people in a process of narrative elaboration. The story is thickened and enriched by the addition of details from many people's experience and also by the addition of thematic reflections from many perspectives. Repeated retelling also results in a reflexive process in which experience is folded back upon itself. It leads to the development of a more explicit reflexive consciousness. Barbara Myerhoff (1986) says this about reflexive consciousness:

> When both the outside and the inner world deprive us of reflections—evidence that, indeed, we are still present and alive, seen and responded to—the threat to self-awareness can be great.

> Definitional ceremonies deal with the problems of invisibility and marginality; they are strategies that provide opportunities for being seen and in one's own terms, garnering witnesses to one's own worth, vitality and being [p. 267].

Myerhoff was writing at the time about a community conflict in Venice Beach in Los Angeles in the 1970s, between a community of elderly Jewish people and an influx of young people attracted to the opportunity to live an alternative lifestyle beside the beach. When one of the members of the elderly Jewish community died after being knocked down by a young person on a bicycle, the local Jewish Community Center became a site for the gathering together of the Jewish community members to protest what was happening to their community. In the process they not only mounted a public campaign for their own interests but also came together and defined themselves afresh as a community. Myerhoff noticed that they galvanized and renewed their collective identity story in the process and drew personal strength and pride from defining who they were and what they stood for. They became more visible to themselves and as a result also became more visible and recognizable to others around them. Reflecting as an anthropologist on what she had observed, she wrote that "unless we exist in the eyes of others, we may come to doubt even our own existence. Being is a social, psychological construct, made, not given. . . . Culture serves as a stage as well as mirror, providing opportunities for self- and collective proclamations of being" (Myerhoff, 1982, pp. 103–104).

According to Myerhoff, heightened self-consciousness, often known as self-awareness, "is not an essential, omnipresent attainment" (1982, p. 100). She does not believe that it always comes automatically with age or experience, nor does she assume that it is critical to well-being. "But when it does occur," she says, "it may bring one into a greater fullness of being; one may become a more fully realized example of the possibilities of being human" (p.100).

How then might mediators produce opportunities for experiencing such heightened self-consciousness in the midst of a conflict? The idea is to create arenas, scenes, or stages in which the different parties involved in a conflict can have the experience of being seen and can come to existence in the eyes of the others. In an entrenched and painful conflict in a organization, this might be a very difficult task to achieve, but not an impossible one.

A Structure for an Outsider-Witness Conversation

As a ritual conversation format, an outsider-witness conversation needs to be carefully structured. The following structure is based on the work of Michael White (2007). First of all, there have to be a couple of rules for what is allowed and what is not allowed in order to create room for a different kind of conversation than the one that has been dominant under the influence of the conflict story. All the persons present have to sign on to those rules and agree to follow them.

The first rule says that *participants are not allowed to discuss or to argue.* The purpose of this rule is to suspend the authority of the conflict story. The reason behind this rule is that the mediator is trying to create a context for listening and for the possibility that the experiences of participants will be seen through the eyes of others and understood by these others, including those with whom the participants might be in conflict.

The second rule is that *participants have to agree to form their responses according to a particular sequence of questions.* Here are the four questions:

1. Which expressions were you drawn to when you listened to the presentation of the person speaking? (It is important that you can quote the specific expressions used by the person.)

2. What images do you get of the person? (It is very important that you listen as a friend and not as an enemy.)

3. Which of your own experiences are you noticing that relate to what the person is sharing? (It is very important that you mention some specific, lived, and embodied experience and not just general similar experiences. Do not try to give direct advice or indirect advice by telling what you did to solve another problem.)

4. Where does listening to the person take you to in your own life? What did you find inspiring? Was there anything you want to hold closer to your heart and share with others?

The ritual process begins with an interview of one person. Other participants are invited to listen to this interview. In this interview the mediator inquires into the person's account of what has been happening in the organization, her concerns about these events, and her values that give rise to those concerns.

Then the attention shifts to the listeners. The first person's telling of her account of things, her story, is reflected on by the listening group. The consultant asks the series of four questions listed previously to invite a retelling of this first story by the listening group. In this retelling they are invited to bear witness to what they have heard but they are not left free to make any old response. Experience led Michael White to carefully design the four questions so they would act as a sequenced scaffold for responses and would enable a new story of relationship to emerge. These questions invite retellings through a series of levels of ascending significance.

First Level of Response

Question 1, the first level of response, asks listeners to relate to what the person in the center of the ceremony or presentation actually said, to the words, phrases, expressions, and metaphors she used. In this first response listeners are asked only to relate to these expressions. They are asked to avoid coming up with interpretations or general statements, advice, criticism, or other comments not relating to the actual expressions. To assist them, they are asked questions like these:

- What were you especially drawn to in the presentation of the person?
- What did you find especially interesting?
- What stood out for you?
- What touched you?

The important thing is that the listeners can repeat some of the actual words, sentences, and phrases that were used and that struck them in some way. In doing this, they should speak only to each other and not directly to the person who first spoke. The aim is that this first speaker gets to experience what it is like to overhear what is being said in response to her own speaking, but without any obligation to respond to any specific utterance.

Second Level of Response

Question 2 invites the listeners to come up with a metaphor that fits with what the first speaker said and what she stands for in her values, beliefs, and principles. For example, a person might say, "I get an image of this person as a flying machine but the wheels are not functioning. She has to keep on flying and is afraid of landing and touching the ground." Here the effort and the intention is to try to give the person in the center of this ceremony an experience of being seen not just through her own words but through another's image. An image is often said to say more than a thousand words. It invites a poetic element into the discourse and unlocks entry into previously unknown territories of meaning. An image also invites listeners to daydream, to see themselves as something they have not seen before. Through the act of calling up an image, consciousness moves into what American psychologist William James (1890/1983) called "the stream of consciousness." The Danish philosopher Ole Fogh Kirkeby suggests that metaphors are stronger than concepts and are like pieces of art created by language. His idea (after Ludwig Wittgenstein) is that metaphors are the pictures painted by language. In these philosophical views, metaphors are more important than factual truths. The late American philosopher Richard Rorty was quoted in 1990 as saying that, "Truth is simply a compliment paid to sentences seen to be paying their way" (Andrews,

Biggs, & Seidel, 1996). Participants in a definitional ceremony might therefore be asked, for example:

- What metaphor, image, or picture do you get of the person?
- Do you have a sense of what is precious to person?
- Do you have a sense of what this person gives value to in life?

Third Level of Response

Question 3 invites listeners to talk about themselves and their experiences in relation to what they especially paid attention to in the expression of the first speaker. In this third level of response, witnesses have the opportunity to speak about the personal resonance that the original expression gives rise to in their own life story. This resonance might arise because a listener has had similar experiences or experiences with similar themes. It is important that each witness is asked to become concrete and to give specific examples from his own life, tell a little story, and not speak in general or abstract terms. It is also important that the witness gets a chance to speak about what it is that he appreciates in his own life in these experiences and memories. For example, a witness might be asked:

- What came to your mind from your own experience as you listened to the first person's story?
- How does that experience relate to the expression you especially mentioned?
- Can you tell a story that conveys a sense of how your own experiences were perhaps a bit similar to the experiences of the first speaker?

Fourth Level of Response

Question 4 leads to the fourth and last step of response, which has to do with the witnesses' experience of being moved, in the sense of experiencing consciousness of movement in their own lives or of being transported by hearing the first speaker's story and by reflecting on their own similar stories. After listening to the first speaker the witnesses may be brought to another place in their own experience and to a new or renewed sense of what is important to them. Feeling this sense is similar to what happens when one is affected by watching a movie or a drama. You are touched by what you have seen, and you are moved to think of important relations and values in your own life. In order to invite the expression of this sense of transport, a mediator or facilitator might ask:

- How is it for you to revisit your own experiences?
- Which of your own values and relationships now seems even more important to you?
- Is there anything you would like to do or is there anyone you feel like talking more to about this?
- What would it mean to that person if you were to talk to him or her about this story?

All the participants are provided with a very carefully described set of instructions for all these responses and each of the steps in this process, both in writing and orally.

Example of a Workshop Using Outsider-Witness Practices

The example that follows is told by Allan Holmgren.

This example derives from an invitation I received to assist in a mediation workshop for the reworking of a conflict story among a group of professionals in a large public hospital. The conflict had arisen among members of one department rather than in the whole organization. This department was the heart surgery unit of the hospital, which performed both emergency and planned surgery. The head of the department, the current chief surgeon, was a former colleague of the other eight senior doctors and a former chief surgeon was still working as a member of the surgical staff.

The actual conflict had been occurring for about four years and perhaps had an even longer story in the department. It was a story about how difficult it was for the leaders to have authority with and respect from the team. The invitation to be involved had come from the chief doctor of the hospital, who had heard of other consultancy work I had conducted.

Before the actual workshop, which took place in the hospital's heart surgery ward, all those involved had to negotiate the ethics around such a consultation (this is described further later). Questions that needed resolving included.

Who should be informed about what is said here?
Will anything said here end up in the staff files?

These are not just procedural questions. They have to do with how and by whom discourses and meanings will be managed in particular practice contexts. These are issues of power; they are more than procedural because they involve participants in building a story of respect and negotiation from the start. Negotiations about these issues can take a long time, but it was very important to spend all the time needed to talk about these matters in order to create as safe an environment as possible for the actual work.

Holding the Initial Consultation

A colleague and I conducted the initial consultation with the chief surgeon and the chief nurse of the department and also the administrative director, the chief doctor, and the chief nurse of the hospital. The purpose of this meeting was to listen to their stories about the conflict and about the difficulties they experienced as a result of the conflict. We also listened to their hopes for what might result from this workshop to address the difficulties that were negatively influencing their team. They all contributed stories about the poisoned atmosphere in the department. The tone of the relationships among the surgeons was described as "warlike." The senior surgeons had been known to threaten each other. Some had complaints about others in their jottings on their desks. The head of the department characterized the senior surgeons as "a gang of Rottweiler dogs." The younger physicians had complained, the nurses had complained, the unions were involved, and it all seemed to be a big problem.

Nobody, however, could give a clear name to this conflict. My colleague and I decided to offer a consultation built around the outsider-witness metaphor, and we explained the principles and the structure of the consultation carefully. We would start by interviewing the senior surgeons and each of the eight department nurses who were part of the team that each surgeon worked with. Thus there were sixteen participants from the surgery department plus the department's chief surgeon, the department's chief nurse, and the three persons from the top administration of the hospital—twenty-one persons in all. Other staff groups could have been represented as well and surgeons from other hospitals at similar departments could have been invited, but the decision was made that these twenty-one were the central persons involved.

Interviewing the Participants

Except for two surgeons, all the health care professionals had agreed to participate, and so a series of interviews of the nineteen remaining participants was conducted. Each interview was built around the following questions, which were sent out in advance in writing to all the participants:

- What would you call the problem(s)?
- What would you call the patterns of communication that have developed in the department?
- What is the effect of the problem(s) on you—on your thoughts, moods, emotions, health, sleep patterns, relationships at home? On the different relationships in the department? And on other people involved?
- What is your position on the effects of the problems and patterns? Are some OK? Do you think some are not OK?
- What does the position you take say about what is important to you?

All the answers to these questions were carefully written down during each interview for distribution among all the participants. All the persons interviewed knew that all the others involved in the consultation would receive exactly the same written documents. Moreover, an agreement had been made that nothing would be sent out to others until it had been accepted by the person being interviewed. This demanded some writing back and forth.

All participants received the interview documents in written form before the workshop was held; however, they put varying degrees of effort into reading these materials beforehand. So how much help the interview itself really was can be questioned. Nevertheless, most of the persons interviewed appreciated the opportunity to express their opinions before the workshop, even though the actual interviews did not appear to create any shifts in their understanding of the issues or any ideas about a way forward.

Conducting the Workshop

On the first day of the two-day workshop the chief surgeon welcomed everyone. I then spoke and commented that the situation seemed very serious and noted that the seriousness was evidenced by the presence of those responsible for the top administration of the hospital. The rule that there would be no discussion and no arguing during this process was reiterated. The purpose of the workshop was described as only to listen in order to create a basis for mutual understanding about what was important for each person present. Separate meetings were held by each of the groups present (nurses, surgeons, administrators) to decide whether people were willing to go ahead with the workshop under these conditions. After meeting for about twenty minutes the participants returned and announced that they had agreed to go ahead.

My colleague and I then explained four more procedural guidelines for which we were seeking participants' agreement. These guidelines would help to create the context in which participants would work together.

- The first guideline specified the activities over these two days. The consultants would regularly ask the participants to work in pairs and smaller groups to keep the process alive and to create opportunities for reflection and listening in smaller groups.
- The second guideline concerned language. If anyone said anything that a listener did not quite understand, the listener would have an obligation to ask about the meaning of the word or sentence.

- The third guideline regarded specific interests and problems that might pop up for the participants during their two days together. The participants had a responsibility to bring up whatever issues they might find important to address and talk about.
- The fourth guideline had to do with ethics. Who should know what was said during these two days? And what would end up in staff files? It was decided, with consensus and support from everyone, that the only thing that could be said to outsiders after the workshop was the text that would be agreed on later by the workshop participants. Those surgeons who were married to nurses working in the department (but not participating in the workshop) agreed not to talk about the specific statements made by specific participants. But they could still talk with their spouses under these terms of confidentiality.

What followed was an exercise in groups of three people each. Each triad was made up of persons from different staff groups, so that nobody would be together with his or her closest professional partner. Each group's task was to bring forth all the problems its members could think of that were existing in the department. It was specified that a person could not be named as a problem. Each person in each triad was interviewed for about twenty minutes by another group member, while the remaining person took notes. These roles rotated around each group. Next, all the problems mentioned in the triads were written on flip charts by the group members, and each group presented its flip chart with further comments in a plenary session. Once the flip-chart sheets were posted, all the walls were filled with all sorts of problems.

Then the participants were given the task of getting into pairs either with a person they probably disagreed with or with someone whose opinions and experiences they were curious about and would like to get to know a little better. Each couple received a piece of paper with the following questions for the couple to discuss and to use to interview each other.

1. Which of the problems listed affect(s) you the most?
2. What words would you use to describe or name these problems?

3. What are the effects of these problems on you, your life, your identity, your relationships, your future hopes, your mood when you go to work, your mood at home?

4. Are there areas where the problems you are talking about are not so dominating as they are in others? What makes these areas less problematic?

5. Is it fair that these problems influence you, and have the effects they have? Is this OK?

6. What are some basic values you hold precious that are incompatible with these problems?

7. Can you give an example from your work experience that illustrates how you have sought to express these values and principles in the past?

8. Who in your experience is connected to these values?

9. What was it like for you to talk about these values and experiences? What shifts do you notice in relation to the recent conflicts?

10. What is important for you that I say about you and your experiences in the plenary? How shall I present you?

These interviews took a considerable period of time, but for many people they served the purpose of the first phase of a definitional ceremony. They created visibility for the personal experience of the conflict and for people's preferred values in the face of the conflict. The interviews also served as an antidote to the marginalizing effects of the conflict. In the midst of conflict, individuals often become invisible to each other, in the sense that only a few aspects of each person's life and intentions are actually seen and referred to—and then most often in problematic and negative ways. These questions therefore promoted the visibility of an alternative story that revealed what people preferred for their workplace and work life. The exercise also allowed each person to listen to and gain a fuller understanding of at least one other person in the organization. In the process each conversation partner became more visible to the other.

The idea behind making the interviews fairly long and thorough was to give each person an opportunity to talk about his or her actual experiences and preferred values. People were encouraged to tell stories about the real effects of the problems on their lives. They were also encouraged to tell stories about their preferred values and about specific actions related to these values. One interview could easily take an hour or more, so it was important that we allowed people sufficient time to do these interviews. The top administrators were, of course, not as directly affected by the problems in the surgery department as the department staff members were, but they still had the opportunity to talk about some of their own experiences in their work and in their relationships.

Conducting the Final Plenary Session

In the plenary session that followed, all the participants were gathered, all the names of the department participants were put in a hat, and one name was selected at random. The person whose name was chosen was then presented by the person who had actually interviewed him or her. This involved a retelling of the telling (White, 2007, p.186). The person at the center of this definitional ceremony (the person presented) heard his or her words again, and the others listened to the presentation also. During the presentation all the listeners took notes carefully to pick up the words and phrases that stood out for them and to which they paid special attention. The participants were reminded about how to do this task. After the presentation the listeners (who were now constituted as witnesses to the first telling) interviewed each other in groups of three or four. One person in each group was assigned to be the interviewer, and he or she was interviewed too by the other group members. This was done to make sure that there really was curiosity and engagement in the retellings of the retellings in the small groups. The consultants asked one person from each group to go through what he or she had just said, to make a summary of what was paid attention to, of the metaphors and images, and of the resonance and transport for the persons who had witnessed the story. These responses were then presented back to the plenary session.

Some of the presentations in the plenary were extremely moving and powerful. A female surgeon had had a terrible time during the previous year, and she almost could not stand it anymore. The male surgeons were shocked. They had not been aware of the real effects of their fights and "wars" and of their way of talking. It was not just a strong emotional experience to witness the testimony; indeed, the strongest part was perhaps that people made connections with each other that had not been possible under the regime of the conflict story. All could relate to similar experiences with feelings of despair, loneliness, and hopelessness in their own lives.

One of the participants had been pointed out by several others as the "bad guy" in the organization. He had come to the seminar not expecting to be moved by what others had to say. In the end he stayed on much longer than his planned early departure and became thoroughly engaged with the process. His respect and attentiveness grew as he listened to others' stories about the effects of the problems and the conflicts and about the other participants' prized values.

The next morning the process was repeated through several more cycles. The seminar ended with a series of interviews in small groups about how the experience had affected the participants. People commented that this experience had given them a much better understanding of each other's intentions, purposes, and values—so much so that they had been moved to a different relational place. They were also asked what ideas had arisen that might be useful in the future to counter the effects of the conflict when the problems showed up again. Each person was given a chance to formulate his or her aspirations for addressing difficulties in the future in a way that maintained heartfelt values and principles. Each person was then asked to form a connection with another person in the group who would act as a friend and ally. As allies, they were asked to support one another in embodying their preferred values in future actions.

Reflections on the Outsider-Witness Practice

The process Allan Holmgren has described in this scenario does not focus on reaching agreement about solutions to a conflict. Neither does it require disputants to engage in dialogue about a conflict. Nor does it establish mutual goals that people can work toward in future negotiations. On the contrary, it focuses on opening the possibility of talking about preferred values in a context that allows for the greatest possible experience of being listened to. The listening is ensured by asking people to become witnesses to each other's tellings.

In the context of an organization in conflict, such listening is not always easy. If participants are having difficulty we sometimes use what Michael White (2007, p. 202) calls *repositioning*. This is a process in which a mediator invites a participant to "borrow" a listening ear from another person whom they know and have had experiences with as a good listener—it might be a grandmother, an old teacher, a friend, and so on, whose ear they can imagine themselves borrowing and listening with.

Working this way creates a foundation for better understanding and for a movement into the territory of cooperation. When people are invited to connect more closely to their preferred values during a period of painful conflict, they get a better sense of who they are, of who they want to be, and of what seems important to them. When participants get an opportunity to witness others' stories in the organization, they seem to get a much better understanding of each other. This improved understanding creates a foundation for negotiating which stories organizational life can be organized around and which meanings can be privileged with regard to topics on which people may disagree—and for doing this without getting into war with each other. Differences seem to have a better chance to live alongside each other and individuals seem better able to avoid becoming attached to particular views and getting into severe conflict when people have a wide and broad understanding of each other's stories and experiences.

This process also stands in contrast to modernist ideas about the split between people's work and the rest of their lives. Rather than maintaining the so-called professional-private split, this process supports the drawing of links between professional life and personal experience. It can support people in the idea that differences can be much better dealt with when there is an atmosphere of mutual understanding based on the sharing of personal stories. We suspect that through such a process, an organization can create really strong communities within itself. In this sense, the workplace might become a new village for people, a new center for social and political life.

Chapter Seven

Employment Mediation

Written with Alison Cotter

In this chapter, we apply the principles of a narrative approach to the context of workplace and employment mediation. The examples of workplace mediation cited in this chapter come from the practice of Alison Cotter in the context of the mediation services of the New Zealand Department of Labour. This is a government-funded service set up by an Act of Parliament (the Employment Relations Act of 2000) to deal with workplace disputes, with mediation as the primary problem-solving mechanism. Although mediators have the power under the Act to adjudicate disputes, this power is used infrequently. Cases that do not settle at mediation may be taken to the next level of employment problem resolution and legal provision, the Employment Relations Authority, where they are adjudicated by an authority member who makes a decision, or a *determination,* about the case. The intention of the Act is that problems in employment relationships be "resolved promptly by the parties themselves" (Franks, 2003, p. 5) and that mediation services be "free, fast and fair" (Franks, p. 6). Signed settlements emerging from mediations are to be legally final and binding. In the years since the passing of the Act, mediation has become the primary method through which employment disputes are resolved in New Zealand (Franks, 2003).

The authors thank Peter Murphy, employment relations adviser of the New Zealand School Trustees' Association, for his helpful comments on this chapter.

Types of Employment Mediation

A range of matters are brought to mediation through this service of the New Zealand Department of Labour. The majority of cases (62 percent) involve personal grievances of one kind or another (Franks, p. 7). Many of these grievance cases involve claims of unjustified dismissal. The dismissed worker is usually keen to have his perspective heard on the events that led to dismissal or redundancy. He wants to clarify misunderstandings and explain the impact of the dismissal decision on him. Both personal and legal issues are considered. Some workers are interested in rein-statement (the first remedy to be considered under the Act). Many want to claim some kind of compensation, monetary or otherwise, for the hurt and humiliation caused by the alleged unjustified dismissal. All kinds of remedies are negotiated at mediation, including financial compensation, making apologies, providing work references, acknowledging what could have been handled differently, and a whole range of creative proposals to ameliorate the hurt caused and to allow the parties to move on from the problem. With the assistance of the mediator, the parties work out the terms (details) of any agreements reached. These agreements are then written up and signed off on by both parties and by the mediator, usually on the day of mediation.

A second category of mediations addresses problems that have arisen in collective bargaining negotiations between an employer and a union. An independent mediator can often assist the parties to work through a problem and then they are able to resume their negotiations without assistance.

A further category relates to problems in ongoing employment relationships (relationships that have not been terminated). Early intervention by mediation can help to get such relationships back on track, and thus these mediations fit with one of the expressed goals of the Employment Relations Act, "to build productive employment relationships." This type of mediation (along with mediation of strikes and lockouts in essential industries) is given priority over other mediations that have been schedule by support staff. The case of Ruby and Phoebe, described in the following paragraphs, fits this category of an ongoing employment relationship.

This chapter explores the use of a narrative approach in this employment context by telling two stories that illustrate different aspects of this practice. One is about an ongoing employment relationship and the other is about an "unjustified dismissal" dispute. Comments are offered on some specific elements in these stories in order to make connections with the ideas presented in the rest of the book. Both stories are told by Alison Cotter.

The Story of Ruby and Phoebe

The conflict story that came to mediation with Ruby and Phoebe involved a merger of two companies in the financial services sector. As a result of the merger, Ruby and Phoebe had continued to work together in the same office, but their roles had changed. Phoebe was both a shareholder and an employee in the company, and she was working in the office three days per week. Her husband was a director of the company. Ruby was a young operations manager in a full-time position who had progressed rapidly in the company since her original appointment as a receptionist. Phoebe had been ill and believed that part of her ill health could be attributed to the stress of her working relationship with Ruby. She felt that Ruby was demonstrating "office bully" behavior toward her and was nervous about meeting with her in mediation in case it would lead to further painful exchanges. As a result of the tensions between them, both Ruby and Phoebe had sought help from professional counselors. It was one of the counselors who had recommended mediation.

Holding Separate Meetings with Each Party

I met first with Ruby and Phoebe separately, along with their respective support persons (both Ruby and Phoebe had brought their professional counselors to the meetings). It is my usual practice to hold such preliminary separate meetings with the participants, with several purposes in mind. One is that I want to ease the tension that invariably builds up as mediation participants anticipate revisiting the problem issues in a new environment. I also want to begin the process of building rapport with each individual without the restraining influence of the other party being in the room.

With each of them, I introduced myself and asked preliminary questions: for example, "What's been your experience of mediation?" I also acknowledged the presence and role of the support persons. I commented on how valuable it was to have that extra pair of ears to fill in gaps of memory or understanding when reflecting during breaks in the mediation or when debriefing afterwards. I did confirm, however, the importance of hearing directly from the participants themselves during mediation, rather than from support people. I showed the group where they could get coffee, tea, or water that they could bring into the mediation room.

I also asked, "What's most important to you at this mediation today?" Ruby wanted assurance that she had a future in the company. She liked her work and would feel bad about leaving but at the moment did not feel good about staying either, given the way things were. Phoebe wanted Ruby's behavior toward her to change so that she could get on with her work without feeling distracted and uneasy.

I then explained to each of them that the first part of mediation would involve unraveling the problem issues and hearing the effects of the problem on each person and on their working relationship. I explained that this phase would involve careful listening on their part and mine to understand the different perspectives. We might all need to ask questions to clarify matters further. Then we would consider what could make a difference for each of them and what might be some ways forward.

Conducting the Joint Meeting

When everyone had been introduced, I took a few minutes to speak of mediation as an opportunity to have a structured conversation across the table about the employment relationship problem that had arisen. I said that the Employment Relations Act sets some principles for mediation that help to make it a safe environment and that I wanted to explain three of these principles. First, I pointed out that mediation is a confidential process. This protects the participants from others' surmises and possible distortions of the conversations that have taken place. I would also keep confidential anything said to me in separate meetings, unless a group specifically asked me to discuss it with the other group. Second, I explained that the mediation process is "without prejudice," meaning that nothing said at mediation can be used against anyone in another legal forum. Third, I outlined my role as an independent facilitator working in an impartial way, rather than as a judge or decision maker.

The next step was to agree on some guidelines for the mediation. I suggested that I propose some core guidelines, check how the participants felt about those, and ask whether there were others they wanted to add. I requested that they listen to each other without interruption (either in words or body language), in order to really hear the other's perspective. I suggested that assumptions and interpretations often contribute to stress in relationships and asked them to be aware of these, both in their own and the other's conversations. I asked that they choose their words with care because words, tone, and manner all make a difference in the way a message is heard.

We were now ready to explore the problem issue and its effects on each of the participants. I invited them to consider some questions about the problem as I wrote the questions on a whiteboard. I also offered a separate space, so that Ruby and Phoebe could discuss these questions with their support people individually before getting together again to discuss their answers. Here are the questions and the answers that Ruby and Phoebe gave.

How Would You Name the Problem?

I asked Phoebe and Ruby, "How would you name the problem?" Phoebe responded to this question with a story. She explained that she felt victimized and bullied by Ruby. It was like being "on a roller-coaster" with Ruby, who was kind and chatty one minute and unpleasant the next. She gave an example in which she, Phoebe, had asked Ruby not to use the fax because she had been on the phone to Australia getting technical support about a problem with the copier and fax machine. Ruby had then turned on the fax "deliberately." When questioned about this by Phoebe, she had answered "in a defiant manner" that Phoebe found offensive. Phoebe observed that Ruby treated her differently from others in the office. She felt that Ruby and another staff member, Susan, the receptionist, had "ganged up" against her. They would laugh and talk together and exclude her in a pointed way. Phoebe believed that management had allowed Ruby to get away with this behavior because she was young—and because they "don't know how to deal with it." Things had come to a head when Phoebe made a written complaint to the directors of the company about Ruby's behavior.

For her part, Ruby described the situation as a "personality clash." She felt that the whole thing was personal, not a business problem, but agreed that both she and Phoebe had taken it to heart. She did not agree with Phoebe's view that she and Susan were "ganging up," but she understood that this was Phoebe's perception. Ruby's explanation was that through the job she and Susan had become friends who took an interest in each other's lives both at work and outside it. Lately, one or the other of them always seemed to be getting into trouble with Phoebe, so they were leaning on each other, which was then perceived as "ganging up."

What Has Contributed to This Problem?

Then I asked Ruby and Phoebe, "What factors do you believe have contributed to this problem that has arisen in your relationship?" This question was designed to get them to expand on their initial descriptions of the problem. It also allowed the discursive context of the conflict to emerge. Not all of this context would be within the control of the disputing parties. These factors could then become material for an externalizing conversation in which the factors themselves could be constructed as contributing to the growth of the problem, thus encouraging the participants to focus less on a blame-oriented construction of events.

Phoebe and Ruby both described the merging of the two companies and how confusing some aspects of their work had become. There was substantial agreement between them on this point. An example was that it had not always been clear who should report to whom. Two new people, with different skills and experience in the newly acquired aspect of the business, had been brought into the company, but there was some confusion about reporting lines and even their individual roles. What was important here was that in the context of a painful conflict, Phoebe and Ruby could sit in the same room and agree on some factors that had contributed to the dispute. In itself, this shared perception was an interruption in the power of the conflict story.

Phoebe also explained that she was both employee and shareholder. She was concerned that other employees might not always understand her dual roles, or that there were some different expectations because of them. Ruby confirmed that no one had explained this clearly to her. In terms of positioning theory a mediator might notice the relational positions produced in the interactions between Phoebe and Ruby as a result of Phoebe's being both a shareholder and the spouse of one of the company directors. The effects of such positioning might be expected to be felt by both parties. Positioning theory may also be relevant with regard to the age differences between the participants. Phoebe, in her forties and a shareholder of the company, needed to learn her operational role (three days per week) from Ruby, in her early twenties, who had been doing this role, but had recently been appointed to a new position in the company.

What Have Been the Effects on You of This Problem?

When I asked the participants, "What have been the effects on you (personal, emotional, at work) of this problem?" Phoebe spoke about the effects of the problem on her health, on her relationships with friends and family, on the quality of her work, and on her self-esteem. She reported an increase in her blood pressure and said that relationships with friends and family had become stressed. It felt to her like the joy had been taken out of her life and her sense of her own self-worth had plunged. "How could I allow myself to be treated like this?" she kept thinking, and she worried about the effects of holding it all inside herself. The problem had also had financial costs for her. She had paid for counseling for herself, and she had stayed away from work on some occasions. In terms of effects on her relationship with Ruby, she reported that they used to be friends and that she felt a sense of loss about the relationship.

For Ruby the main effects of the problem had been on her work performance, on her self-regard, and on her friendships. She reported feeling sometimes reluctant to go to work. "I have to force myself," she said. The interactions with Phoebe had left her feeling shocked and hurt and sometimes angry at herself and at Phoebe. She had noticed that her performance at work had slipped because she was distracted. She was also concerned that Jake (Phoebe's husband, who was a director of the company) was avoiding her. The whole situation had left her confused, and she was disappointed at the loss of friendship with Phoebe and had missed that relationship. As she had reflected on her own behavior, she had been led to try apologizing to Phoebe for her part in the conflict, but Phoebe had brushed this off. She had found herself thinking, "What's the point?" when her sincere effort to address the problem in this way had ended up seeming futile. Moreover, the whole problem, including the sense of being accused of doing things to Phoebe, had had an impact on her personality and style. It had almost produced in her the behaviors she was accused of. She described her style as being usually quite loud, bubbly, and outgoing, but this had changed to not wanting to talk to people because she was always upset. Her friends would invariably suggest that she leave the job but she didn't really want to do that. Now she just wanted to be by herself and wasn't even interested in having a joke.

Opening the Counterstory

Having heard these frank expressions of the effects of the problem on each of the participants and having recorded them on a whiteboard so that both could see them, I invited Phoebe and Ruby to identify some common themes. They both identified the loss of friendship, and they noticed that both had been experiencing reluctance to go to work. They also joined together in feeling very unhappy about the situation. They volunteered this shared agreement about their unhappiness with the current state of affairs, so I did not have to ask them whether they liked the way things were.

This step in the mediation conversation does not simply ask the participants to speak from within the conflict stories that they have been experiencing. It also asks them to step outside of their positions within the conflict story. Phoebe and Ruby took up something of a meta-position in relation to this story and began to comment on the conflict itself rather than on each other. In the process the power that the conflict had been having over their perceptions of each was shifting.

The opportunity was now there for the development of some openings to a new story. I took the opportunity to ask about some unique outcomes that did not fit with the conflict story. An obvious opening to explore was the theme of previous friendship. I asked these questions: "Was there a time when your relationship was different?" "What was happening then?" and, "What did that mean to each of you?" Such questions have an effect on the context in which the conflict story is placed. Rather than being constructed as defining the relationship between the two parties, the conflict is by implication now constructed as one story among other stories. These other stories can then be explored in terms of both plot and theme. Using Jerome Bruner's (1986) terminology (further developed by Michael White, 2007; and referenced in relation to mediation by Winslade & Monk, 2000), one might see these questions as alternating between the *landscape of action* and the *landscape of consciousness* (also known as the landscape of meaning or of identity). On the landscape of action both Ruby and Phoebe could narrate examples of friendship between them. On the landscape of meaning each could express appreciation of the other and of their previous more friendly relationship.

What emerged was that each could tell a story of the other as capable, efficient, and organized and could recognize that they had similar efficient working styles. They had liked working together and had sometimes joined up for a walk together after work on a fine evening. Phoebe described it as "not a confiding relationship, like a peer friendship, but an enjoyable extension of their working relationship." Telling these stories connected them, and built up a pool of goodwill that had its roots in the past. In the process the power of the conflict story was further deconstructed, and its totalizing effects were somewhat diminished. I hoped that this alternative story might be drawn on as the mediation developed and as other tensions in the relationship were worked through.

Inviting Further Developments in the Alternative Story

Next, I asked both participants to reflect on the picture described so far and to individually consider the following question, discussing it, as previously, with their support person as a sounding board. I said, "What strategies or ideas could you put in place that would make a difference to your relationship? What do you want of the other?"

Each took time to talk through her ideas with her support person, and then they came together again with me to discuss their ideas. I invited them to put forward ideas alternately. In this way, neither was positioned as responding to all of the other's ideas before being able to initiate her own. Phoebe asked first that if a problem were to arise in future between them, Ruby would raise it directly with her but also book a time to discuss it later, so that she had time to think it through. She also asked that such matters be kept confidential between them.

Ruby asked that Phoebe, in order to avoid misunderstandings, give her time to check out that she had been understood correctly. She wanted Phoebe to check out any assumptions and clarify things if necessary rather than react quickly.

Phoebe said that she would like to be treated with a level of respect by Ruby and that there be no "ganging up." In return, Ruby asked that she and Susan the receptionist, who had become her friend, be dealt with separately and not "lumped together" by Phoebe. They explored the "ganging up" idea further, and Ruby agreed that she would be watchful of having negative conversations with anyone in the company. She agreed to have only business conversations with Susan when at reception, saving personal discussions for when they went out together for lunch.

When Ruby suggested that roles and reporting lines had not been clear since the merger and needed to be sorted, Phoebe agreed, and they began to talk about what might be needed. I continued to capture their ideas on the whiteboard. They agreed to put in a joint request to management to define roles and reporting lines in the new organization. This clarification was to include making transparent Phoebe's different roles and conditions as an employee and a shareholder, as well as the extra flexibility she had in work hours. Phoebe would develop the memo and check it with Ruby before sending it.

As this discussion developed, Phoebe and Ruby had begun to work together against the problem. They were positioned within this conversation as collaborators rather than as contestants.

Both agreed that they wanted to reestablish a good working relationship. When asked what would make a difference to this relationship, they each had something specific to ask of the other. After hearing Phoebe elaborate on the "roller-coaster" of not knowing what Ruby's mood might be, Ruby said she was prepared to make a commitment to be conscious of her moods and their possible impact on others and to behave more carefully in response to that. She would make an effort to be cheerful in the mornings and to treat everyone similarly, but she reiterated that what had been interpreted as moodiness was really a result of the tensions between her and Phoebe. If these tensions were sorted, she expected to return to her previous outgoing style.

My concern at this point was to firm these relational intentions into actions. Only as they became fully fledged plot developments could they take their place in a viable story that could be sustained. I asked, "What can you put in place that will give these intentions developed today the greatest chance? What would each of you need to do?"

Reaching an Agreement

I explained that I would type up a *memorandum of understanding* listing the agreements reached (as recorded on the whiteboard), which could be a useful reference point for the future. I explained that such agreements are not the end point of the mediation story because they still have to be carried out and lived. They were the latest events in the ongoing story of Ruby's and Phoebe's working relationship.

In the agreement that was then negotiated and drawn up in writing, Ruby and Phoebe agreed that they would set up a meeting with the company managers and ask for roles and reporting lines to be defined more clearly. They would propose that there be a monthly staff meeting to discuss any issues that had arisen. Phoebe thought it would be useful to ask the directors to redefine expectations about staff use of e-mail. Each of them also agreed to commit herself to a "good working relationship." Ruby would also approach Susan and suggest that she wanted to make a new start on having better relationships in the office. She would say that she wanted to set some new boundaries and to pull back from talking about personal matters in office time. She could see the benefit of each of them being more self-contained in the office, while still enjoying their occasional lunch outings. A series of intentions about better communication was then spelled out. This list included things like being cheerful in the mornings, being conscious of moods and their possible impact on others, checking out that one has been understood, keeping personal stuff out of office time, facing each other when talking, avoiding recruiting others to gang up on either of them, and treating each other with respect.

I offered them the opportunity of reconvening the mediation in a month or two if both agreed that they wanted this. They agreed that this was a good idea.

"So what will you tell anyone asking about today's mediation?" I asked. I was concerned with how the new story might be knitted into other relationships in the workplace. "Who, if anyone, needs to know the outcome of this conversation?" Ruby and Phoebe agreed that they would set limits around any account of the personal story that they had been working on. They would say only, "We've made progress. We agree on a lot. And we're keeping it confidential."

Growing the Story in a Later Meeting

A month later we all met again. This time Phoebe and Ruby attended without support people. I welcomed them and aired my curiosity about how the working relationship was developing. Such review meetings provide a special opportunity not just to look back at the agreement and how it has been kept but also to develop and strengthen the relationship story represented in the agreement.

"It's four weeks since we met," I said initially. Then I reviewed the details of the problem and its effects, using externalizing language as follows: "In that meeting you identified the problems each of you was experiencing in your employment relationship and the painful effects resulting from that, some different for each of you, some in common: for example, reluctance to go to work, stress—physical, mental and emotional—loss of friendship, and loss of any pleasure in your working relationship."

Next I reviewed the steps toward an alternative story that had been taken at our previous meeting. "Then together you worked out some steps for rebuilding your relationship. Relationships are shaped by small steps such as greetings and interactions over the photocopier or e-mail, as well as by organizational expectations."

I suggested that they take a few minutes to reread the memorandum of understanding developed at the first mediation meeting, as a reminder of the steps they had agreed to take. In all of this review of our previous meeting my intention was to situate the story of the relationship in the context of the alternative story that they had developed, rather than back in the original conflict story.

"As we did at the previous mediation meeting," I said, "I want to ask you to consider some questions, and then we'll share the answers." These were the questions I gave them:

- "In which areas do you think you've made progress?"
- "What particular efforts have *you* made that have contributed to that progress?"
- "What have you noticed about the other person's efforts? In what circumstances? What effect did that have on you?"
- "What hasn't worked so well? What would it be helpful to focus on today?"

In any event, Ruby and Phoebe were reluctant to keep to the format I was proposing in my role as mediator. They were excited and wanted to pour out the stories of the last four weeks. I went along with this. They talked about how knowing and understanding their respective positions and roles had made a huge difference. "A 100 percent difference," said Ruby.

"Knowing what's acceptable and what's not has mattered too," said Ruby. Phoebe agreed that now there was no confusion, no grey areas. There had been an agreement to have a monthly staff meeting with all the female staff and to keep minutes of this meeting. Out of this meeting an action plan had been developed.

Ruby said, "I tried to keep to all the things we agreed on." She also reflected back on her shock and horror at finding herself involved in a mediation. "It doesn't feel like me," she said.

"And learning to back off was important too. It's so easy to be reactive." I asked her to tell me more about this idea, and she spoke of a book she liked that suggested that "you can choose your attitude." She said that if she feels angry at work or home she applies this idea and tries to consciously change her attitude.

I commented that it seemed that management also deserved some credit for doing their bit and getting onto the issues in a prompt and positive way, as did Ruby and Phoebe for turning around the situation so quickly. "What has happened that has surprised you?" I asked. I was not content for a new story to exist. It needed to be accounted for. I had a number of other questions to ask in this regard: "What would others in the team have noticed?" "How have these subtle changes in your relationship affected the rest of the team in the office?"

I also asked Ruby and Phoebe to think about what had made a difference in creating the changes they had managed. They were almost jumping with enthusiasm as they answered, "What made a difference was that we were both willing to commit to changing things."

"And also that management did what they were asked."

"And it made a difference that we each had counseling for support."

These comments added to the story of change by adding new layers of significance to the events of the previous month. It was now not just on the landscape of action that the new story existed. It also was being accounted for on the landscape of meaning.

In response to the momentum that was being generated, I asked whether there were any new issues that either person would like to talk about. Both thought about it but neither could identify any new problem. They kept referring to the memorandum of understanding developed at the first meeting and how they had kept to it, especially with regard to their interactions with each other. Together, they spoke of the usefulness of the mediation process, and commented on how the process had flowed from the questions asked and how well it had worked. Phoebe could not imagine where it would have gone without the three questions at the beginning and the chance to discuss those separately with her support person. Both spoke of being nervous about coming to mediation and of not knowing what to expect, but they said that they had not really found it threatening after all. It was, they said, "a respectful, well-structured process which we couldn't have come up with on our own." It had also been good for Susan (in her interactions with Ruby) as an example of how to make relationships work better in the office.

Phoebe concluded by saying, "I've learned a great deal about myself. I'm the one who let it go on. I'll never let something like this escalate ever again."

The Story of Rosa and the School Board

The second story of employment mediation relates a situation in which Rosa, formerly the principal of a school in a rural area of New Zealand, was alleging unjustified dismissal by her employer, the school's board of trustees.[1] Rosa, through her legal representative, Oliver, had taken a personal grievance for unjustified dismissal to the Employment Relations Authority, the next level beyond mediation for dispute resolution of employment matters. Oliver had submitted a very detailed *statement of problem* to the Employment Relations Authority. He had received back a *statement of reply* of similar volume from Matthew, the board's legal representative. Both of these statements had served mainly to endorse the differences in perspective between the two parties.

When it was realized that the issue had not been to mediation, the authority directed that the two parties attempt to mediate the issues in good faith. If they were unable to resolve matters at mediation, the case would return to the Employment Relations Authority for a full hearing and adjudication.

Moreover, interwoven with the problem issues of the dispute were cultural issues, because Rosa was Maori, as were a number of the school board members. Maori are the indigenous people of New Zealand, and they have distinctive cultural traditions of conflict resolution that need to be accorded honor and priority. They also have assumptions about the ways conflict should be managed within a community and these assumptions depart in key places from modernist Western assumptions that individuals are negotiating the resolution of their own interests.

In addition, in rural districts of New Zealand, such as the one where this school was located, it is more likely than it is in large urban centers that Maori groups will have close connections to longstanding traditional *marae*

---

[1] In order to protect those involved in this story from easy identification, it has been necessary to change the details, including the location, considerably. It did not actually take place in a primary school, for example, but it was in an educational institution.

affiliations and to highly respected tribal elders. A *marae* is a sacred meeting house where the culture can be celebrated, Maori language spoken, intertribal obligations met, customs debated, family occasions held, and important ceremonies performed (Mead, 2003). Rural areas are also often sparsely populated and anonymity is difficult to maintain in organizational disputes. Narrative mediation in this context needs to invite forward the local knowledges (Geertz, 1983) that are indigenous to the community and needs to treat them as valuable resources to be drawn on in the process of finding a way forward.

Beginning the Mediation

I entered the conference room of the motel booked for the mediation in a rural town to see a group of about twelve people waiting there. Some were gathered around the large table in the middle of the room. Some were sitting in armchairs around the walls.

I moved around greeting people, asking their names and their roles in relation to this meeting. I became aware that people were not grouped in the usual two distinct groups of employer and employee. Instead, a mix of different groupings was scattered around the room. This was a dispute that affected and involved a community in all its complexity, rather than a dispute that could be isolated to two sides, or two individuals.

A majority of the board members were present, as was the former principal, Rosa. She had with her some *whānau* members ("extended family," or family group) (Taonui, 2007) as support people. For Maori, a slight against an individual is held to be a slight against a whole *whānau*. They all had an interest in this issue, not only Rosa. It also became obvious that a number of board members had a strong allegiance to the dismissed principal. Other current board members were gathered in a different part of the room, and there were also some former board members present. They had been on the board at the time of the incidents under discussion but had not been reelected at the recent election (held every three years). Also attending were two lawyers, Matthew, representing the employer, the board, and Oliver, representing Rosa.

I invited the employer and employee groups to meet with me separately. The recently appointed chairperson of the board, William, stood immediately to lead his group to a motel unit reserved as a *breakout* room. I went with them, and in the breakout room I explained that I had a number of questions to ask of each group. First, I asked the members of this group, "Can you each explain to me your position on the board and how you see your role today?" Answers varied from those wanting to be fair to both sides, to those expressing strong allegiance to the board and its right to make decisions and stick by them. There were also two board members who mentioned that they were related to Rosa. They were protective of her, believing that aspects of the way she had been treated by their own board were unfair.

Matthew, the board's legal representative, summarized helpfully by saying, "Board members have a range of views about this situation. I've suggested to them that I'll summarize on behalf of the board but will invite their participation on specific matters. We're going to ask for regular breaks so that we can come in here, discuss what's been said, and plan our response to it."

I endorsed this as a good plan and asked my next question, "How do you want to begin the mediation? For example, do you want to start with a traditional *karakia*?" (a Maori form of prayer or incantation that invokes a blessing on the meeting and a consciousness of spirituality; Turner, 1960). Asking questions about procedural issues invites the parties to buy into the process by participating in its design. In narrative mediation this is considered a reflexive, balanced approach to the power of the mediator.

The group members assured me that they did want to have a *karakia*. When I asked who was willing to lead it they all looked at William, the chairperson, who was Maori. He nodded. Recognition of *mana* (broadly, status, influence, and reputation) in the Maori community is important. Such cultural recognition is more than the personal recognition advocated by Folger and Bush (2001). It is about acknowledgment of community and its distinct patterns of ascribed authority. In order to acknowledge *mana* in the mediation context, I explained that I would need to check out the board group's proposal with the employee group. As long as both parties to mediation could agree on a process, we could proceed with it. They accepted this.

I then asked, "What's most important to you in this mediation?" They answered spontaneously, "Fairness"; "Putting this behind us and moving on"; "Getting our focus back on education— what we were appointed to do"; "Spending trust board money on the right things." In addition I asked, "How do you wish to be addressed? Would you be comfortable with first names or do you want us to be more formal?" All preferred that we use first names.

Next, I took the same questions to the employee group. They were much more united in their views, with some strong feelings of injustice on Rosa's behalf and a common dissatisfaction with the board and its treatment of Rosa. They agreed without question to the *karakia* proposal and accepted that William, would lead it.

I asked Rosa, "What's most important to you in this mediation?" She answered, "The board acknowledging that what they did to me was wrong. And giving me back my *mana*." *Mana* is a Maori term that encompasses a person's reputation and social status, and also a person's spiritual distinctiveness and dignity. A person's *mana* is conferred by ancestral descent but may also be enhanced or damaged by the person's own actions, by roles the person takes up in the community, or by actions of others that affect the person (Durie, 2000).

I confirmed that the employee group was also comfortable with the use of first names. Both groups then returned to the mediation room, and all attended respectfully as William led the *karakia*.

Introducing the Mediation Process

As this was a personal grievance mediation, I needed to make some extra introductory points, beyond the points described in the account of the mediation with Ruby and Phoebe. First, I explained that mediation is an opportunity to have a structured, thoughtful conversation across the table about the employment problem that had arisen. I said, "It's an opportunity to unravel and discuss both the personal and the legal issues around this employment relationship problem." I wanted everyone present to understand that mediation is more than a legal process; that I would want to hear something of the history of the relationship, the highs and lows, and the impact on each person of the particular problems that had arisen. Signaling a broader approach like this can lead to the first shift away from a fixed interpretation of the situation and toward an understanding that there may be different perceptions of the same events.

I then explained the concepts of confidentiality and "without prejudice" and also the mediator role under the Employment Relations Act. I added, "It may be possible for you to reach resolution if together you can find ways forward. If such agreements are reached, they are written up and then signed by both parties and the mediator. They are recognized as full and final and binding under the law."

They continued to listen keenly and then began to nod as I asked, "Are you willing to work to some guidelines?" I then went on to request that they listen without interruption, try to be open to new information and different possibilities, and choose their words with care in the best interests of the relationships and the community represented here. Everyone nodded in acceptance. I asked them all if they had any further guidelines they would like to add. One of the board members glanced at the board's lawyer, who encouraged him to speak. "I'd like to add," he said, "that we treat each other with respect and dignity." There was a murmur of assent to this.

Unraveling the Problem Story: Rosa's Story

I invited Oliver, the legal representative for Rosa, to take us through Rosa's perspective on the problem issues that had arisen in the disputed employment relationship. Oliver outlined the history. Rosa had been appointed six years earlier as the principal of this rural school. She had gained considerable teaching experience in other parts of New Zealand and had been very excited to return as principal to her own community, which included her *whānau* ("family group") and *iwi* ("tribal group"). In the years since then, the school had gained a reputation for its innovative and successful reading program. Rosa's leadership in getting staff, parents, and children behind this program had been praised by the New Zealand Education Review Office in its audit of the school, and she was highly thought of in the community.

"Things changed," said Oliver, "when within a period of just a few months three board members resigned for personal reasons." New members were elected to the board for the four months remaining until the next board of trustees' election (held every three years). The new members were nominated for their financial and managerial backgrounds and were naturally keen to make a contribution in the run-up to the election of a new board. Rosa's understanding was that at the first meeting of the board after the membership change, issues were raised about the budget, especially the proportion of money being spent on the reading program compared with proportions spent on other curriculum areas. After some discussion, a motion was made that a subcommittee be appointed to work with the principal to try to reduce reading program costs over the next four months and to apply the savings to other curriculum areas, ones in which the standards being achieved were less consistent. Although only a small number of board members were present at this meeting, this motion was passed and a subcommittee of two members was appointed. Rosa, as the principal, was a member of the board but was absent from this meeting. She was shocked to learn of this decision and challenged it vehemently, first by speaking to her cousin on the board and then through Oliver, her legal representative, in a formal letter to the board.

Oliver alleged that there were some irregularities about the way this subcommittee had been formed, and that the subcommittee had confused governance and management boundaries in the directions given to Rosa since then. He questioned whether these instructions were lawful and stated that as a result of them Rosa had found herself in an untenable situation as an employee. She had been given serious responsibilities as a principal and a member of the board, but had been struggling to carry them out because of the actions of the subcommittee of the board. In the meantime, there appeared to be an internal struggle going on within the board itself.

Oliver argued that Rosa's obligation was to report to the board as a whole and not to this "self-formed" subcommittee. He had advised the subcommittee on Rosa's behalf that she would not be attending its meetings until the questions raised about whether or not the subcommittee was properly constituted had been addressed. The board had considered this challenge inappropriate and had called Rosa to a subcommittee meeting, alleging that she was in breach of her obligation as an employee to follow lawful instructions and that she had damaged the trust and confidence essential in an employer-employee relationship. Rosa had been given the opportunity to explain her actions, had submitted a written statement on the issues, had been suspended while the board investigated the matter, and had been later dismissed.

Oliver explained the legal expectations that an employer must meet in making a dismissal and also explained why he believed that in this case the dismissal could not be justified either from a substantive or a procedural point of view. He believed that options other than dismissal had been open to the employer, and he outlined them. "I believe," he said, "that the actions taken were not those of a fair and reasonable employer in all the circumstances of this case."

Mapping the Effects of the Problem on Rosa

After listening to the legal perspective, I asked Rosa, "Would you like to tell us about the effects of this situation on you and on your work?"

Rosa spoke from her heart: "I gave my very best to this job and this board for six years. These are my *whānau* and *iwi*. This is my community. I've watched young people come into the school shy and uncertain and I've seen them leave with increased skills and confidence. I've watched them become enthusiastic about further learning. I've worked hard for the students and the staff and the community. I would not have expected it to come to this. Now the school's reputation has been threatened and some of the people who were my friends have become distant towards me. It's been very stressful for me and my *whānau.*"

Rosa faltered, and then continued: "I've been blamed unfairly and the final straw" (she became distressed as she held up a newspaper) "was this article in the paper about my falling out with the board. I was made a public spectacle in our community. How can I recover my *mana* after that?" She answered her own question strongly, "I want a public apology and an explanation from the board to be published in the same newspaper." This demand was to become a sticking point later in the mediation.

In summary, Oliver stated that this was an unjustified dismissal and that it had resulted in a high level of hurt and humiliation for Rosa. In order to resolve this matter, he proposed remedies close to what Rosa might be awarded if she were to win her case at the next level of employment law, the Employment Relations Authority. However, she did not want to be reinstated to her position as principal, the first remedy under the Employment Relations Act. Instead she was seeking payment for wages lost in the traumatic period since her dismissal, compensation for the distress caused, and a contribution toward her legal costs. "And," he added, "Rosa expects a public apology to make up for the public humiliation she has suffered."

Unraveling the Problem Story: The Board's Story

Matthew, the employer's representative, described events from the board's point of view. Following the resignations of three members, three competent, experienced people had been elected to the board to serve until the next election. The board had legal, financial, and educational obligations to fulfill and had begun discussions about restructuring the way it worked in order to address these obligations more effectively. It was correct that concerns had arisen about the level of expenditure on the reading program. Spending on this program was disproportionate, and it was apparent that other areas of the curriculum were being neglected. Accordingly, a decision had been made to appoint a subcommittee of two board members to work closely with the principal to address these issues. Matthew affirmed (challenging the view expressed earlier by Rosa's representative) that this was a legitimate committee, appointed by a board with the authority to do so and at a meeting that was properly constituted. In the period following this board action, the board had become concerned about the level of distraction, stress, and absenteeism among staff at the school, which they believed was resulting from Rosa's challenges to the board's governance. There was also the threat that the board's right to govern could be revoked by the Ministry of Education if there were unanswered questions about the quality of its governance.

Rosa had been asked to attend a meeting of the subcommittee to hear the board's response to the questions she had raised around governance and management. Matthew stressed that Rosa had been "invited to bring a support person or a representative. The purpose of the meeting was made clear to her, as were the possible consequences. In spite of this, she refused to meet with the subcommittee." He did not comment on the fact that Rosa had prepared a written statement for the meeting. However, her nonattendance had been considered willful and in breach of her obligations as an employee. The board believed that Rosa had overstepped the mark in her challenges to her employer and had refused a number of lawful instructions to attend meetings to discuss these matters. The board made the decision, first, to suspend her while board members investigated the matter further and, later, to dismiss her.

"I believe," said Matthew, "that the board was entitled to take the actions it took. The board had obligations to the students, to the staff, and to the New Zealand Ministry of Education. It acted as a fair and reasonable employer in all the circumstances of this case."

I asked Matthew and the board members present, "What were the effects of this employment situation on the board and the community?" Mathew glanced at the group and waited for group members to answer if they wished. Several of them voiced their thoughts, saying: "These issues have taken up a lot of time and it's meant that other aspects of our work have been overlooked." "We've had to have extra meetings with Matthew and have incurred legal costs." "Some of us are *iwi*, we're related, but sometimes we've been pulling against each other in a painful way."

I acknowledged that what I had heard indicated that this employment problem had had a significant impact on individuals, staff, the board, and the community.

Opening the Alternative Story

After hearing the conflict story from both sides, I was interested in asking some questions that would elicit aspects of a counterstory to the story of the problem and its strength. I wanted to break down the sense of apparent impasse and to recontextualize the problem story.

First, I asked board members, "Were there occasions in the past when the relationship between the board members and principal was working well? If so, what was happening then?"

"Rosa was a highly competent educator," said one board member after a short silence, and there were nods of agreement. "She led the new reading program," said a second. "It became well known in education circles," added another; "We had requests from teachers in other areas who asked if they could observe the program." "The kids loved it too," said another.

I asked Rosa, "What do you recall about times when this relationship was working particularly well?" Rosa spoke quietly at first, and then more firmly of the glowing reports the school had received from the New Zealand Education Review Office over a number of years. She spoke of building a team of dedicated staff and of the positive relationship she had had for years with the board.

In asking these questions I was trying to destabilize the conflict story and to remind participants that their relationship had not been one solely of conflict. It had a much broader, richer history. Already I could see some of those present recognizing that there were a number of different ways of interpreting the events within this employment relationship.

At this point I made some observations to the whole group, "In spite of the differences in legal interpretation expressed by the two representatives, it is clear that from a personal, human perspective, the two groups [the employer board and the employee principal] have much in common. This is a small rural community of Maori and Pakeha [a Maori term for New Zealanders of European heritage]. There are *whānau* and *iwi* members as well as Pakeha on either side. You are all feeling hurt and under threat. Both parties have incurred legal costs. Neither side intended to create the divisions that have occurred." My intention in these observations was to draw attention to the big picture beyond the employment problem that had arisen. I also wanted to move from focusing on the differences between the parties to acknowledging what they had in common.

I said that I wanted to talk with the employee and employer groups separately to hear their response to some questions, which I now wrote on a whiteboard for all to consider:

- Is there a way to restore the *mana* (reputation or personal standing) of both parties?
- With the benefit of hindsight, can you see aspects that each of you might have handled differently?
- What will be some of the advantages if you can come up with a plan to resolve the issues coming between you?
- What will it look like if you *can't* get this matter sorted at mediation?

The first and second questions were intended to open up discussion of how to address the personal, relational, and community effects of the problem story. The third question asked the parties to consider the advantages of working to create an alternative story.

The fourth question was designed to ask them to discuss with their legal representatives the possible effects of the Employment Relations Authority hearing that would follow if there was no resolution at mediation. Such a hearing would be public, with likely delays in the legal process. It would lead to an uncertain (adjudicated) outcome in favor of one group or the other. It would incur further financial costs for both parties, the ex-principal and the board, and most important, it would prolong the stress on the people involved and on their families and community. I wanted everyone to weigh up carefully the possible costs and benefits of proceeding further in the legal system.

I suggested that while I was following up the questions with one group, the members of the other group should take the opportunity to get some food and fresh air. I allowed twenty minutes before rejoining the first group I would question, the employer group.

Developing the Counterstory

As I entered the room the members of the employer group were engaged in intense discussion. Matthew, the lawyer, took me through the board's views on the questions I had put to them. He said that the board wanted to try to resolve the issues.

There were family members on both sides of this employment problem. Board members maintained a strong belief in their respective positions, but a number also had a strong desire to resolve the situation in the interests of their broader *whānau* and *iwi* in the district.

William, the chairperson, spoke up, "I want us to put the troubles behind the board and move on." He and some other board members mentioned that they were not afraid to say, "We didn't get it all right. We could have taken things more slowly. We can learn from this."

Among some board members there was a level of goodwill toward Rosa, whereas others were still resentful of what they saw as her stance against the board. In terms of restoring *mana*, they were prepared to offer a statement of reconciliation and a payment to seal this, but they were adamant that the payment would not be in the realm that Oliver, Rosa's legal representative, had proposed.

I commented on their conciliatory approach, and then suggested that they refine the details of a proposal for resolution that could be given to Rosa. In the meantime I needed to hear Rosa's answers to the questions I had raised.

Rosa's response contained themes in common with those expressed by the board. She too was conscious that there were family members on both sides of this employment problem. She recognized that the problem was having a negative impact on both her *whānau* and on the community. Rosa stated that she would like to find a resolution on that day but that it would need to include a published apology for the public humiliation she had experienced and a meaningful payment close to what her legal representative had proposed.

Negotiating a Shared Story

I invited the two groups to come together again and acknowledged the thoughtful way in which they had addressed the questions given to them. I commented that in moving between the groups, I had heard ideas discussed about restoring *mana*, or reputation, and to the credit of each group, some acknowledgment of specific aspects that each might have handled differently. I had heard both lawyers lead discussions about the potential merits and disadvantages of pursuing the case in the legal forum of the Employment Relations Authority versus continuing to work toward resolution through mediation. I had been asked by each group to add my independent view of those risks and costs and had shared my views. What was now being expressed was a desire on both sides for a coming together around a resolution. At this point the relational conditions existed for the formation of a new story that could go forward. But the details of this new story still needed to be negotiated.

At this point I invited the board to present its proposal for settlement. The board was offering a written statement of reconciliation that would include expressions of regret about the article that had appeared in the newspaper, and an acknowledgment that aspects of the board's management of the employment problem could have been handled better. The board was also willing to endorse Rosa's high level of competence as an educator. In addition, the board was willing to pay Rosa the equivalent of three months' salary to acknowledge that she had suffered stress and hurt as a result of the board's actions and decisions. Proposals for resolution (*terms of settlement* in more formal mediation terms), could be written up clause by clause. These terms of settlement would be kept confidential by the parties and could not be publicized in any way.

Rosa and her legal representative and supporters were relieved that discussion was now focusing on possible resolution but were insistent that a public apology was a key part of potential resolution and that the compensation figure to be paid needed to be increased. At this stage the board was prepared to reconsider the level of financial payment, but not the public apology. There followed an intense period of discussion with waves of goodwill alternating with active resistance.

As the possibility of resolution seemed to falter and failure to achieve resolution began to seem likely, William, the board chairperson, said firmly, "This is not the Maori way. Our way is to talk things through until we get it sorted. Let's not give up!" This appeal to cultural tradition was powerful and caused a shift in the mood and direction of discussion.

The board members were prepared to increase their original financial offer. They were willing to acknowledge that the previous year had been an unsettled period in the board's history because of the loss of three experienced board members. They were willing to express regret for the impact of this on Rosa. They were also willing to make an oral or written, but not a published, statement of reconciliation.

Achieving a Breakthrough

It was one of the new board members who speculated quietly across the table that an apology in the newspaper might rebound on either or both parties by opening up the issues again in a public way. There could be no certainty about how it would be received or interpreted in the community, and there was a possibility that it could damage both the board and Rosa. He thought that there might be other ways of achieving what Rosa and the board both wanted, which was to reclaim their *mana* and respect in the community and be able to move on from these events.

"Why don't we," he said, "organize a special *hui* ["community gathering"], a ceremony to acknowledge Rosa's services to the people of the *iwi*, the school, and the board. If we were to advise the local newspaper of the event, they would most likely attend and report on it favorably of their own choosing. It would be an opportunity to restore the *mana* of all involved and to demonstrate that the board is moving forward in a positive manner."

Rosa and her legal representative took time out to consider this idea. While they were out of the room, board members started talking about who could be invited to the *hui*, where it could best be held and what *taonga* ("gift") they might present to Rosa. There was a huge sense of relief in the room when Rosa and Oliver returned, and Oliver stated that Rosa would accept this final clause alongside the agreements already reached.

I wrote the clauses of agreement (terms of settlement) on the whiteboard, so that everyone would have a chance to see that the wording reflected accurately the decisions that had been made. The proposal still needed to be typed and taken to the full board for formal acceptance, but the hard work had been done. With a majority of the board present at mediation and committed to this resolution, there was confidence that it would be passed by the full board. William planned to call a special meeting for this purpose the following week. Anticipating this, I needed to confirm that both Rosa and William, who would, we all hoped, be signing the final terms of settlement, understood the legal implications of having a mediator sign off on this document. I explained that the terms would be full, final, and binding and also enforceable by the Employment Relations Authority. Except for enforcement purposes, this employment problem could not be raised in any other legal forum nor could the terms of settlement be appealed. Both Rosa, as employee, and William, on behalf of the board, confirmed their understanding of these conditions.

As the group began to chat more openly across the table, one of the board members commented that Maori ways of working had finally prevailed, that they had kept talking until they had reached resolution. Another was heard to say, "I'm glad this is behind us. It's a new day for us all tomorrow."

William led another *karakia* to conclude the mediation. He ended with the repetition of an old Maori proverb, *He aha te mea nui o te ao, he tangata, he tangata, he tangata* ("What is the greatest thing in this world? It is people, it is people, it is people").

There were tears and hugs as the group of twelve moved out, chatting and laughing as a single group.

Reflections on Employment Mediation

A colleague of Alison's who is also a mediator with the New Zealand Department of Labour is fond of saying that being a mediator is like going to the movies every day. It is an opportunity to witness the working through of significant dramas. A narrative perspective emphasizes the artistic aspects of this practice more than the scientific ones. The mediator's role is about facilitating and bearing witness to the crafting of a viable story. In the denouement of such a story, there are often visible differences in individuals' appearances. This was certainly true for Rosa and her fellow community members. They left the mediation looking decidedly more relaxed than the tense and nervous protagonists who had entered the room. Participants in other mediations have sometimes disclosed that they expect to have their first good sleep for ages.

In order to reach this point, people have had to let go of well-rehearsed and well-sealed stories that they have repeated to their friends and family members many times. Narrative mediation asks them to dig deeper into their repertoires of story fragments and to open up their construction of a coherent account to include story elements contributed from the other party. This takes effort and is not easy.

A well-known Maori leader in New Zealand, Sir Tipene O'Regan (2008, personal communication), has commented on this difficulty, saying, "We let go of our dreams easily. It's a much harder thing to give up on our grievances." This chapter has told two major stories about people in employment contexts who have had the courage to let go of accounts of events that fashioned a story of grievance and to open up new stories of shared understanding, mutual commitment, and changed ongoing relationship. Lest this sound too good to be true, we should in ending acknowledge that mediation is not a perfect process. Not all conflicts end with people hugging each other, resolutions can also come unstuck, and making mistakes is part of human nature. Mediation is, nevertheless, a dignified way of working through employment problems and redesigning the future that might be.

Chapter Eight

Restorative Conferencing in Schools

One of the limitations of mediation as a practice lies in the isolation of two parties at the center of a conflict. Built on the assumption that everything can be reduced to individual interests, the habit of identifying two people as the protagonists in the drama of mediation, and working only with them, shapes the story of what will happen in a conflict resolution process in powerful ways. It may lead to an outcome that actively involves only those two people, no matter how many others are affected by that outcome. Conflict situations commonly cast a shadow over the networks of relationships around the protagonists, and the actions of those who are under that shadow can either exacerbate or ameliorate the effects of the conflict. In short, mediating between two people only often leaves out many who have a stake in the outcome of a conflict resolution process.

When there is an imbalance of power between the two individuals at the center of a conflict, a two-party-only mediation preempts possible balancing moves through the inclusion of more voices. There are, moreover, many conflicts that grow and fester among groups of people rather than primarily between individuals. In such cases, constructing a two-party mediation may profoundly distort the conflict story and may produce "resolutions" embodied in an alternative story to which there is only a very narrow commitment.

In this chapter we explore some options for altering the lens through which conflict is viewed, for zooming back and working with the larger picture. We do this within the context of some work we are familiar with that is often described as (among other names) *restorative conferencing.* A conferencing process takes as one of its starting principles the idea of including the community of care around a problem and knitting that community of care into whatever resolution processes emerge. There are a variety of approaches to such conferencing work, and we have been involved in the development of a restorative conferencing approach built on the use of the narrative metaphor. We outline that approach in this chapter and locate it in the broader context of other, similar approaches.

Restorative Justice

Various innovative conflict resolution practices have coalesced in recent decades under the heading of restorative justice. Howard Zehr (1990, 2002) has been a leader in articulating what is distinctive about a restorative approach to the concern for justice after an offense has been committed. He finds that an emphasis on understanding offending behavior from a relational perspective is central to a restorative justice approach. In contrast to what he calls *retributive justice* (the mainstream approach in the justice systems of most modern states), restorative justice directs people's focus away from the demonstration of the authority of the state and the protection of rules through punishing those who offend. Instead, it asks people to look at any offence as primarily an offense against other persons. A criminal act in the end causes harm to others, to relationships, and to communities. Mainstream legal systems have paid little attention to addressing the harm done by an offense. They have concentrated on restoring the authority of the rules and of those in charge of the rules. Thus victims of crime may experience some satisfaction from seeing offenders punished but usually receive little else by way of benefit from the administration of justice. If they have lost money, for example, they do not get it back. If they have been humiliated and hurt, they do not receive emotional support. If they have been left with a legacy of fear by an assault, for example, they do not have that fear reduced by state-administered courtroom practices and the imposition of jail terms on offenders who show little remorse.

Restorative justice processes, in contrast, focus on addressing the harm that has been done by an offense. This may be accomplished by setting right the damage that has been done to a relationship or to a community. Restorative justice necessarily involves granting prominence to the voice of the victim of an offense, and asking him what he needs in order to minimize the damage. This restorative aspect differs markedly from an emphasis on either punishment or rehabilitation. Rather than working to effect change in the person of the offender alone, as rehabilitation is intended to do, a restorative approach requires the offender to make a relational move and to take up some measure of responsibility toward the victim. Rehabilitation has been criticized on the grounds that it does nothing for the victims and—if the search for an explanation for offenders' actions produces sympathy for their difficult life circumstances—that it may convey a sense of justification to offenders that diminishes their responsibility.

A definition of *restorative justice* that reflects a consensus view has been published in a United Nations handbook. It states that "restorative justice refers to a process for resolving crime by focusing on redressing the harm done to the victims, holding offenders accountable for their actions and, often also, engaging the community in the resolution of that conflict" (Dandurand & Griffiths, 2006).

Early restorative justice processes in the United States were referred to as *victim-offender mediations* (Umbreit, 1994), and they now have a twenty-five-year track record. They have focused on creating meetings between adult offenders and their victims for the following purposes: "the victim is able to tell the offender about the crime's physical, emotional, and financial impact; receive answers to lingering questions about the crime and the offender; and be directly involved in developing a restitution plan for the offender to pay back any financial debt to the victim" (Bazemore & Umbreit, 2001, p. 2).

Gordon Bazemore and Mark Umbreit (2001) have counted 320 victim-offender mediation programs in the United States and Canada. Lorraine Amstutz and Judy Mullet (2005) claim that there are over 500 programs in the United States alone.

Indigenous Practices

A different emphasis grew in New Zealand and simultaneously in Canada as a result of initiatives from indigenous peoples. In New Zealand, in response to a request from the Maori population that Maori be authorized to deal with their own young people when they committed crimes, the government set up an pilot process for a form of conferencing through the *Matua Whangai* movement. This model for dealing with young Maori offenders was deemed so successful that it was embodied in New Zealand law in 1989 as the primary method of dealing with all youth crime. Rather than being sent directly to court, young people in New Zealand—for all but the most serious offenses—are dealt with through the *family group conference* process (MacRae & Zehr, 2004; Maxwell & Morris, 1993, 2006; Morris & Maxwell, 1998, 2001). This approach calls together immediate and extended family members, victims and victims' rights group members, the police, and social workers in a conference that aims to address what has happened. The family members, and not just the individual offender, bear the primary responsibility for devising a plan to address the task of restoring what was damaged by the offense. This plan, however, must be acceptable to the victim and the police. This process did not come out of nowhere. It was drawn from a long tradition of Maori practice in which *hui* ("community gatherings") have been used to resolve conflict (Durie Hall, 1999; Macfarlane, 2000).

The restorative justice approach in Canada is also acknowledged to have its roots in the cultures of aboriginal peoples (Cormier, 2002). The *sentencing circle* (Stuart, 1997; Cormier, 2002), a process similar to the family group conference, developed from indigenous practices. In these sentencing circles people sit in circles and speak in turn to address issues in a community. In contrast to the process developed and then mandated in New Zealand, however; the process developed in Canada has not been uniformly applied, mainly because it has not been mandated for use across the board as a method for dealing with all youth crime.

Rapid International Growth

Interest in using conferencing processes for restorative justice has spread to many quarters of the world, and not only as a means of working with youths but also as a function of the adult courts (Morris & Maxwell, 2001). In part such interest is a response to the increases in many countries in the numbers of offenders being imprisoned. In New Zealand a pilot program that extends the use of restorative justice conferencing to referrals from the adult courts is being conducted (Triggs, 2005). In Australia the family group conference has been taken up under the name *community group conference* (Hyndman, Thorsborne, & Wood, 1996). In the United States many local jurisdictions have implemented programs offering family group conferences (Mirsky, 2003, counts 150 of them) or have developed similar programs under different names, such as *community reparative boards* (Karp, 2002), *family group decision-making* (Mirsky, 2003), and *family unity meetings* (Mirsky, 2003). In Canada, programs using much the same process are being referred to as *community justice forums* (Cormier, 2002).

There are also many European developments in restorative conferencing. For example, England, Scotland, and Wales have many family group conferencing initiatives running (Mirsky, 2003). The Scandinavian countries, Norway, Sweden, Finland, and Denmark, have all established family group conference programs (Mirsky, 2003). Other projects are underway in Belgium. International conferences on the subject were held in The Netherlands in 2003 and Hungary in 2007 (and also in Australia in 2005). One report claims that over 800 restorative justice programs are underway across Europe (cited by Gavrielides, 2005). The idea of restorative conferencing is also spreading in Asia, Africa, and South America, judging by the territories and countries represented at the 2003 Netherlands conference. They included Hong Kong, South Africa, Japan, Argentina, Thailand, and Papua New Guinea. In 2007, an international conference on restorative conferencing was held in Jamaica (Wachtel, 2007). Countries with active restorative justice programs include South Africa, the Czech Republic, Lesotho, and Ireland (Dandurand & Griffiths, 2006).

Many of these projects are restorative justice initiatives designed to respond to youth and, to a lesser extent, adult criminal offending, often (but not always) at the lower end of the scale of offense seriousness. They have often been associated with police-run youth diversion programs. The concept of restorative practice has also been translated into comparable formats in other domains (for example, in workplaces; Thorsborne, 1999a). A major domain of restorative justice application is as a response to school disciplinary offenses. School discipline systems often parallel criminal justice systems. Offenses that would be handled by the police if they occurred outside the school are frequently handled by teachers and administrators when they occur within the school. The usual approach, in schools as in the community, emphasizes isolation of the offender, assignment of guilt, and the administration of punishment and retribution. As in the criminal justice field, it is uncommon to pay attention to the restoration of damage done to relationships or to the community of the school. Prominent New Zealand judge and advocate of restorative conferencing Fred McElrea (1996) argued for schools to take up the same practices that were being applied in the youth justice context. Restorative conferencing began to be applied in school contexts in Australia in the 1990s (Blood & Thorsborne, 2005; Hyndman et al., 1996; Thorsborne, 1999b) and in New Zealand a few years later (Drewery & Winslade, 2005; Restorative Practices Development Team, 2003; Winslade, Drewery, & Hooper, 2000). We were both involved in a restorative conferencing pilot project undertaken for the Ministry of Education in New Zealand between 1998 and 2000 (Winslade et al., 2000; Gerritsen, 2001). In North America restorative practices in schools have been taken up in Canada (Zammit & Lockhart, 2001) and in many parts of the United States. For example, in California one community has established parallel restorative conferencing processes in youth justice and school contexts (Nash, 2004). *Restorative discipline* (Amstutz & Mullet, 2005; Elton, 2007) has been argued for as a new approach to the management of misdemeanors in schools that teaches responsibility and addresses inappropriate behavior. There are also pockets of enthusiasm and some projects underway to introduce restorative conferencing in schools in Ireland and in the United Kingdom (McGrath, 2002).

School systems are applying the principles of restorative practice at a variety of choice points along the continuum of responses to disciplinary offenses. In Queensland in 1994, restorative conferences began to be used when young people committed serious criminal offenses, such as arson, against a school (Morrison, Blood, & Thorsborne, 2005). In our pilot project in New Zealand the principle motivation of the Ministry of Education and the Crime Prevention Unit of the Prime Minister's department (who together provided project funding) for introducing restorative conferencing in schools was to try to reduce the number of suspensions being recorded in secondary schools. Suspensions in New Zealand rose sharply during the 1990s (Ministry of Education, 2003), as they did in many other countries in response to the increasing application of market-led values in schooling policies. The restorative conference was therefore implemented as an alternative to a suspension hearing. Many New Zealand schools used the restorative conference for that purpose at first but soon began to see its value in a number of other instances. Often a conference would be called to head off a trend in a student's behavior that appeared to be leading toward a future suspension. Some schools use conferencing after a suspension to reintegrate a student who has committed an offense back into the school in a way that will lead to changes in behavior. Sometimes a whole class is identified as being in crisis as a result of relationship problems among its members, and instead of assigning a retributive punishment, a restorative classroom conference is set in place (Restorative Practices Development Team, 2003). Circle processes have also proved productive in classroom conflicts in various locales (Amstutz & Mullet, 2005; Pranis, 2005). Alan Jenkins (2006) illustrates the use of restorative practice to address instances of sexual assault and sexual harassment in schools. In a Utah program for "truancy mediation" (with a process that resembles conferencing more than straight mediation), 276 cases of truancy were processed in 2003 and 75 percent of the children improved their school attendance (Amstutz & Mullet, 2005; Elton, 2007). Sometimes a full-blown conference is not justified and smaller *restorative conversations* involving three or four persons are used (Restorative Practices Development Team, 2003). This process may be referred to as a *restorative interview* or a *restorative chat* (Margaret Thorsborne, personal communication, 2006).

Increasingly, however, restorative practices are being conceptualized as heralding a substantial cultural shift in how relationships in schools are envisioned. The idea of a community that operates in a way that makes relationships central to its functioning, and that works to restore those relationships when ruptures occur, is being touted as fundamentally transformative of institutions like schools (Drewery, 2004; Drewery & Winslade, 2005; Morrison, Blood & Thorsborne, 2005; Shaw, 2007). Nothing less than a major culture change is being contemplated. This change might lead a school to view all aspects of institutional communication through a restorative lens. Morrison, Blood, and Thorsborne (2005) argue that this would likely affect "how management speaks to, and about, staff; how staff speak about the management, particularly in their absence; how management and staff speak to, and about, students and parents; the patterns of communication within staff meetings and what is said immediately after meetings; how criticism and disagreement are handled; how the school invites, promotes and supports initiatives and vision; how the school responds to identified needs amongst students or staff" (p. 339).

The same authors also argue that it is relationship networks such as these that constitute and construct the social capital that the school is transmitting to its students. They provide students with a hidden curriculum that is learned, or absorbed, through the practices of the school.

Evidence of Effectiveness

Evidence is beginning to mount of the effectiveness of restorative practices in schools and communities. Maxwell and Morris (2006) have compiled the most comprehensive reports on the effects of the New Zealand family group conference process with young offenders and their families. They find that since 1989, over 90 percent of family group conferences have resulted in plans that include accountability tasks. Over 80 percent of these tasks have been aimed at repairing harm done by the offense, and in 80 percent of the cases the tasks were completed by the young persons. Family group conferences have also resulted in a decrease of two-thirds in the incarceration rate for young offenders. Canadian research has demonstrated marked drops in recidivism following restorative justice programs addressing youth and adult crime (Cormier, 2002). Satisfaction rates have been very high among both victims (89 percent) and offenders (91 percent) participating in Canadian victim-offender mediation programs (Cormier, 2002). Joan Pennell (2006), in a North Carolina study, has also reported high levels of participant satisfaction with the process and the decisions reached. Australian research has found that the presence during conferencing processes of remorse in offenders for their actions was significantly predictive of reduced reoffending rates (Hayes & Daley, 2003). And in Indianapolis, a study of first-time offenders over a two-year period found that offenders who attended a family group conference had significantly lower rates of reoffending than offenders in a control group did (McGarrell & Hipple, 2007).

In schools, effectiveness has often been noticed in terms of reduced referrals to school administrators for disciplinary offenses. For example, after adopting a whole-school approach to *talking circles*, a Utah school demonstrated a 72 percent decrease in referrals to the school office (Elton, 2007). A school in Arizona that made a similar commitment to restorative processes noticed in one year a drop in office referrals from 3,786 to 945 and in truancy rates from 16 percent to 5 percent (Wipple, reported by Zammit, 2001). And a St. Joseph, Missouri, school reported a significant reduction of unexplained absences (Elton, 2007). In the United Kingdom a residential special school introduced an extensive program of restorative circle conversations and experienced reductions from a previous year of more than 50 percent in "negative incidents" and "incidents of damage" (Boulton & Mirsky, 2006, p. 91). Finally, a series of studies show that offending students who have been part of restorative conferences have reduced rates of reoffending and a lowered likelihood of school suspension or expulsion than before intervention of restorative practices (Adair & Dixon, 2000; McGrath, 2002).

Principles of Restorative Conferencing

Some generic principles of restorative conferencing fit well with a narrative perspective on conflict resolution. We outline these principles here and then go on to suggest some specific narrative principles and practices that give our approach to restorative conferencing its own flavor.

Increase the Number of Voices in the Conversation

Conventional justice-seeking approaches are usually aimed at identifying the individual at fault and then isolating this person under a judicial or administrative spotlight. The accusative gaze functions to pin the person to a place of shame and requires the assumption of moral guilt. The individual is required to respond from within a narrow range of remorseful and submissive behavior and to acknowledge the authority of those with the power to punish. In contrast, restorative processes wrap the individual in a network of those who matter to her. Responsibility for addressing the harm done by the offense is frequently shared, even though the person at the center is made significantly accountable. The accountability element is often stronger in restorative than in retributive justice approaches but it is also situated in a more relational context. At their best, restorative conferences can be very creative in devising a plan for addressing the harm done. The range of perspectives represented in these conferences and the additive effect of including a number of voices can lead to the development of ideas that would never be contemplated by authority figures. If two minds are better than one, then fifteen or more minds can be exponentially more creative still. The likelihood that the plan will be tailored to address the particular needs of both the victim and the offender can potentially be increased manyfold.

Integrate the Offender Back into the Community

Incarceration in the criminal justice arena and suspension or expulsion in the school context both work to remove the individual from participation in the community against which she has offended. Restorative processes aim in the other direction. Rather than being aimed at isolation and separation, they are aimed at the repair of relationship and community. The offender is offered the chance to be knitted back into the community, not on the basis of guilt for committing the offense but on the basis of her work to redress the effects of the offense. In schools this means that a school community can adopt an attitude of inclusion that is not so much soft and neglectful in overlooking the seriousness of offenses as it is demanding of appropriate responsibility taking as a condition of community membership. The boundaries around the community are therefore allowed to remain porous rather than rigidly constricted. Schools that take up this attitude can be argued to be more socially responsible than those that simply exclude offenders and effectively pass the buck of dealing with an offender who has never been held significantly accountable to other institutions in the community. There is a distinction here between being morally righteous and being effective and responsible. Policies of righteous exclusion have been popularized under the rubric of *zero tolerance* in recent discourse. But it is worth noting that an American Psychological Association task force on zero-tolerance policies (Skiba et al., 2006) has recently argued strongly that these policies have no effectiveness or value in schools. The report of the task force concluded bluntly that "zero tolerance has not been shown to improve school climate or school safety." The evidence "consistently flies in the face of . . . beliefs" that removing disruptive students from school will improve the school experience for others. Instead, zero tolerance has been shown to effectively increase disruptive behavior and dropout rates and to lead to higher rates of misbehavior among those who are suspended. The report recommended that more attention be paid to restorative practices as an alternative to zero tolerance.

Integrating offenders back into school through a restorative process means dealing with the experience of shame that goes with being found to have committed an offense. John Braithwaite (1989) has argued that the shaming of offenders cannot be avoided completely but that it can be constructed carefully within a reintegrative framework through a restorative process. He argues that conventional court processes are often ceremonies focused on the degradation of individuals' status as a prelude to these individuals' exclusion and that shaming plays an important role in this process. Restorative processes concentrate on reintegrating offenders into full inclusion as community members, rather than on degrading them.

Wendy Drewery (2004) argues that restorative practices in schools herald something much larger than a better disciplinary technique. They are in the end about the expression of an ethos in the wider society. They pose the question of whether a society can handle diversity in an inclusive way. They suggest an approach to education that is more about the creation of a community of care for young people, and for the kind of adults they might become, than it is about measuring test scores on a narrow range of subjects. Such care can never be about dividing society into those worthy of success and those to be consigned to the margins. It must instead be about creating ways to continually knit people into their schools and their wider communities, even after they have offended against relationships in those schools and communities.

Address the Need for Relationship Healing

Adopting a restorative perspective requires a shift in thinking away from conventional discourse. In the dominant discourse of Western justice, the individual who offends is assumed to have a moral or mental health deficit. Either punishment or treatment is required to address this deficit condition. In contrast, a restorative perspective views things in terms of the relationship between people and identifies the offense primarily as a rupture. It sets about identifying the harm done to the relationship and then endeavors to set things right. This emphasis does not preclude attention to the harm experienced by the individuals involved, but it views individual damage from an interpersonal rather than intrapersonal angle. It may consider the damage done to the personal integrity of the perpetrator by the offense as well as the damage done to the victim. Then, as Zehr (2002) suggests, it concentrates on the meaning of the offense, not so much in terms of what that offense says is wrong with the offender but in terms of the obligation it creates for the offender to repair the harm done. Restorative practices encourage offenders to understand the consequences of their actions for others, not just for themselves, and then to act responsibly on this understanding.

Restoration to address the harm done by an offense may be actual or it may be symbolic. Often it is not possible to completely restore what has been damaged. In such instances there may be more emphasis on symbolic acts of restoration. There is frequently a degree of relational healing that takes place, but often *healing* is not the most accurate term (Zehr, 2002), particularly for more serious offenses. For many victims it is important to be assured that the offense will not happen again, either to themselves or to others. To this end, offenders need to address the causes of the offense in their own patterns of response to the world. Many have themselves been victims of other people's harmful actions. It is here that the community of care around an offender can act to support and encourage the taking up of responsibility in the offender to address the circumstances that have led to his offending.

Principles of Narrative Restorative Conferencing

The principles of restorative conferencing explained in the previous section of this chapter are compatible with a narrative approach and may be shared with other approaches to restorative practices. The narrative approach to restorative practices that we are advocating specifies further principles, which we outline now. These principles articulate the use of some particular discourses and intentional language practices. We then outline in detail a narrative method for restorative conferences.

Adopt Respectful Language

The person is not the problem;
the problem is the problem.

We referred to this aphorism, derived from Michael White (1989, p.7), in Chapter One. Often the person facilitating a restorative conference will write it on a whiteboard as a motto for the process. The principle that is summed up in this motto is one of profound respect. It says to an offender from the start that those involved in this process will treat you as a person worthy of respect and will separate your actions from your identity. Actions may be criticized as harmful but the person who did those actions will not be called a bad person. Nor will she be labeled as a sick person. Rather she will be treated consistently as an agent who can think for herself and can be invited to take responsibility for her own actions. Another message contained in this aphorism is that those involved in this process will work hard to see a person as having a range of possible identity stories and will assume that some of these identity stories have no connection with the offense committed.

Avoid Deficit Discourse

Conveners of restorative conferences who base their practice on this principle of avoiding *deficit discourse* will take care to separate the person from the action in the way that they speak. They will therefore avoid the kinds of language that fall under the sway of this discourse. Deficit discourse is rife in mental health and education contexts (Gergen, 1990); it occurs when people locate the origin of problem issues in an offender's personality. It involves the placement of persons in relation to some scale of assessment and finding them less than normal. It is commonly used by authorities of various kinds to assign spoiled identities to young people, as a way of managing their problematic behavior. Examples in schools are the labeling of students as "behavior problems," "attention deficit disordered," "emotionally disturbed," "dyslexic," or "from a dysfunctional family." The problem with these descriptions of young people is that frequently they render everybody helpless to effect change. If a problem is understood to emerge from a person's nature, then it becomes hard for anyone to imagine change, including the person with the problem. Such descriptions may be said to "naturalize" problems into people. We are not necessarily disputing the "truth" of these descriptions so much as the value of them. They have often been criticized for their stigmatizing effects (see, for example, Braithwaite, 2001). But beyond this tendency to stigmatize, when they create an indelible image of a person in other people's minds or in the mind of the person labeled, they do not facilitate responsibility taking. Rather than empowering people, they enfeeble them (Gergen, 1990). Therefore we urge that they not be used in restorative practices.

Avoid Totalizing Language

Another type of language that interferes with the goals of restorative practices is *totalizing language*. Deficit descriptions are one example of totalizing language but there are many others. Totalizing language seeks to summarize the whole nature of a person under one heading. It takes one aspect of a person's actions and treats it as the person's essence. For example, a person tells a lie and is then referred to as "a liar" by nature. Totalizing language often employs universalizing words like *always* and *never.* For example, "She never makes any effort," or, "He is always aggressive." The problem is that no one is ever a liar or aggressive or failing to make an effort all the time. Totalizing descriptions are usually based on a narrow band of experience, but once in place they render invisible the many exceptions that would otherwise be found to the problematic description. Totalizing language and deficit discourse are examples of essentialist thinking, which we critiqued in Chapter One. When totalizing language is used by people in positions of authority, such as teachers, psychologists, or administrators, it has particularly powerful effects and is often felt by students to be unfair. Totalizing descriptions of students have powerful effects on the stories by which students are known in a school and eventually on the stories by which a student comes to know herself. They block from view other possible stories about a person, thereby blinding people to the exceptions to the story being told.

Because both deficit descriptions and totalizing descriptions are efforts to ascribe actions to the natural core in the center of a person, they are often said to use *internalizing* language. Narrative practice seeks to counter these internalizing effects with the use of externalizing language. In restorative conferences this means that the facilitator seeks to structure the conversation so that actions and behaviors are described as the problem but persons (students or teachers or parents) are not called problem persons. Externalizing language is a grammatical and syntactical expression of the kind of respect that we talked about earlier.

A Narrative Method for a Restorative Conference

In this section we detail a method facilitators can use for structuring a restorative conference in a narrative mode. This method can be adapted to construct simpler forms for a smaller interview that involves a fewer number of participants. The steps in the process are outlined in summary form in Exhibit 8.1.

Exhibit 8.1. A Narrative Restorative Conference.

1. Engage with participants, and invite them to attend the conference.

2. Begin with a welcome that acknowledges the cultural backgrounds of all present.

3. Write on a whiteboard, "The person is not the problem; the problem is the problem." Speak to this concept.

4. Ask each person to introduce himself or herself and to say one thing he or she hopes will come from the meeting.

5. Ask the administrator to explain the purpose for which the conference was called.

6. Name the problem. Ask each person to name it from his or her own perspective. Draw a circle on the whiteboard and write all these names inside it (see Figure 8.1).

7. Map the effects of the problem. Go around the circle of participants, and ask each person to speak about the effect the problem has had on him or her. Draw spokes radiating out from the circle on the whiteboard containing the list of problems, and list each effect on one of the spokes (Figure 8.1).

8. Map the counterstory. Begin by saying that any story tells only part of the picture. Ask everyone to think of any times, places, or relationships where the problem story is not present. Note these examples down in relation to a new circle on the whiteboard, starting this time with the spokes on the outside of the circle (see Figure 8.2).

9. What other qualities that would not be noticed if people paid attention only to the problem story now become visible about the offender? Write these qualities in the center of the second circle (Figure 8.2).

10. Ask the offender to choose the story she would like to be the one that everyone knows about her in future. The problem story or the counterstory? Point to the two circles in turn as you ask this.

11. If the offender chooses the counterstory, ask the whole meeting what will be necessary to do to make sure this story goes forward. Turn first to those harmed by the offense, and ask what they would need to have

Figure 8.1. The Problem.

Mapping the Effects of the Problem

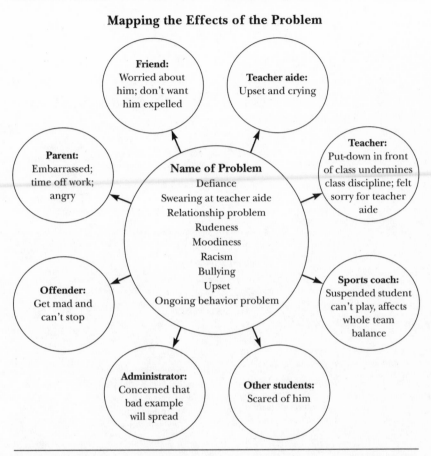

Note: This map is drawn by filling in the center of the circle first; the spokes and outer information are added later.

happen in order to feel that the harm caused by the problem has been addressed.

12. Formulate a plan drawn from the ideas of all present for addressing the harm done and ensuring that the counterstory is advanced.

13. Assign responsibility for carrying out the plan and for reviewing to see that it has been completed.

Figure 8.2. The Counterstory.

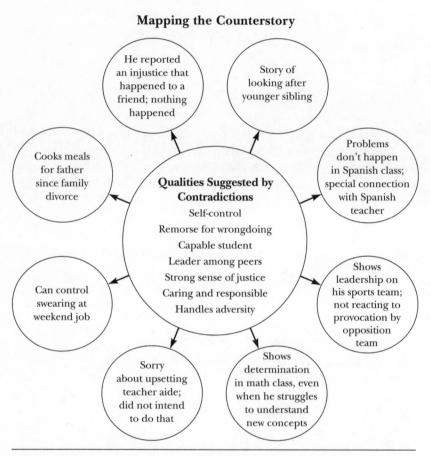

Mapping the Counterstory

Note: This map is drawn by supplying the spokes and outer information first; the center is filled in later.

We explain these steps in more detail in the following discussion. A fuller description of the detailed facilitation of a restorative conference built on narrative assumptions is available in a booklet published by the Restorative Practices Development Team (2003) at the University of Waikato (and available from http://education.waikato.ac.nz/research/pages/item.php?id=89).

Making Arrangements Before the Conference

The story of what will happen at the conference will be set in motion by the way people are invited to participate and by the context expressed by the venue selected. Such choices exert a structuring effect on what will be spoken about during the conference. Care should be taken to ensure that this process is situated in a markedly different narrative than the one that might be expected in a more punitive or retributive process. This means that people should be invited to attend, rather than summoned by someone in an authoritarian position. And they should be invited in a respectful way, rather than being sent a cursory note in the mail or an automated phone call. A personal invitation and a full explanation of what will happen is needed from someone whom the person invited can trust. This means sometimes thinking carefully about the cultural background of the stakeholders and taking care to address this background.

Similarly, the room in which the conference is to be held should not be one that reeks of the authority of the school. It should not, for example, be the room where suspension hearings are held or the teacher's lounge. Sometimes a neutral venue off campus is useful, such as a local community center. What is important is that the venue should be a comfortable place for both the offender and the victim and one where they are able to speak without intimidation. The venue should speak to the difference between a restorative approach and a more punitive or retributive process.

Articulating Hope

The facilitator of a restorative conference should aim to invite each participant to speak early on in the process. Through speaking, each participant is constructed as having a voice in the context of the conference. This is most easily accomplished with a round. Preliminary introductions of the process should be kept brief and not too formal so as not to establish an impression that most of the authority of the conference lies with the facilitator. We favor an introduction round in which all those gathered are invited to introduce themselves and then to state one thing that they hope will come from the meeting. Most people come to such a conference with some hope in mind, and it sets the meeting off on a positive footing when this hopefulness is articulated early on, before the problem story has been specified.

As we outlined in Chapter One, one of the effects of this approach is to constitute the problem story as restraining the achievement of hoped-for outcomes. In other words, the trajectory of the alternative story is constructed from the start as the prime focus of the conference, and the problem story is set up as something to be dealt with in order for the alternative story to be advanced.

Using Externalizing Language

The next step is to specify that the problem story exists as an obstacle to the hoped-for outcomes. The problem story may be introduced by a school administrator explaining why the conference was called. The justification may lie in the seriousness of the offense or in the trajectory of relations that appear to be heading for more serious trouble. Either way the reasoning needs to be spelled out. The story of what happened should be sorted out in advance so that the conference does not degenerate into a court case about the facts. The focus of a restorative conference is not on establishing the facts so much as on putting things right after the fact.

In order to avoid falling into totalizing or internalizing language, a narrative restorative conference builds an externalizing conversation in which the problem is talked about as separate from the persons in the room. One way to develop such an externalizing conversation is to invite people to name the problem that the conference is gathered to address. As we said, the conference is not about establishing the facts, but the facts of what happened can always be viewed from multiple perspectives. A number of voices are gathered together in a conference situation, and each person present will have his or her own stake in defining the problem and in setting things to rights. The naming of the problem needs to include these multiple perspectives, and the problem will have multiple names. Therefore another round is initiated in which each participant is asked to name the problem from his or her own perspective. Each name offered is recorded on a whiteboard in the middle of a large circle (Figure 8.1).

It is important that each suggestion be honored, accepted, and recorded. The only proviso here is that a suggestion may need to be phrased in externalizing language before it is recorded. It should be an action or situation that is described in the name, rather than a person or a deficit inside a person.

In accordance with the philosophy of restorative practice, the first opportunity to name the problem should not be accorded to the professional voices of school administrators or teachers. It should be given to the victim or victims of the offense. Sometimes the word *victim* does not easily apply, or perhaps some people do not choose to think of themselves as victims. It is therefore often preferable to talk about those who are most affected by the offending action. They should be given the chance to name what it was that affected them. If they are nursing anger about the offense, they might name the person as the problem. In this circumstance, we would not engage in argument with them but would simply ask, "What did this person do that caused a problem for you?" The response to this question can be turned into a noun and described in externalizing language. For example, if the response is, "He hit me," it can be written down as "hitting." It is also important to ask the student who has committed the offense what she would call the problem. If she responds in a way that is blaming, either of herself or of others, the same kind of question can be applied. Externalizing language interrupts blame and shame and simply describes the action or situation that is experienced as a problem.

After the problem has been named, the conference facilitator should then continue to refer to the story that the various names represent as a story about the offender, rather than as the truth about the offender herself. The advantage created by externalizing language is that it leaves a potential, a space, for everyone in the room, including the offender, to describe events in other terms. If these other terms can be developed in a way that is associated with being accountable and responsible then it becomes easier to move toward addressing the harm done by the offense.

Mapping the Effects of the Problem

Once a list of names for the problem has been generated, the next step is to explore the effects of the problem on each person in the conference. These effects can be collected through conducting another round of the participants and asking, "How has this problem [*pointing to all the words in the circle*] affected you?" Once again, each person's response is recorded on the whiteboard. For each response, a spoke is drawn out from the circle and the effect of the problem is recorded at the end of the spoke (Figure 8.1).

Once again, it is important to ask those who have been the primary victims of the offending behavior to speak first. They need the chance to express how they have been affected fully enough to feel that their voice is heard. Often feelings are strong, and these feelings need to be acknowledged and recorded. But it is also important to remember that the emotional effects of any problem are probably only part of the total effect. Therefore the facilitator should not ask, "How does this problem make you feel?" A problem story may have many other costs than the emotional effects. Actions may have been required, bodily pain experienced, monetary costs incurred, social consequences noticed, time demands created. The acknowledged and recorded effects of the problem story need to include the full range of the actual effects, rather than focusing exclusively on the emotional effects.

It is also important to ask the person who has perpetrated the offense the question, "How has this problem affected you?" This question assumes that the offender is also often a victim of his own behavior. Asking it can help the participants to break up totalizing stories about the offender.

What is created from this round of questions is a visual map of the problem story and its effects on a network of relationships around it. Because everyone's attention is drawn to the diagram rather than to the individual student, the process of separation of the person and the problem through externalization is enhanced. Seeing the range of the effects of the problem can be very instructive to all present. It breaks up individualistic assumptions about an offense and makes visible the networks of relationship in which people's lives are lived. For the offender, it is often chastening to see how many people have been affected by one action. For the victims, it is often comforting to realize that they are not alone in experiencing the effects. For the conference as a whole, the diagram created on the whiteboard shows where actions need to be focused to put things right.

Mapping Exceptions to the Problem Story

Because life is complex, there are always exceptions to any story. There are always gaps in any account of who a person is. A person who is totalized as a criminal has many instances that can be found of honest law-abiding behavior. Someone who is called a behavior problem at school has many moments when her behavior is not a problem to anyone. The question that a narrative approach seeks to answer is, "How might everyone involved in this process think of such gaps and contradictions?" Rather than ignoring them and treating them as insignificant or irrelevant, we prefer to make the choice of granting them significance through growing a story around them. Narrative restorative practices, therefore, separate contradictions out into distinct stories and do not seek to integrate them with the problem story so as to form singular, or totalizing stories. We start from the assumption that people's lives are not single-storied but multiply storied.

Before developing a new story about an exception, the facilitator needs first to hear it and notice it. The difficulty is that dominant stories about a person, by their very dominance, make it hard to hear exceptions and to grant them any significance. Therefore, in our restorative conferencing, we deliberately start with the problem story and record it for all to see on the whiteboard. Then we deliberately say, "No one story captures all that can be known about a person. We assume that the story of these problems [as externalized] gives us only a very thin picture of [name of offender]'s life." We go on to ask what each person present knows about the offender "that does not fit with this problem story?" Are there times when the problem story is not present or places where it does not follow? Or are there particular relationships where it does not show itself? Each story of an exception collected is noted and recorded on the whiteboard on spokes around a second circle, which is drawn alongside the circle that maps the problem story. In the process of drawing this second diagram (Figure 8.2), a contrast is gradually built up.

This time the facilitator works in the opposite direction on the diagram. On the problem story diagram the facilitator started by listing names of the problem inside the circle and then listed the effects of the problem story on the spokes around the outside.

This time the facilitator collects examples of how the offender is known by those present that do not fit with the problem story and records these instances on the spokes outside the circle first. The facilitator goes to the inside of the circle in the next stage of the process.

Developing an Alternative Story

As the instances of contradiction to the problem story are assembled, the facilitator can then ask about the conclusions those present might draw from these examples about the qualities the person has within him that stand in contrast to the problem story. For example, if the participants have heard a story of how the young person in trouble for speaking offensively at school regularly exhibits kindness and responsibility in caring for an elderly grandparent, they might conclude that there is a story here about kindness and responsibility. These two words might then be written down in the center of the second circle.

There is here no intention to negate the problem story. It still happened and is still serious, but the contrast enables all to see that the problem story does not have to continue. There is at least one other alternative. The facilitator is therefore able to frame the existence of these contrasting stories as a choice point for the offender. After both stories are fully fleshed out, the facilitator asks the offender, "Which one of these two stories would you want to be the one everyone knows about you in future?"

Offenders often have a history of being frequently talked to in terms of totalizing and deficit descriptions, so it is usual for an offender to be quite relieved to be able to say that he prefers the alternative story to be the one people know about him in the future. This choice is easy enough for him to make with a single word, or even by just pointing to the chosen diagram, but it is a significant step toward an alternative story. The choice that has been made has been witnessed in public by those who care about him. The facilitator is then in a position to ask all those gathered to suggest what needs to be done to set right what was damaged by the offense and to strengthen the alternative story that has been mapped out on the whiteboard.

The final part of the restorative conference involves the formation of a plan to strengthen the alternative story. After the offender has chosen the counterstory to be the one that he would like everyone to know about him in future, the facilitator asks everyone gathered, "What will be necessary to ensure that this story does go forward from here?" It also needs to be underlined that the problem story has had the effects listed on the first diagram and that these cannot be ignored. The counterstory needs to address the problem and the effects it has created. The participants therefore need to be asked about the harm done by the offense and what they would like to see done to address it. This part of the conference often generates a brainstorming session. Care should be taken to ensure that the voices of victims are heard first here. They can be asked specifically, "What would you personally like to see happen in order to feel that your needs and concerns have been addressed?" The next priority is that family members of the offender get a chance to speak about their proposals for addressing the problem and that the voices of professionals do not get to dominate. At this point many conferences can get quite creative. Because time has been taken to map the effects of the problem in detail, there is plenty of opportunity for generating ideas that will address each of these effects.

Often apologies are offered or sought out at this juncture. Care needs to be taken with them. Sometimes people assume that giving an apology ends the matter. For this reason, victims are often understandably mistrustful of apologies if they do not match the obligations for accountability created by the offense. A narrative perspective can help here. Thinking in terms of stories as accounts that move through time, the facilitator can inquire about the actions an apology might lead to. What actions might follow that would allow everyone present to know that the apology was not just empty words? As this question is answered, the facilitator can build an apology into something that is lived out, rather than just spoken at one moment in time. It can become part of an ongoing story of accountability, rather than remaining an isolated event with insufficient meaning to be sustainable.

The plan that is developed in the last stage of the conference needs to contain a number of features. It should be detailed and time limited and it should be reality tested. It should also be culturally appropriate. As much as possible, it should be related to the nature of the offense. It should specify who will be responsible for doing what and by when. Such specifics should obviously include the responsibilities that the student who offended has agreed to take up. But there also might be other responsibilities that others have volunteered to take up. For example, parents might assume responsibility for making sure that the offender does what she said she would do. And teachers might take on supervising and reviewing functions at the school. Sometimes problems suggest changes in school procedures in order to ensure that in the future similar problems are less likely. One school, for example, agreed to review its process of lunchtime supervision in order to improve the protection of all the students from possible bullying incidents. This is one of the advantages of a conferencing process over an individual accountability process. In responsible and responsive hands a conference can generate an impetus toward systemic shifts as well as personal ones.

Finally, the conference itself should not be regarded as a one-off event that exists somehow outside of time. It should, ideally, be knitted into the ongoing narratives of the school and of those who have participated in it. To this end it is imperative that the decisions made at the conference be followed up and some sort of review conducted to see that decisions made were acted upon. Before the conference ends (with some sort of ritual celebration ideally), the participants should decide on the process of review and the people who will be responsible for it.

Reflections on Restorative Conferencing in Schools

What we have outlined here is a process for a restorative conference in a school context. It embodies a strong narrative focus although we acknowledge that there are a number of other approaches around. We have witnessed this approach having profound and moving effects on all participants. We have talked with a number of school administrators and teachers who have begun to use this process, at first cautiously, and then later enthusiastically. Some schools have often surprised themselves with how much energy they have been willing to devote to restorative practices. What we have outlined here is a full conferencing process that can be used to address significant problems that cry out for powerful interventions. Creative schools have adapted this process to smaller versions for use with problems that are less advanced.

Those who catch on to the spirit of this process often find that their relationships with students in schools are reenergized and they begin to see the potential for a different vision of an educational community. It is a vision of schools in which problems are attended to in ways that actually address them (rather than just remove them) and that bring about significant change, sometimes very quickly.

Chapter Nine

Conflict Resolution in Health Care

In this chapter we describe narrative mediation practices we have applied in health care settings over the last five years. These settings include perinatal patient safety training in conflict resolution, conflict resolution work in a health care labor management partnership, and work with health care ombudspersons (or ombuds) who mediate conflicts between health care professionals and the patients and family members who have suffered real or perceived, unanticipated adverse outcomes. We describe specific narrative mediation techniques used in these settings and show how they have been implemented in real cases (as elsewhere in this book, names and some other details have been disguised to ensure confidentiality). Finally, we review narrative strategies and techniques that can be used with health care professionals who exhibit high-conflict behaviors with their colleagues and their patients. We also demonstrate how these same narrative applications can be used to address high-conflict behaviors of patients and their families.

Before engaging in this discussion, we provide the reader with some contextual information about the unique challenges facing health care professionals in the United States today. This contextual backdrop takes account of recent transformative changes in health care and shows why conflict resolution and mediation have become essential to both patients and health care professionals in addressing health care needs.

Culture and Conflict in Health Care

William Ury, a leader in international conflict resolution, once remarked during the Cold War that "a hospital makes U.S.-Soviet relations look like a piece of cake" (Marcus & Roover, 2003, p. 17). In health care settings many people have significant but ambiguous levels of authority and power, and issues are so complex and potentially divisive that many issues emerge as explosive conflicts. Simple conflict in health care is rare. Decisions and actions are intertwined. Every move made by a health care professional necessarily affects numerous other people (Marcus, Dorn, Kritek, Miller, & Wyatt, 1995).

The unique culture of health care delivery places unique constraints on conflict resolution among health professionals. The most significant barriers relate to the power imbalances produced by traditional hierarchical structures in health care. However, there are numerous other obstacles, such as clashes in clinical and operational priorities, differences in experience and education, practice variations in the delivery of clinical services, and diffusion and lack of clarity of professional roles. Lack of time and fatigue also play a part in preventing health care professionals from having opportunities to address important problematic issues when they arise.

Recent Changes in the Culture of Health Care

There have been extraordinary changes in health care delivery over the last two decades. The world that physicians and senior health professionals once inhabited no longer exists. Physician autonomy, both in the delivery of health care and in its financing, has become anachronistic. Once clinically and financially autonomous professionals, physicians and other senior health care providers are now forced to integrate with major health care provider organizations for whom teamwork and cost savings are of central importance. Because of the move toward managed care and the tremendous power that insurance companies now wield, the professional judgments and recommendations of physicians are often queried. Changes in service reimbursement coupled with the prospective payer system have forced health care providers to completely reevaluate the way they deliver health care (Schwartz & Pogge, 2000).

The hierarchical patterns and demarcations of authority in health care have been permanently disrupted. This change has led to numerous turf battles. In recent times, conflict has grown among specialists and between specialists and generalists, and conflict between nurses and physicians has also escalated (Marcus et al., 1995). Traditionally, physicians have been reticent to concede a meaningful role to patients in determining the course of their care because physicians were held ultimately accountable for patient outcomes. In the current environment, patients' and their families' concerns have to be taken more seriously because of the potential for litigious action. In multidisciplinary health care teams, senior medical personnel have been threatened by the encroachment of nursing staff and other nonphysicians into their professional domain. In addition some physicians have been incensed by the expanded role of insurers in the determination of medical necessity. Questions about decision-making responsibility are a great source of conflict for physicians who have been used to functioning autonomously. Traditional physician behavior was independent, individualist, and detached. In the current climate, interdependent, managed, and connected behavior has become a valued skill set (Marcus et al., 1995).

The challenge for physicians and other senior health care providers is to be able to move back and forth from one-on-one patient-physician interaction to negotiation with the wider system, which requires an understanding of organizational behavior, timing, constituencies, the environment, and negotiation skills (Schwartz & Pogge, 2000). Some leaders in health care believe that it is essential for physicians to determine when outside expertise, collaboration, and empowerment are necessary for successful team functioning, in order to anticipate, manage, and resolve conflict.

The Consequences of Conflict

Unresolved conflict in a health care environment can prove at the very least highly stressful and at the worst deadly. Tess Pape (1999) noted that conflict that is not addressed can escalate to such an extent that patient care is jeopardized owing to reduced productivity and poor coordination of efforts. According to a 1999 Institute of Medicine report titled *To Err Is Human: Building a Safer Health System,* medical errors cause between 44,000 and 98,000 patient deaths in U.S. hospitals each year (Houk & Moidel, 2003). These figures make medical error in hospitals the eighth leading cause of death in the United States. Not only may unresolved conflict contribute to patient death but it also exacts a day-to-day cost in the severe toll it takes on health professionals and on the health care system as a whole. Unresolved conflict in health care leads to medical malpractice, litigation, interference with health professionals' ability to practice, staff stress, increased staff sickness and sick leave, high staff turnover, loss of confidence, and the undermining of morale (Marcus et al., 1995; Pfifferling, 1997; Pape, 1999; Dauer, 2002; Marcus & Roover, 2003; Gerardi, 2004).

Internal Institutional Demands for Conflict Resolution Skills

In 1999, apprised of the need for high-quality education in the new skill sets needed in the current health care environment in the interest of safe patient care, the Accreditation Council for Graduate Medical Education (ACGME) began explicitly directing medical residents to develop communication, networking, team-building, and conflict resolution competencies. Medical residents must demonstrate effective communication and caring, respectful behaviors in their interactions with patients and their families. They are required to work collaboratively with professionals from other disciplines, use effective listening skills, and elicit information using effective nonverbal, explanatory, questioning, and writing skills. Despite the recognition of the importance of these competencies, there are enormous challenges to be met in their implementation.

Current Restraints on Implementing Conflict Resolution Programs

Traditionally, health care personnel received limited training in achieving collaborative working relationships between medical and nonmedical personnel in health care, and such relationships were a low priority. In general, few mentors or role models for effective conflict resolution skills have existed in health care (Gerardi, 2004). There is now an expectation of collaboration, but little guidance on how that collaboration should be conducted. Organizational barriers, a shortage of collaborative mentors, inconsistent feedback, and avoidant behavior all make it unsurprising that unresolved conflict is prominent in clinical settings.

Another potent challenge to collaborative relationships and healthy approaches to conflict resolution lies in health care professionals' work as individual advocates for their patients. Only in clinical emergencies do they truly work together. The physician's fear of doing harm to the patient continues to create a need for control of the patient and undermines the development of true collaboration and partnership (Gerardi, 2003). Because mistakes can be lethal, it is difficult for health care professionals to consider that they could be wrong with any judgment. This characteristic of health care professional discourse carries over into conflict situations, where people believe they have the correct answers and find it difficult to listen to and acknowledge other solutions. Developing openness across the professions and up and down hierarchies is difficult but necessary for patient safety.

Despite these obstacles, there are significant shifts in attitude taking place and a growing interest in the need for training in communication, conflict resolution, and team-building skills among some health care providers. As a result, a variety of programs, classes, seminars, and retreats teaching communication and conflict resolution skills have been offered to health care professionals, residents, and students. There are now dedicated graduate programs offered by universities on the topic of conflict resolution in health care.

Conflict with Patients and Their Families

Patients and their families consistently request specific psychological health care needs from health care professionals. Providing for these needs can diminish conflictual issues for all concerned. The foremost health care need reported by patients and their families is the desire to be listened to and respected. In the hurly-burly of a health care environment, nurses, physicians, and other caregivers can be distracted by the sheer physical demands and burdensome loads placed on them. Yet when patients' and families' concerns are ignored, anxiety, fear, and distress quickly escalate.

Informing patients and their families about what is happening to the patient during assessment and treatment also makes a significant impact on patient well-being. Patients want to know what kinds of treatments they are receiving and when these treatments will occur. Regular updates on health care processes alleviate much patient anxiety and reduce fear of the unpredictable and unknown. When patients feel that health care professionals are doing their utmost to provide the best treatment possible, patients and their families typically feel that they are important and that their lives matter. If health care professionals make mistakes, are culturally inappropriate, or are unintentionally neglectful, and yet do their best to make amends, most patients and their families will respond favorably to a sincere apology. Patients want to know that their concerns are taken seriously and that health care professionals can learn from them so that future patients do not have to suffer from inattentive care. A recent qualitative study by Coby Anderson and Linda D'Antonio (2004) noted that physicians sometimes have significant blind spots with regard to the effects of their behavior on patients and their families. The study documented instances of dissonance between a doctor's experience of an interaction with a patient and the patient's self-report.

Conflict and Conflict Resolution Between Health Care Professionals

Anderson and D'Antonio (2004) interviewed sixty health care professionals, thirty at each of two teaching hospitals in Southern California, to learn about perceptions of conflict among health care professionals. The professionals included MD administrators, nursing administrators, in-house counsel, risk managers, patient advocates, and ethicists. This study revealed a great deal about health care professionals' views of conflict in their own work context. Only 10 percent of respondents believed that the doctor-patient relationship was the greatest source of conflict;

whereas 80 percent identified the doctor-patient relationship as the domain of conflict that physicians are most competent at addressing.

A majority of the participants identified the doctor-administrator relationship as the most fraught. The respondents explained that physicians did not like to be told what to do by administrators. The respondents also estimated that 45 percent of a doctor's day is spent in conflict or in imminent potential conflict. The authors of the study reported that a lot of conflict is created or perpetuated because doctors do not know how to deal with it effectively. They also asked health care experts what skills, styles, or concepts would enable doctors to deal more effectively with conflict, and with this information, they identified three themes: listening, communication skills, and empathy. Listening was the skill the health care experts thought was most required to improve a doctor's conflict management.

Discursive Shifts in Relations Between Doctors and Nurses

Numerous studies have reported on conflict between doctors and nurses. About a third of U.S. nurses have difficulty speaking frankly and directly to physicians, and another third of nurses have difficulty disagreeing with a physician. Historically, their training has encouraged nurses to be nurturers, to make things right, smooth things over, and work in a subordinate role. Most of all, nurses are trained to avoid creating trouble or provoking conflict with physicians. Kathy Baker (1995) has reported that nurses overuse techniques of avoidance as a conflict resolution method and under stress revert to a subordinate role in multidisciplinary teams. Baker also found that nurses increase their use of avoidance when placed in subordinate roles but can harbor emotions about the conflict and can act out those emotions in covert and harmful ways. Avoidance of conflict can produce a passive or apathetic approach to difficult problems that need resolving. Using avoidance to deal with conflict in health care is potentially lethal because safe clinical practice requires open and direct communication.

Physicians have, historically, been trained to be immediate problem solvers and to practice in an autonomous, directive, and tough-minded manner. Their typical conflict style can be described as confrontive or competitive. Physicians are also trained to exhibit confidence and firmness in making decisions. Historically, if nurses challenged a physician's assessment of a medical situation, they risked being blamed, shamed, ridiculed, or scapegoated. When one party to a conflict has a confrontive or competitive style of resolving conflict and the other has an avoidant style, relations between them can become a breeding ground for miscommunication and potential medical disaster.

The existence of such communication challenges is hardly surprising given the long-established and differential training of nurses and physicians and the differential status conferred on each professional group, both during training and in the practice of medicine. Patient safety can be seriously compromised when nurses and doctors fail to communicate directly. Because doctors and nurses now work more closely together in multidisciplinary teams that require more collaborative than hierarchical functioning, high-quality communication is even more essential for effective problem solving.

Many health care providers have identified the communication problems between physicians and nurses and have made a concerted effort to address these concerns in, for example, perinatal multidisciplinary teams. Effective perinatal units require a high level of professional teamwork and interdependence. In this environment, things can go seriously wrong in a short time. Medical specialists with a particular skill set must rely on the expertise of other team members with a different skill set, and team members must communicate clearly about the potential for impending medical emergencies.

Today nurses on perinatal teams receive training in giving specific and direct communication to physicians at a level seldom adopted in the past. Nurses fearful of the wrath of tired medical specialists unnecessarily called to examine a struggling patient are now required to be direct, clear, and bold. Their current training directs them to systematically survey the patient's situation, make an assessment, and then make a recommendation to physicians.

These professional behaviors are very different from those seen in the past, when intimidated nurses might have hinted that something was seriously wrong and hoped the physician would make the decision to come to the patient's bedside. Now required to make recommendations to senior medical personnel, nurses may sometimes make inaccurate recommendations and then may be exposed to negative consequences from their superiors. Some hospitals and health care providers offer them training in assertiveness skills. Nurses and junior medical staff are more likely to be assertive in a culture where the consequences for doing so do not subject them to threats, abuse, ridicule, or humiliation.

Obstacles to a More Just Culture in Medicine

It is challenging in health care settings to introduce new cultural practices that contradict accepted norms of medical practice. In a time-honored tradition, physicians are at the pinnacle of the medical totem pole. Customarily, doctors are people who have been selected from among the best and brightest students to undergo brutal training that ultimately turns them into an elite cadre of professionals. Physicians typically have high personal standards and high expectations of their own professional performance. In fact, established protocols in health care have relied on perfect performance from physicians. Most physicians trained in an environment that denied the damage done by factors such as fatigue, task overload, distraction, stress, and incorrect data. The culture of medicine has reinforced the notion that the best people do not make mistakes. Doctors are all too aware of the consequences of making a mistake—punitive sanctions, loss of status, and loss of job. However, research on medical error makes it clear that no matter how skilled doctors may be, they are still negatively affected by systemic faults, hierarchical cultural practices, and a history of closing rank and remaining silent when things go wrong.

Promotion of a Just Culture

Paradoxically, doctors are also affected by the general malaise in the discourse of health care that assumes medical errors are inevitable because of the complexity of what is performed and human fallibility. However, current research in *high reliability organizations* (Weick & Sutcliffe, 2001)—such as nuclear power plants or air-craft carriers—demonstrates that most error can be eliminated by building a complex array of human and technological checks and balances into a system and by promoting a just culture where mistakes can be analyzed in the open and addressed (Kerfoot, 2007). Some providers are now promoting a just culture (von Thaden & Hoppes, 2005) in health care, a culture in which a hierarchical, chain-of-command leadership style is changing to a style of interdisciplinary leadership. A just culture in health care ensures that all health care employees, at all levels of the organization, have a right to be treated with respect. It allows health care specialists to review their practices without censure in order to better address medical errors. In a just culture, errors will not be used as the basis for discipline, except in the rare cases where punitive discipline is indicated, such as when the identified employee is alleged to

- Be under the influence of drugs or alcohol
- Have intended to cause harm
- Have engaged in egregious negligence

A just culture in health care invites a shift in professional relationships from a hierarchical to a collegial orientation. This shift in the way health care services are being organized and delivered in hospitals is not always welcomed by practitioners who are in well-established routines. Resistance is common among both senior and junior medical personnel who have worked under the hierarchical chain-of-command approach for years. It is within this environment that we have been invited to apply collaborative conflict resolution strategies and narrative mediation practices.

Roles for Mediators and Ombuds in the Health Care System

In response to the move from hierarchical management toward the flatter organizational systems required for interdisciplinary teamwork, increasing numbers of health care organizations are investing significant resources in conflict resolution systems. Many health care providers in North America are becoming more motivated to build quality communication and conflict resolution systems at the micro- and macro-levels. Some are making a concerted effort to reduce medical error and unanticipated adverse outcomes for patients and families by improving communication and conflict resolution processes.

Over the last five years, we have been providing organizational input and specialized health care training for mediators and ombuds to improve the quality of services to patients and their families. As a result, more patients and their families have opportunities to hear from health care providers when things go wrong or when there is serious communication breakdown. Rather than closing ranks and hiding information from patients and their families when medical error occurs, health care providers can do the opposite and help families learn about unintentional errors that have caused harm. Training helps mediators assist families to deal with unanticipated adverse outcomes for their loved ones. Mediators can facilitate patients and their families in discussing concerns with health care experts. Such concerns might include, for example, a medical error, a delayed diagnosis, or the perception of an error or delay. The health care providers involved are making sincere attempts to make amends to patients and their families and to fix problems so that they do not reoccur. This open, honest, and proactive approach to potential health care conflicts requires specialized and wide-ranging mediation skills. We have trained mediators to perform in this specialized domain. Such mediators have a lot more to attend to than breakdowns in communication between health care personnel and patients and families. Health care trainers and mediators in an open system and a just culture have to fulfill multiple and complex roles.

In our training of mediators we focus on the identified goals of the disputing parties, exposing underlying issues and exploring the impact of conflict stories on the parties. One of the aims of mediation is to identify the underused resources each of the parties may possess. The ultimate goal is to create options and assist parties to reach sustainable and mutually satisfying solutions. To be effective in reducing the level and intensity of health care conflicts, mediators must intervene at the earliest possible time.

We train health care mediators to be evenhanded, appropriately confidential, and technically neutral and impartial, although achieving these goals is difficult in practice. Neutrality and impartiality are particularly tricky when mediators and ombuds are paid by health care organizations. However, despite the perceived lack of impartiality produced by the payment of health care mediators by health care providers, patients and their families experience great relief from mediation processes when professionals make sincere efforts to make amends and fix problems.

In our training health care mediators learn to coach parties to express concerns or show understanding without inadvertently escalating the interaction. When an apology is required from a health care professional for incorrect action, we train mediators to coach health care professionals to take responsibility and express an apology. Mediators also learn to coach patients and families to challenge authority figures in a safe and structured way. Through role-play exchanges, mediators practice assisting parties to express distressing thoughts and feelings in a controlled fashion, without escalating conflict. Mediators can also promote shared decision making, facilitate constructive feedback between health care personnel, use shuttle diplomacy where necessary, and provide a safe caucusing environment for managing high-intensity emotional expressions.

Health care mediators can also be very effective in resolving patient concerns about coordination of care problems. A mediator can help the hospital leaders to gain a better understanding of what is taking place in their organization. We train health care mediators and ombuds in informal system change interventions independent of the formal investigations conducted by the hospital's risk, quality, and member services departments. Although health care mediators support senior medical personnel in addressing system failures, they do not participate in formal root cause analyses of problems, in order to protect their role as evenhanded agents for patients, families, and health care personnel. Our mediation training supports health care mediators (both as internal and as external practitioners) to advocate for fair processes for patients, providers, and the organization as a whole. Our training focus is also systemic. Systemic issues in an organization can have a wide influence on how physicians and nurses interact with patients and their families. Table 9.1 displays an example of a systemic analysis that also describes ways to address conflictual systemic dynamics early on. This chart, devised by two health care mediators, emphasizes interventions to avoid escalating conflict.

Table 9.1. Causes of Conflict with Patients and Families and How Medical Teams Can Respond.

Issue	Family Perception	Family Responses	What the Patient Is Saying	Interventions	Benefits to Provider
MD communicates only if there is a serious deterioration or significant change of treatment.	Feeling not cared for & unimportant. The MD does not care. There is something wrong & everyone is hiding it.	Insecure. Suspicious. Angry.	Making up stories: Patient & family make up a story about what is happening in the vacuum: "The doctor is avoiding me." "There must be something wrong" Demanding: "I demand to see my doctor." Accusatory: "Nobody tells me anything. I want to see my chart." "What are you hiding?"	Demonstrate respect for patient & family. Provide information to fill in the void. Develop a communication schedule. Allow time for patient's/family's questions. If you can't answer all questions at one time, schedule a time to return & keep that appointment. If you have to cancel, apologize for the delay.	Builds/restores trust in provider. Reduces the number of pages from family because they know the patient is being seen. Allows faster access to patient's/family's real concerns so they can be addressed quickly before they escalate.
Patient hospitalized for extended period & cared for by hospital-based services (HBS).	No one is coordinating the patient's care.	Abandoned. Insecure. Angry. Loss of confidence in MDs.	Demanding: "I don't want anybody other than last HBS physician to care for me."	Demonstrate continuity of care by introducing yourself to the family (give them your card).	Builds/restores trust in provider. Reduces questions about communication between providers.

			Increasingly questioning care. "I just answered that question yesterday for the other doctor. Don't you doctors ever talk to each other?" "Who knows what is going on with me?"	Explain the process of rotation & identify period of time when you are responsible for patient care. Convey knowledge of patient's history by commenting on chart review or problem. Request information. "I am here for XYZ. Could you tell me more about that?" Go over plan of care.	Builds/restores trust in provider.
Differing definitions of generic terms. For example, "The patient is fine."	Patient is getting better & will be as good as new when he/she leaves.	Initially relieved. Feels betrayed later if patient doesn't make a full recovery.	Accusatory: "But you said he would be fine." "Why did you lie to me?"	Manage expectations: Be specific when talking about the patient's condition. Check the patient's level of understanding. "When I say the patient is . . . What does that mean to you?"	Reduces the number of pages from the family because they are not surprised that the patient is still ill. Reduces the likelihood of upset if patient still requires treatment.

(Continued)

Table 9.1. Continued

Issue	Family Perception	Family Responses	What the Patient Is Saying	Interventions	Benefits to Provider
Patient & family expectations are unreasonable.	Perception that the patient is not getting better.	Frustrated. Frightened. Angry.	Accusatory: "Why is this taking so long?" "I read on the Internet that I should be getting X treatment. Why aren't you doing that?" Confrontational: "How can you sleep at night knowing that you are not helping me?" "How can you be so uncaring?" "You should quit!"	Demonstrate respect by taking time to introduce self to everyone in the room. Acknowledge feelings & perceptions & ask open-ended questions. Demonstrate willingness to work with them by asking them to describe their expectations. Acknowledge that their experience has not been what they anticipated. "I'm sorry things aren't going the way you expected. Let's talk about what I can do to help you understand what has happened so far & what will happen in the future."	Leads to less confrontation. Builds/restores trust in provider. Allows identification of false expectations so they can be addressed quickly before they escalate.

Differing opinions by physicians.	"Who can I trust?" Has the physician been wrong all the time?	Insecure. Suspicious. Frightened. Angry.	Confrontational: "But the last physician said I should be getting better." "Dr. New Physician told me your treatment is wrong."	Do not discuss difference of opinion with another physician with patient/family. Acknowledge there may be differing opinions or preferences for treatment. Demonstrate a willingness to explore other options & concern for patient's feelings.	Maintains trust/respect in the relationship with the providers. Develops a treatment team. Builds/restores patient's/family's trust in provider.

Source: Louise Aguilar, Kaiser Permanente, Orange County, & Leny Ambruso, Kaiser Permanente, Bellflower. Reprinted with permission.

A Narrative Mediation Protocol for Use in a Health Care Setting

- We instruct health care mediators to follow a specific narrative protocol when bringing together patients, their families, and health care professionals after a serious breakdown in communication or when distrust is present. Generally, our protocol includes four stages, although this structure can be adapted to the specific needs of the parties. Stage 1 involves separate meetings with the patient and family members and with the health care professionals. Stage 2 involves bringing the parties together in a joint session. Stage 3 is about following up with patients and families and with health care personnel to support positive outcomes and address further issues requiring attention. In stage 4, health care mediators work with senior management to explore possible system changes in response to mediation outcomes.

The first stage addresses specific purposes. In the separate sessions the mediator can join psychologically with each party and explore problem issues in confidence, rather than in front of the opposing party. The separate sessions also present the mediator with an opportunity to defuse intense affective responses produced by the conflict. In these sessions the mediator works to understand and gain clarity about issues of concern for each stakeholder, and the parties have an opportunity to reflect on the effects of the problem story and to build their own motivation to act constructively for change. The mediator can also identify possible avenues for building a narrative of cooperation and understanding. Effective separate sessions set the stage for a productive joint session that can be highly focused on addressing problem issues creatively.

Stage 1: The Separate Sessions

Here is a list of the specific tasks to be performed in the separate session.

Meeting with Patient and Family

The health care mediator introduces himself or herself and explains the mediator role to the patient and family members.

- Discusses with parties how she will conduct the meeting.
- Explains he is not a judge and does not have power to determine outcomes or impose an agreement.
- Explains that mediation is a voluntary informal process in which parties explore options and possibilities to help solve the problem.
- Tells the parties the meetings are confidential and that information shared in the meetings is inadmissible in court.
- Informs the parties that everyone will have an opportunity to express his or her concerns and requests in the meeting.
- If paid by health care provider, explains that the mediator's role is to serve the needs and concerns of the participants and facilitate a process that is evenhanded and fair.
- Although the meeting is confidential, discusses at the end of the meeting the possibility that the parties may want information shared with others.

The mediator discusses the nature and purpose of meeting.

- Invites the parties to speak frankly about their concerns.
- Explores with the parties whether there is interest in participating in a joint session with the other party (or parties) to the conflict.
- Acknowledges willingness to try and resolve the conflict.
- Searches for occasions when health care personnel have behaved in helpful ways.
- Helps the parties rehearse their requests and concerns to health care providers in a respectful and clear fashion.
- Checks back about information to be shared with others.

Meeting with Health Care Personnel

The health care mediator introduces himself or herself and explains the mediator's role.

- Covers the same information shared with the patient and the family about the role of the mediator. Helps prepare the health care professional for a joint session with the patient and the family.
- Discusses how to explain medical interventions in a language that the patient and family can understand.

- Plans with health care professional how to express an apology for any miscommunication.
- Discusses how to ease family fears resulting from misunderstandings or confusion.
- Discusses specific steps to ameliorate outstanding concerns.

Stage 2: The Multiparty or Joint Session

In the joint session the scene is set for the parties to build mutual understanding and perhaps agree on a specific course of action to follow. Ground rules are established, and hopes for the mediation are identified. The mediator invites the parties to give an overview of their concerns and develops an externalizing conversation about these concerns. The conversation is particularly focused on identifying what is at the heart of the matter for the participants. The mediator then maps the effects of unfulfilled hopes and externalized problems on the patient, the family members, and each of the other parties. The health care professional (or professionals) may apologize for any miscommunication or may take responsibility for any incorrect or harmful medical procedures carried out. He may also provide the patient or family with further information about any medical procedure that was previously misunderstood. As the session moves toward completion, the mediator summarizes understandings reached and outcomes agreed upon. Sometimes further separate and multiparty meetings are scheduled to ensure that agreed-upon milestones have been reached or proposals to make amends for some error have been realized. To illustrate this process, here is a conflict scenario between a patient and staff in a hospital's emergency room (ER).

Conflict Scenario

A patient, Matt Hodges, met with a urologist, Dr. Carl Bondi, because he was suffering from erectile dysfunction following surgery. The urologist proposed a treatment using papaverine, which is injected into the penis to artificially produce an erection. Matt agreed to the treatment. The dose was too high and the erection failed to subside after four hours. Matt had been told by Dr Bondi at the time of receiving the injection that if the erection did not subside after four hours, he must immediately go to the ER and seek treatment. Matt followed the doctor's orders and checked himself into the ER. After waiting seven hours to be seen, Matt finally received treatment. Matt explained that he was so traumatized by the experience that he contacted Patient Services. He wished to confront his health care provider because he believed he had received poor and disrespectful treatment.

Roberta Owens, a health care mediator employed by the health care provider, offered to meet with Matt to hear his concerns and to offer assistance. Matt met with Roberta twice. She was also trained to help patients and families connect with other appropriate resources if need be. Roberta would even support Matt 's transfer to another health care provider, if that was what he requested.

Roberta followed the protocols described previously and sought Matt's permission to ask the ER staff about the night that he was awaiting treatment. Roberta wanted to be fully informed about the issues that led to the service failure before holding a joint meeting with Matt and the ER personnel. Roberta met with the physician involved in treating Matt that night. Because there had been numerous complaints about this ER unit, she also requested a brief discussion with the ER staff physician and the assistant chief of ER services. After this meeting, the assistant chief of services sought to meet with the chief of services to discuss some of the systemic problems that kept occurring in the ER. Independent of this particular mediation, this ER unit was to engage in a series of reviews of procedures for interfacing with patients and dealing with complaints.

After Roberta's meetings with ER personnel, it was agreed that Dr. Spooner, the physician who had treated Matt that night, would attend the mediation session. These separate meetings set the stage for the joint meeting.

Beginning the Joint Meeting

Our discussion of the joint meeting begins with introductions covering the partiess' names, roles, and involvement in the situation, and Dr. Spooner's authority to speak for the ER unit. Roberta has already addressed the ground rules and explained the process that the mediation will follow. After the introductions, she begins to elicit the stories about the events that gave rise to the conflict.

Roberta: While I have met with each of you and spoken to you at some length, you may not know each other very well, so I'd like to start by asking each of you to tell us a bit about who you are and your role, and what your hopes are for what might be achieved in this meeting.

Dr. Spooner responded by explaining that he was the physician on duty that night and had overall responsibility for the care of Mr. Hodges. His hope was expressed as a desire to understand what Mr. Hodges had experienced, so that he might be able to understand it and offer any information that could be of assistance. Matt explained that he wanted to know why he was treated so badly and whether anything could be done to help him come to terms with the events of that night. He said that he never wanted to go through another experience as awful as this one and didn't want this experience to occur to anybody else.

Roberta: So we're here to today to address [*turning to Matt*] what happened to you. We are here to understand how each of you sees the situation and to look at how to address what occurred. Do you agree that this is our purpose?

The parties agreed. With consent from the parties, Roberta briefly summarized the main issues she had garnered from the separate meetings with Dr. Spooner and Matt. She mentioned the communication issues, the misinformation given, and the co-pay Matt had made of $250.

Then she asked Matt to tell his story of what happened and asked Dr. Spooner to listen without comment.

Listening to Matt's Story

Matt explained that the hospital visit amounted to a series of horrendous experiences that felt like "being in hell" for seven hours. He said it was galling to have to pay the $250 co-pay for what amounted to a traumatizing experience. He described being frightened and anxious throughout the experience and deeply concerned that his body would be badly affected by the drug papaverine. He had watched advertisements on television speak of serious side effects if an erection lasted longer than four hours.

He also reported being distressed by the nonchalant attitude of the receptionist, who didn't seem to care how long he was going to be there. A patient information message on the TV monitor in the ER waiting area had suggested that help was available if the pain got worse and yet he could see no medical staff ready to help.

After a long wait he had been ushered into the examination room. He had felt humiliated by two male nurses, who had looked mildly amused with his condition. It was at about this time that Dr. Spooner had arrived. Dr. Spooner told Matt he would have to wait to see a urologist in about thirty minutes. Matt had thought that Dr. Spooner had appeared very casual and had not realized the urgency Matt had felt. After two further hours, he became beside himself with anxiety, and a nurse placed him on a sedative drip. It irked Matt that when the urologist had arrived, he had said cheerily that he was quite within the amount of time to treat somebody with this problem. Matt felt offended by the urologist's comment that he was "within the standard of care." If only somebody had reassured him that permanent damage was not being done, he said, the experience would have been much less traumatizing. Matt's final concern was that the urologist had invited two nurses to observe the priapism treatment, which involved removing six to eight vials of blood from his penis. He had he felt part of an involuntary experiment and had felt further humiliated. Matt concluded by saying:

Matt: This whole episode was not of my making. It was caused by a medical procedure that was potentially harmful, physically and psychologically. The level of anxiety I suffered that day was very upsetting. I hope you can understand why it would feel so galling and unjust to have to pay for a treatment that was harmful, and then again for the negative medical consequences. I was perfectly healthy when I walked into my appointment with my surgeon. I was very distressed and physically compromised as I departed in the middle of the night on that same day.

Roberta briefly summarized the themes expressed in Matt's story. She externalized the feelings of fear, anxiety, trauma, and disrespect and linked these themes with the negative effects for Matt. It was then Dr Spooner's turn to speak.

Listening to Dr Spooner's Story

Dr. Spooner explained that the ER unit had often been under-staffed recently and had often been overwhelmed because it was one of the central ER units for a wide geographical region. When shootings or multiple serious car accidents occurred, the unit was quickly flooded with patients. Matt's condition had been a minor medical emergency in comparison with what the ER team was dealing with that day. In the separate session Dr. Spooner had nevertheless told the mediator that although Matt was tech-nically treated within the standard of care for this medical prob-lem, he did acknowledge that Matt had a legitimate concern. In the joint session he recognized that Matt had indeed suffered from an experience in the ER unit that was unduly negative. The health care provider Dr. Spooner worked for was committed to promoting a just culture and supported physicians and health care personnel in taking responsibility when things went wrong, apologizing, finding some way to make amends to the patient, and conducting a root cause analysis to ensure such a problem would not occur again.

Dr. Spooner sought to apologize to Matt for how he had been treated. Roberta had used the separate meeting to encour-age Dr. Spooner to take responsibility on behalf of the ER team and as an individual and to express regret and apologize. In this instance Dr. Spooner offered what is technically called a *protected apology* (Lazare, 2006). This form of apology includes a benevo-lent statement of sympathy but cannot be used in a legal claim as an admission of guilt. He made the following statement:

Dr. Spooner: Mr. Hodges, I am deeply concerned about the level of distress that you suffered in our ER unit. I hear your feelings of trauma, disrespect, agita-tion, and stress. I want to acknowledge that you did not deserve to be treated in this manner. I deeply apologize for the experiences you have suffered at the ER. We do not want to hear distressing stories like yours again. Specifically to that end, we have begun to review our communication procedures in the ER. In particular, we have met with the recep-tionist staff and they are going through a specialized

communication training to learn to attend more
appropriately to patients in crisis. Please accept
my heartfelt acknowledgment of your unnecessary
distress.

Dr. Spooner went on to explain the other events that were
unfolding on that night and why the specialist had taken so long
to attend to Matt.

Negotiating a Shared Story

Roberta then asked Matt, "What difference does it make to
hear what Dr Spooner has said?" Matt was relieved to hear
Dr. Spooner's apology and seemed pleased that Dr. Spooner had
acknowledged the effect of the situation on him. Furthermore,
Matt appreciated hearing that there were specific actions being
taken to address the poor communication of the receptionist staff. However, Matt was adamant that more was needed in
addressing the operations of the ER. He also made it clear that
he wanted a reimbursement of the $250 co-pay, given the shabby
treatment he had received.

Roberta said she would follow up on a request for a waiver of the
co-pay from Patient Services. Matt wanted immediate action, and
Roberta said she would have an answer within two business days.

In order to grow the alternative story, Roberta asked Matt
to identify any elements of his experience of the mediation conversation that might be helpful in coming to terms with a difficult experience. He said that he was grateful for the chance to
be taken seriously and heard. It had lessened his anger at being
humiliated in the ER.

Roberta then asked, "How have you managed your own internal resources and marshaled them to maintain resiliency through
this entire difficult process?"

Matt thought for a moment and then spoke of his determination to see things through when he starts something. He added,
"I can be very responsive to working things out when people who
have acted badly apologize and take responsibility. I don't hold
onto a grudge."

Not all conflicts can be resolved in one session. When there
are issues of a more serious magnitude, the mediator needs to

lay out a specific plan about what to do next. A series of meetings may need to be scheduled. In closing, Roberta summarized the progress achieved in the session, with a specific future date for further contact identified if needed. Roberta committed to Matt that she would make a follow-up phone call to let him know the outcome of the discussion with Patient Services about the co-pay.

Stage 3: Follow-Through

The mediator's next responsibility is to track the implementation of decisions reached in the mediation. Matt Hodges was reimbursed for the co-pay and was informed about ongoing improvements undertaken in the ER unit. Roberta also checked later with Dr Spooner about his satisfaction with the process and outcome of the mediation. He said that he had come away from the process more committed to good communication with distressed and anxious patients and had shared this focus with the ER nursing staff.

Stage 4: Exploring Possible System Changes—Some Suggested Protocols

Many conflicts in a health care environment result from poorly organized communication systems. In our health care training, we emphasize engaging senior hospital and health care providers to pay attention to system change requirements to preempt conflict. In the following sections, we outline some protocols we highlight. They include suggestions for addressing the systems change issues identified by Ken Cloke (2006, pp. 15–18).

- Conduct a conflict audit and identify chronic sources of conflict within the system or communication culture.
- Identify conflict management systems that are working and build on those.
- Develop multiple approaches and creative systems to address potential conflict.
- Arrange conflict resolution procedures from low cost to high cost.
- Encourage early informal problem solving.

- Include a full range of options from process changes to binding arbitration.
- Create feedback loops for informal problem solving and negotiation.
- Use coaching and mentoring to alter entrenched behavior patterns.
- Develop ongoing training programs in conflict management and resolution and preventative programs.
- Simplify procedures and policies and adopt measures to encourage widespread use of resolution procedures.
- Continually evaluate why interventions succeed or fail and improve their design.

Facilitating Apology Conversations

Some further comment about apology conversations is warranted, given their significance in situations like the one described in our previous example. On the one hand, Margaret Lee Runbeck (quoted by Image-e-nation, 2004–2007) comments that an "apology is a lovely perfume; it can transform the clumsiest moment into a gracious gift." An apology contains recognition of another's story and has the potential to communicate a degree of respect that can serve to defuse antagonism in conflict situations.

On the other hand, apologies are often difficult to make for a variety of reasons. Professionals often live in fear of accusations of malpractice and of subsequent litigation. But it is not only potential future narratives played out in the legal arena that exert influence on the present. Professional identities are also linked with personal narratives. Medical professionals are also accountable to their own stories of professional pride and are keenly aware of how their reputations are treated by others. Feeling shame or guilt about not providing the care that one hoped to provide can make it hard to apologize.

Professionals who are committed to an ethic of service can also develop resentment toward patients and family members who act in entitled and disrespectful ways toward the very values to which professionals are committed. Professionalism and expertise do not develop without effort. They are hard-earned and require personal commitment and sacrifice. Professionals often feel disrespected when people treat them in an instrumental way and complain about comparatively trivial matters.

Concern about possible litigation can be eased by developing the skill of making a protected apology (Lazare, 2006). As described earlier, this is an apology that conveys recognition of and sympathy for another's distress and takes up a degree of responsibility but stops short of legal culpability. Here is another example of a protected apology: "I am very sorry that your family has been through so much pain and worry this last week."

The law protects benevolent expressions of sympathy from being used in a legal claim as an admission of guilt. Contrast the previous statement with another one that would be admissible in court: "I am so sorry that I did not have the nurse bring those lab results directly to my office when she first got them so I could have gotten you to the hospital sooner."

In this statement an admission of negligent action is made in the process of explanation. The law does not protect explanatory statements from being admissible in legal action. In situations where there has been medical error, professionals can be encouraged to

- Describe the error and its impact on the patient.
- Take responsibility as an organization, team, or individual.
- Express genuine concern and regret for the situation.
- Outline steps they or the organization will be taking to reduce the chances that the problem will occur with other patients.
- Offer assistance to patients and families, or put them in touch with appropriate resources.
- Offer to transfer care to another provider.
- Honor the patient's decision-making rights.

Apologies of this nature are indicated when an investigation has concluded that medical or systems error is involved. When an apology is specifically sought and expected, its absence can itself be inflammatory to a patient and family.

Preparing for an Apology Meeting

Mediators can facilitate an apology process through developing a clear protocol for a meeting that has an apology as its goal.

Such a meeting needs careful preparation and a mediator should arrange to first meet privately with the patient and with the health care professional. The goals of these separate meetings are, first, to learn each party's point of view by hearing the individuals' stories. The mediator can then use externalizing language to talk about the "situation" and can ask how each person was affected by it. The meetings can also canvas preferred outcome possibilities and work at scheduling further individual meetings or a joint session as appropriate.

As the mediator listens to the patient's problem-saturated story, she should bear in mind some process goals. First, she should liberally use the listening skills of paraphrasing, acknowledging, and summarizing to check for accuracy and to communicate a desire to understand. Second, she should use externalizing language about the "situation" to avoid ascribing blame to persons. Third, she should thoroughly explore the effects of the situation on each person involved. Fourth, she should be on the lookout for hints of any positive interactions between the patient and the health care representatives. Fifth, she should facilitate the shift from complaint narrative to preferred narrative by asking, "How would you have wanted to be treated?" Sixth, she should help the patient identify strengths and resources by asking open questions such as, "How have you coped with this for so long?" Finally, she should help the patient develop questions to be asked of the health care representatives at the joint session. For example, she might ask the patient, "What do you need to know from the medical team about the situation?" Before the meeting ends, she also needs to check with the patient about what information she can convey to the separate meeting with the health care representatives before the joint meeting.

When the same meeting is held with health care personnel ahead of a joint session, the process is largely similar, with only some minor differences. Careful listening and communication of understanding is still necessary. Externalizing the situation still helps. Mapping the effects of the situation will probably require less emphasis on the personal domain (although that still might apply) and more emphasis on the domain of systems and professional service delivery. The mediator may have information to pass on from the patient meeting. And more time will be spent on assisting the health care worker to formulate answers that will adequately address the concerns. Another task is to decide who should be present at the upcoming joint meeting and what role each participant should play.

Deciding who should attend the joint meeting to represent the hospital involves a consideration of the seriousness of the event and its likely impact on the hospital service involved. It also involves taking care to select someone whose presence will convey sufficient concern and regret and someone who can accurately answer the clinical and administrative questions. Generally, the personal or attending physician can take the lead, but this person must be able to respond empathically and nondefensively.

Recovering from a Breakdown in Communication

Some narratively informed conflict resolution protocols were introduced to a labor-management partnership division of a large health care organization. The purpose of these protocols was to help the organization transition from its traditional hierarchical chain-of-command leadership style to a more collaborative and interdisciplinary style of leadership. The emphasis was on assisting personnel in a labor-management partnership to conduct difficult yet respectful conversations in conflict situations. The aim was for both sides in the conflict to come away feeling that their problems were addressed, they were respected, and the process was completed with their dignity intact. There was consensus among the members of the management team to agree on ground rules, focus on the common goal of the organization, and keep quality care and patient well-being in the forefront in all circumstances. Team members agreed to be hard on the problem and not the person.

Our first goal was to show participating staff in the labor-management partnership that there are techniques and strategies that can be used to limit the damage and disruption conflict can cause. Our purpose was also to show how difficult situations could be addressed in productive ways to promote collaboration. We aimed to assist the manager to support her staff in resolving workplace conflict and in making conflict resolution an integral part of everyone's job. Rather than letting disagreements get out of hand and escalate conflict in the organization, we introduced a negotiation protocol for averting and defusing conflict and for helping disputing parties to build greater understanding and perhaps agreement on future actions.

Using a Negotiation Protocol

The negotiation protocol was informed by narrative concepts. It was suggested to employees for situations where people showed a willingness to attempt to resolve conflict without involving a mediator. If the strength of the conflict issues was such that either party was concerned that he or she could not maintain a respectful stance, then mediator involvement would be preferable. However, if both parties thought they were able to have a courageous dialogue and deliver their thoughts and feelings clearly, cleanly, and succinctly, a two-party negotiation could occur.

Here are the steps we suggested the parties to the negotiation could use:

1. The first step is to request a meeting with the other party and negotiate a realistic time and place to discuss the issue. The meeting should be held in a private place so that both parties can feel comfortable addressing their concerns. It is helpful in these initial interactions for each party to identify a desire to resolve the difficulties that have produced the conflict. To overtly state, "I really want to get into a better place so we can work more effectively and comfortably together," is a powerful first move in resolving a conflict. It establishes a preference for an alternative story right from the start.

2. The next step is to be aware that body language, posture, facial expressions, and most particularly, voice tone communicate much about any person's experience of being positioned in a conflict story. People can make major advances in addressing problematic issues when they stay calm, quiet their voice tone, and show a nonaggressive and open body posture. When one party displays nonthreatening nonverbal communication, that positions the other party in a story of dignity and respect. If the nonverbal communication is strident, explosive, or intimidating, it is better to call off the meeting immediately and either

reschedule it when emotions are less inflamed or seek assistance from a mediator to work through the conflict.

3. Next, it is useful for the parties to negotiate their own ground rules to promote the likelihood of a respectful exchange. Essentially, each person needs an opportunity to express briefly and without interruption his concerns about the way the problem situation has affected him. Telling somebody how you were affected emotionally takes courage and yet can be quite disarming and influential. If it is done in an open and nonattacking way, the results can build a stronger story of intimacy. It is very powerful to describe the effects of the conflict on yourself. For example, "Those comments in front of Judy made me feel somewhat humiliated and ashamed, and I have been quite self-protective ever since."

4. The next step is to name the problem issue, using externalizing language rather than language that finds fault with the person. The narrative concept that "the person is not the problem, the problem is the problem," applies in this kind of interaction. Here is an example: "Jackie, I want to talk about this way of talking you have used with me that I sometimes find upsetting." As each party names the conflict issues, a specific example of the problem behavior and a description of how the party was positioned by it is helpful. For example, "The other day, when you were giving me feedback about the report, I felt like I was under attack. Your voice tone sounded scolding to me and I felt myself shutting down." A brief example of a problem behavior is preferable to going on and on about a series of problem issues all at once. This approach could overwhelm a person and lead to her disengaging. It is better to deliver this information in a dialogical, or back-and-forth, way, rather than as a long monologue. Each person should give space to the other to say what he wants to say. The person listening can reflect back to the person speaking the essence of what she is expressing. For example, "So I would like to understand how you came to this conclusion. May I tell you what I am hearing? I want to make sure I have understood."

It is helpful to describe intentions and share the thinking behind actions. A direct request that seeks understanding of the other person's viewpoint is respectful and adds a positive dimension to the conversation. "I want to understand what is happening from your perspective. Please talk to me about how you see the issues. I probably see things a bit differently, so please explain what you intended, so I can make sense of things."

5. The next guideline is to use *"I" statements* so you each have an opportunity to explain your overriding goal of improving your working relationship. Explaining what is at stake if the conflict is not resolved shows commitment to resolving the issue. Paradoxically, saying what there is to lose from each party's perspective can galvanize both parties' efforts to resolve the conflict. Here is an illustration of naming what is at stake: "We are on multiple projects together and I want our efforts to be successful. I think our collaboration on these projects will be threatened if we don't address the difficult dynamic that seems to have formed between us." What is at stake has a positive emotional impact when expressed in a calm and nonthreatening manner.

6. The next step in negotiating through a conflict is counterintuitive. It involves each party identifying his own contribution to the conflict. In almost all situations, the way individuals are responding to problematic behaviors is part of the dynamic that needs addressing. Naming one's own contribution creates an unexpected opening. It is a unique outcome in a conflict story and one positions the other party in a place of respect. It is rare for anyone to take responsibility for part of a conflict that she initially believed was all caused by the other person. So naming one's own contribution, no matter how small, adds a new dimension to the dialogue and may shift the whole discussion onto a more positive footing. Here is an example: "I don't think I have helped by not speaking openly about addressing our difficulties or taking active steps to improve the situation. I have a tendency to withdraw in the face of uncomfortable conflict."

7. Next, each participant uses open questions and listens for and acknowledges the emotions that accompany the other's position in the conflict story. The focus here is on understanding the other person's interests and intentions. These intentions may contain absent but implicit preferences for an alternative story. It helps if each person summarizes the experiences of the other and checks for unexpressed assumptions.

8. Next, invite each other to suggest what would resolve outstanding concerns. Brainstorm ideas, and then discuss how each idea would work or not work.

9. To complete the process check to see if there are any unexpressed concerns it would be helpful to share before ending the conversation. For example, you can ask, "Has anything been left unsaid that needs saying? How can we move forward from here, given our new understanding?"

Reaching a decision with a plan to go forward toward a shared goal is a great outcome of a successful negotiation. When an agreement has been reached, determine how each of you will hold the other responsible for keeping it. Even if an agreement has not been made, a partial but still worthwhile outcome might be that each of the parties is better informed and more under-standing of the other's views, perceptions, and motivations.

Working with People Who Exhibit High-Conflict Patterns of Behavior

In working with couples and families who engage in the most serious types of conflict, Bill Eddy, an attorney and social worker with over twenty years of experience in this field, noticed that very often the participants had been affected by serious mental health issues. Eddy (2006) coined the phrase *high-conflict personality* to describe a group of people who escalate conflict because of a *personality disorder*. There is now an increasing focus in the con-flict resolution field on diagnosing these *conflict personalities*. The presence of these personalities is usually confirmed by psycholog-ical testing tools. One text commonly used for this purpose is the *Diagnostic and Statistical Manual of Mental Disorders (DSM)*, which labels particular classes of behavior as evidence of a personality disorder.

People are comforted by this kind of analysis. It seems to explain why some people become very difficult in conflict situa-tions and why they actively escalate conflict rather than diminish it. It also explains why some individuals seem to fail to respond to conventional conflict resolution techniques, despite the best efforts of mediators. Eddy's work on high-conflict personalities is now being used by family court judges and family law attorneys for making sense of high-intensity conflict.

These ideas are also being introduced into the health care field. In situations where multiple professionals are working with a client, Eddy has described how clients with particular personality disorders seek to enlist professionals in taking sides, some for and some against the client. In effect, he suggests that clients with high-conflict personalities can split a team of professionals and draw health care workers into conflict with one another. He suggests that multidisciplinary teams need to have clear protocols in place to avoid being caught up in prolonged and difficult conflicts with clients and other professional colleagues.

There are some helpful practices based upon Eddy's work that we have used to help train health care mediators and ombuds to grapple with intransigent conflicts. However, we have not used the personality disorder constructs associated with the phrase *high-conflict personality* but rather have focused on difficult problematic behavior. We have been very cautious with this work, as some of its philosophical underpinnings are in direct contrast to the philosophical underpinnings of narrative mediation.

The Problem with Essentializing People as High-Conflict Personalities

Before turning to what we find helpful in Eddy's work, we will identify some of the problems we see with viewing people as high-conflict personalities. Such descriptions have their appeal because they simplify in order to explain. But they also come with the cost of excluding complexity. More complex explanations may capture richer, more nuanced understandings of people. Very simple explanations may omit too many variables to be reliable. In working from a narrative perspective we would not want to essentialize individuals as embodying a psychological disorder in order to account for their participation in conflict. If mediators explain the cause of a conflict as simply one individual's psychological deficit, they can easily pay less attention to the parties' real concerns, blame one party for the cause of the conflict, and discount the role of other parties in the conflict escalation. In other words, such explanations can lead mediators to be disrespectful and therefore to make ethically questionable decisions. Instead of focusing on the conflict occurring between the parties and the contextual issues supporting the conflict, mediators can be distracted by the notion that the problem is caused by the personality disorder. From there they can easily be seduced into inappropriately blaming others when it is their own conflict resolution strategies that are failing them. Rather than finding a creative way forward, they diminish their creativity by incorporating as facts assumptions of psychological disorder that are in reality contestable.

Instead of describing individuals as high-conflict personalities, we prefer to use more tentative and fluid descriptions. We suggest that people may adopt difficult interactional styles or patterns of relating in particular situations. Some individuals, under stress, can engage in extreme and hard-to-deal-with behaviors. They can become overly preoccupied with their own issues and chronically adversarial and blaming; they can express totalizing views of others or divide the world into a binary system of enemies and allies. Some people may seriously distort events or display rigid responses to a wide range of events while also demonstrating significant appeal and charm. Other people may consistently fail to take responsibility for their behaviors or actions and may sometimes be protected from the consequences of their actions by family members. Such interactional styles or patterns of behavior can become habitual and often difficult to set aside. Despite our concerns with analyses of personality disorder, we still find value in considering strategies for responding to such difficult or challenging interactional styles.

Sometimes health care personnel can be hooked into believing the content of a complaint before investigating it because of the complainer's emotionally persuasive display. A health care professional may start believing in the validity of a patient's concerns about another health care professional even when these concerns are exaggerated and seriously distorted. Such responses can create hostilities between health care professionals. In addition, the distortions and misrepresentations can cause health care professionals to become angry and judgmental and abruptly terminate contact with the patient. And this abrupt cutting off of relations with a person with a difficult interactional style may lead to a new set of problems.

Working with Specific Problematic Patterns of Relating

Although there are numerous ways to name difficult interactional styles, we have identified two particularly problematic patterns of relating that can be exhibited by both patients and their family members and also by the very health care professionals whose job it is to help patients. They are often described as *borderline* and *narcissistic* behavior patterns. At least, these names are the current fashions in mental health discourse. It needs to be remembered that health discourses are constantly changing. For example, it has become less likely than it used to be for people to be described as *hysterical.* Such descriptions are often gendered too. Descriptions of persons as hysterical or borderline are alike in that both have tended to be applied more to women than to men.

The Borderline Pattern of Relating. The problematic pattern of relating that often attracts the borderline description can be driven by an underlying preoccupation with being rejected or abandoned. There is a tendency for this pattern to push any limit or boundaries set by others. In this relational style, people often demonstrate extreme idealization or devaluation of health care staff. They can exhibit dramatic mood swings and frequent anger. Sometimes they see relatively innocuous events as catastrophes and become impulsive, clingy, seductive, or self-destructive. People caught in borderline patterns can also rapidly become suicidal. The most difficult situation occurs when these extreme responses are mixed with blaming, indirectness, and manipulation.

Helpful Strategies. There are helpful strategies mediators can use to respond to somebody who exhibits borderline patterns of relating. From his work with divorcing couples in a family court setting, Eddy makes a number of suggestions about responding to displays of this relational pattern. Some of them amount simply to respectful listening in constructive helping relationships. Others are designed to help mediators avoid being so affected by problematic patterns of relating (problem stories can have effects on mediators too) that they lose the ability to be helpful. Here are some of Eddy's suggestions:

- Listen to and empathize with fear and anger without getting hooked.
- Anticipate a crisis.
- Provide reassurance and validation to the person—not necessarily validating the complaint.

- Allow brief venting and contain emotion by focusing on tasks.
- Choose your battles and maintain a healthy skepticism.
- Recognize distorted information—jointly examine events that have transpired.
- Set relationship boundaries and provide structure and limits.
- Be absolutely consistent and follow through.
- Do not abruptly terminate the relationship.
- Be modest and matter of fact, without being critical or getting angry.
- Work with the person to develop realistic expectations based upon what is going on at the time.
- Explain your course of action to undermine the tendency to jump to conclusions.
- Work as a team and assign management tasks.

There are a range of narrative techniques that build on Eddy's guidelines and that can assist individuals troubled by these borderline patterns. Externalizing relationship styles and mapping the effects of a particular relational pattern can help people separate from relational styles that have become habitual. Holding externalizing conversations can assist in managing blaming and emotional attacks. In order to build an empathetic alliance with a person exhibiting borderline patterns, mediators can discuss the effects on him of negative behavior exhibited by somebody else. Then he can be invited to externalize and reflect upon his own styles of response. Once these patterns of response are identified, their effects can be studied through asking him about the consequences of the problematic relational pattern on his well-being, safety, and feeling of being respected or cared for.

Talking with people about the effects of their own problematic relational patterns can at the same time provide acknowledgement of other relational styles and open up room for intentionally adopting these other styles. From a narrative perspective it is important always to bear in mind that any person is more than any single description of who she is or any single pattern of relating. Helping the person focus on how a particular relational pattern is influencing her own behaviors interrupts a tendency to focus completely negative attention on the other person.

Once some space has been opened up, it is possible to help people connect with their ultimate goals, aspirations, intentions, and hopes. They can then be asked whether being captured by reactivity to the other person takes them further away from their preferred outcomes. The mediator needs to proceed gently and respectfully in scaffolding people's attention to the links between their own explosive or untrusting responses and another person's negative responses. These interventions must be done in a nonthreatening and straightforward manner.

The Narcissistic Pattern of Relating. The narcissistic style of relating is also challenging for mediators. Although all individuals can be preoccupied at times with themselves and their needs, excessive involvement with their own experiences overtakes some people to the point that it becomes an enormous struggle to take others' opinions and viewpoints into account or to demonstrate empathy. When narcissistic patterns are prominent, an individual can be very demanding of health care professionals, requiring repetitive attention and exaggerated respect. Sometimes this pattern requires people to expect special treatment and to feel they should be the exception to the rule.

When people are under stress, this style of communicating can come across as arrogant and disdainful of others. On other occasions it produces manipulative and exploitative behavior. A person who practices this style of relating might be easily hurt or insulted and very quick to take offense. When these behaviors escalate, people can become highly enraged and even violent. The underlying driving concern is a fear of being perceived as inferior to others. As a result, people caught up in this relational pattern might devalue and criticize health care staff and engage in excessive blaming and faultfinding. They may make frequent suggestions to health care professionals and insist on the correctness of their own viewpoints.

Helpful Strategies. Eddy suggests a number of strategies to help mediators manage this kind of behavior:

- Recognize strengths and be reassuring.
- Provide structure and limits to the relationship.

- Allow brief venting.
- Empathize with people's frustrations.
- Avoid being critical and getting angry.
- Provide tasks, educate, and include.
- Acknowledge and give credit for successes.
- Gently reduce expectations of easy success and the need to be special.
- Be consistent and follow through and do not abruptly terminate the relationship.
- Do reality checking.

A powerful narrative method of responding to a narcissistic relational style is to methodically track the person's resources and abilities as demonstrated in recent interactions. For example, a mediator might say:

Mediator: I can see that the behavior of this person is deeply offensive and disrespectful. I am wondering what ideas or resources you have that have helped you in the past to address the problem, let go and move on, and not let this person's behavior derail you?

Helping the individuals struggling with a narcissistic relational style to track their competency, strengths, resourcefulness, and creativity in dealing with difficult obstacles serves to acknowledge their level of importance and value. Essentially, the mediator focuses the conversation on the sparkling moments and unique outcomes of strength to manage difficult situations and constantly works with alternative narratives of capacity and capability to productively address problem situations.

Eddy talks about family members who enable, invite, or reinforce these difficult relational patterns. He identifies their motive as wanting to help and yet they often inadvertently escalate the difficult communication style by believing false information or tolerating inappropriate or out-of-control behavior. Family members may feel intimidated by their sibling, parent, or child and try valiantly to cope, hoping that problems will go away. When they become highly ritualized and habitual, difficult relational styles are often exhibited by more than one family member.

Working with Professionals Who Exhibit Difficult Relational Patterns

Of course it is not just patients and their families who can generate difficult to manage interactions. When borderline and narcissistic behaviors are exhibited by health care professionals themselves, serious damage can be done to health care teams. Difficult inter-actional styles among physicians, surgeons, and other senior health care personnel can undermine morale, heighten turnover in a health care team, and lead to ineffective and substandard practice. These behaviors can also intimidate, threaten, or harm others and can produce chaos and distress in the work environ-ment. The narrative techniques used in working with professionals are the same as those that mediators would apply to working with patients and their families. Specific and discrete goal setting and linking people's behaviors with the successful completion of their identified goals and aspirations can give people a helpful momen-tum in addressing problems and direct them away from flailing around in misdirected and volatile actions.

There are sometimes limits to the conflict resolution capac-ity of health care mediators when difficult relational patterns are exhibited by a health care professional. When management and containment skills have been applied and not been successful, health care policy and management protocols may need to be invoked, and that may result in a professional's termination. It is important for health care organizations to provide clear com-munication expectations and guidelines to health care teams and develop clear assessment tools to routinely measure appropriate and respectful communication among health care professionals. Such leadership greatly improves the quality of communication in an organization and promotes a just culture. In addition, when health care professionals breach the organization's code of con-duct, it is important that they can receive a fair and open exami-nation of the issues and that due process is ensured. Combining these practices with good quality training in conflict resolution skills will go long way toward improving both the quality of the health care team's environment and the quality of health care delivery.

Epilogue

To conclude this book, it remains to reiterate our intentions and to draw together the main themes we have been pursuing. We have sought to elaborate the ideas presented in our earlier book on narrative mediation and to consolidate the work we did there. Our hope is that a narrative approach to mediation can be understood and appreciated as a viable stance amid the range of approaches to conflict resolution. To us it feels like a distinctive approach, built on some principles that are robust and coherent, even though they may chart a course different from that of other established perspectives. We have sought here to sharpen our descriptions of a narrative approach and to both spell out our intentions and show them in action.

In Chapter One, we outlined nine hallmarks of narrative practice. Some of them represent background assumptions for practitioners to digest in order to practice in a narrative mode with integrity, and some are about the embodiment of these assumptions in practice. Among these assumptions are that stories are to be taken seriously and that they affect the subjectivity of people in dispute. The stories we are referring to here are both personal and cultural. Stories exert a structuring effect on who each person is and what each person does, but no one is completely in control of them. Nor are stories completely out of anyone's control. Human beings are storytelling beings. They are also potential authors of new scripts that can diverge from the rehearsed cultural stories, which in some instances diminish and constrain preferred and enlivened options for the ways people live life.

Embedded in these assumptions is the tension between two views of life: one in which individuals are assumed to be completely free and therefore responsible for the decisions they make and always capable of acting in their own interests, and another in which individuals' lives are determined by the forces at work in the structuring of both their cultural worlds and their personal experience. The latter perspective bears down too heavily upon individual freedom, and the former one too lightly assumes that all have equal opportunity to negotiate their individual interests. We believe that there are very real constraints on the kinds of interests that people can even imagine and that these constraints are produced out of the dominant discourses that all people live with. Individuals are never completely free to make up their own minds. At the same time they are never completely dominated by these same discourses. We believe in the possibility of agency, of resistance to dominant discourse, of self-creation in the moment, and of community solidarity against sometimes considerable odds.

Like Joseph Folger and Baruch Bush, the developers of transformative mediation, we believe that mediation can be transformative of persons and of relationships. It can signify much more than the simple doing of a deal. However, we have talked about this goal of transformation in a different language from that employed in transformative mediation. Instead of personal recognition and empowerment, we are focused on the transformation of relationship through the authorship of stories that can serve as counterstories to the dominant narratives that have shaped a conflict. If narratives and discourses serve to constitute subjective experience and to structure relational domains in powerful ways, then why not work directly on these narratives and discourses? Why not build on the assumption that shifts in the story of relationship will lead to shifts in the lived experience of the relationship? Why not expose the work that dominant stories do, so that they do not continue to work behind people's backs?

We believe people are most empowered when their voices and their actions are located in a robust and coherent alternative story. And the discursive location of these voices must be recognized for their power to be influential. At the same time as people are engaging with dominant discourses or narratives, they must be able to think about how they are being positioned and to make powerful decisions on their own behalf to reject or modify the effects of dominant stories in their lives. We believe our job as mediators is not so much to empower them, in the sense of spooning out dollops of our own power, as it is to treat them as capable of writing and rewriting at least parts of their own scripts.

In the end it is an ethical stance that we hold. Narrative practices of externalizing and of curious questioning are efforts to communicate profound respect. It is, however, important to answer the question, Respect for what? What we seek to convey is respect for people's hopes and best intentions; respect for the stories through which they act upon their intentions; respect for the painful effects that conflict stories produce for them; respect for their ability to edit the stories into which they have entered; and respect for the kernels of desire for cooperation, mutual understanding, peacemaking, greater justice, and resolution that always exist somewhere in the hearts of disputing parties.

We believe that positioning theory holds much potential for analyzing in detail just how people can negotiate their way through the effects of powerful discourses. Hence we have sought to spotlight the idea of positioning in Chapters Two and Three. Discursive positioning is a theoretical scalpel that allows mediators to slice through complex conversation and trace, moment by moment, the nuanced subtleties in the operation of power relations. In the process, positioning theory helps release everyone in a mediation from blunter analyses of power that always stress relations of domination and, in the end, discourage the possibility of negotiation. We have included a strong focus on positioning theory because we believe it promises increased sensitization to the work done through language to weave stories that encase people in conflict. Loosening the grip of conflict entails loosening the authority of the positioning that occurs through such language use.

Mediation is about the facilitation of negotiation between people or between groups of people and is therefore about the facilitation of power relations in the moment. The outcomes of mediation conversations are a measure of how people have succeeded in influencing each other to take seriously their concerns, how much they have been prepared to give away in order to press their own agendas, and how much they value mutual decision making, social cooperation and peaceful community relations. Each of these outcomes is a manifestation of the working out of power relations. We believe that mediators need to have a sound analysis of how power relations work. In Chapter Four we have outlined a view of power relations that is cultural rather than individual. It is based on the insights of a poststructuralist analytics of power rather than on the dominant liberal-humanist agenda.

Effective mediation relies on the mediator's possession of an ethical perspective on the working out of power relations on the ground. It is not enough to have neutrality as the main ethical principle on which one's mediation practice stands, because mediators cannot ever achieve complete neutrality toward the substance of the discourses that dominate the communications between people in dispute. Every time they speak, mediators position themselves and those with whom they work in a particular discourse position. What is needed, rather, is a deliberate and reflexive opening of these discourses to curious inquiry, to deconstruction, and to transparent practices of accountability.

An ethical perspective also requires a clear focus on the production of greater social justice. Jacques Derrida (1994) has offered a tantalizing definition of such a focus. He refers to justice as something that cannot be deconstructed and defines it as the affirming of the other: "If anything is undeconstructible, it is justice. The law is deconstructible, fortunately: it is infinitely perfectible. I am tempted to regard justice as the best word, today, for what refuses to yield to deconstruction, that is to say for what sets deconstruction in motion, what justifies it. It is an affirmative experience of the coming of the other as other" (p. 36).

The expression of hospitality toward and affirmation of the other is what distinguishes ethical negotiation from an instrumental process of facilitating the doing of a deal solely on the basis of satisfying underlying interests. Derrida's statement reads as an appealing goal for mediation practice: to create the conditions in which disputing parties can reach the position of affirming the other as other, rather than attempting to colonize the other with one's own perspective.

Mediators might also borrow from Derrida the idea that deconstruction aims at the creation of an improved democracy. Derrida spoke often of *démocratie à l'avenir,* usually translated into English as "democracy to come." What is lost in the translation is the play in French on the double meaning of *l'avenir,* which can refer to what is always arriving as well as to the future. Narrative mediation is an effort to create a vision of a future in which democracy is improved through professional practice. We do not refer here to democracy in terms of electoral representation, of course, but in terms of the creation of greater freedom for people to have a say in the creation of their own lives. At its best that is what mediation is about. It is about releasing the potential for cooperation and for peace. It is about valuing what people can do together rather than on their own. It is therefore about creating relational formats that are sustainable and satisfying and that can stand up to the common assumption that destructive conflict is inevitable.

We do not agree that the destruction and havoc wrought by war, violence, injustice, and domination is produced out of inevitable and essential elements of human nature. It is easy to find evidence for the case that this is so, given the prevalence of such destruction and havoc in the world around us. But if one looks more carefully, one can see other stories all around as well. In the gaps between wars, valiant efforts are made by many people to create peace. These efforts are often successful, even if they lack any guarantee of permanence, and they are just as representative of human experience as is violent conflict. In the face of bloody violence, moreover, there are always those who work for healing. In response to injustice and domination, there is always resistance and the assertion of a more just world. In the presence of personal pain, there is always the possibility of compassion. Even when they are embroiled in divisive conflict, people often retain hope for resolution.

In short, there is always a story of difference, and this story is just as inevitable and speaks just as strongly of human nature. People are therefore always faced not so much with the task of accepting the fact of destructive conflict as with the task of making a choice between pursuing a narrative supportive of violent acts or one committed to peaceful resolution. Mediation as a practice stands in proud defiance of the inevitability of conflict at its most destructive and in a posture of hope for something better. It gestures toward a different future than previously envisioned and beckons to others to choose between a present conflict and that more peaceful future.

It is easy enough to pronounce on these heady ideas. It is another thing to develop them into viable practices that are effective and that make a difference. Hence the second half of this book has focused on the elaboration of such practice. We have sought to develop narrative mediation by sending its tributaries into further domains of practice than we have written about before and showing how it can work in many contexts. These additional domains of practice are employment disputes, organizational conflicts, school-based restorative conferences, divorce mediation and collaborative divorce, and conflicts in health care settings. In each context the specific demands of the field of practice lead to mediation adaptations and elaborations. Practice also develops differently in the hands of different practitioners. We have shown this here by asking Alison Cotter, Allan Holmgren, and Chip Rose to serve as chapter coauthors, and there are other practitioners whose work we have referred to along the way.

Our aim has been to show that a narrative perspective is not suited just to narrow bands of practice. Some have suggested that it is all right for family mediation, which is closer than some other forms of mediation to the therapeutic background on which we have drawn, but not so relevant to mediation in other domains. We think that narrative assumptions are more robust than that and that there are many domains of practice that can be explored with a narrative framework. Assigning particular approaches to particular practice demands is in any case much too instrumental an idea, one that devalues philosophical rigor and demeans the field of conflict resolution in general. What we have provided is a series of examples of narrative practice in different domains. These examples are by no means exhaustive. However, we believe that they serve as reliable signposts, pointing practitioners toward creative practice. No doubt others can see opportunities for journeys into territories beyond those we have explored here. We hope this book will stimulate such further explorations.

References

Adair, V., & Dixon, R. (2000). Evaluation of the restorative conferencing pilot project: Report to the Ministry of Education. Auckland, NZ: Auckland Uniservices.

Amstutz, L. S., & Mullet, J. H. (2005). *The little book of restorative discipline for schools: Teaching responsibility; creating caring climates.* Intercourse, PA: Good Books.

Anderson, C., & D'Antonio, L. L. (2004, Fall). Empirical insights: Understanding the unique culture of health care conflict. *Dispute Resolution Magazine,* pp. 15–18.

Andrews, R., Biggs, M., & Seidel, M. (1996). *The Columbia world of quotations.* New York: Columbia University Press.

Appiah, K. A. (2005). *The ethics of identity.* Princeton, NJ: Princeton University Press.

Baker, K. M. (1995). Improving staff nurse conflict resolution skills. *Nursing Economic$,* 13, 295–317.

Bakhtin, M. (1981). *The dialogic imagination* (C. Emerson & M. Holquist, Trans.). Austin: University of Texas Press.

Bakhtin, M. (1984). *Problems of Dostoevsky's poetics* (C. Emerson, Trans.). Minneapolis: University of Minnesota Press.

Bakhtin, M. (1986). *Speech genres and other late essays* (V. McGee, Trans.). Austin: University of Texas Press.

Bazemore, G., & Umbreit, M. (2001, February). A comparison of four restorative conferencing models. *Juvenile Justice Bulletin* (U.S. Department of Justice). Retrieved December 19, 2007, from www .ncjrs.gov/pdffiles1/ojjdp/184738.pdf.

Benhabib, S. (2002). *The claims of culture: Equality and diversity in the global era.* Princeton, NJ: Princeton University Press.

Billig, M. (1998). From codes to utterances: Cultural studies, discourse and psychology. In M. Ferguson & P. Golding (Eds.), *Cultural studies in question* (pp. 205–226). Thousand Oaks, CA: Sage.

Blood, P., & Thorsborne, M. (2005, March 3–5). *The challenge of culture change: Embedding restorative practice in schools.* Paper presented at the sixth international conference on conferencing, circles and other restorative practices: "Building a Global Alliance for Restorative Practices and Family Empowerment," Sydney, Australia.

Boulton, J., & Mirsky, L. (2006). Restorative practices as a tool for organizational change. *Reclaiming Children and Youth, 15*(2), 89–91.

Bowlby, J. (1969–1980). *Attachment and loss* (3 vols.). London: Hogarth Press.

Braithwaite, J. (1989). *Crime, shame and reintegration.* New York: Cambridge University Press.

Braithwaite, J. (2001). Youth development circles. *Oxford Review of Education, 27*(2), 239–252.

Bruner, J. (1986). *Actual minds, possible worlds.* Cambridge, MA: Harvard University Press.

Bruner, J. (1990). *Acts of meaning.* Cambridge, MA: Harvard University Press.

Bruner, J. (2002). *Making stories: Law, literature, life.* New York: Farrar, Straus & Giroux.

Burman, E. (1994). *Deconstructing developmental psychology.* New York: Routledge.

Burman, E., & Parker, I. (1993). *Discourse analytic research: Repertoires and readings of texts.* New York: Routledge.

Cameron, N. (2003). *Collaborative practice: Deepening the dialogue.* Vancouver: Continuing Legal Education Society of British Columbia.

Chouliaraki, L., & Fairclough, N. (1999). *Discourse in late modernity: Rethinking critical discourse analysis.* Edinburgh: Edinburgh University Press.

Cloke, K. (2006). *The crossroads of conflict: A journey into the heart of conflict resolution.* Penticton, BC: Janis.

Cobb, S. (1993). Empowerment and mediation: A narrative perspective. *Negotiation Journal, 9*(3), 245–259.

Cobb, S. (1994). A narrative perspective on mediation. In J. P. Folger & T. S. Jones (Eds.), *New directions in mediation: Communication research and perspectives* (pp. 48–66). Thousand Oaks, CA: Sage.

Coontz, S. (2005). *Marriage, a history: From obedience to intimacy, or how love conquered marriage.* New York: Viking/Penguin.

Cormier, R. B. (2002). *Restorative justice: Directions and principles— developments in Canada.* Ottawa: Public Works and Government Services Canada.

Dandurand, Y., & Griffiths, C. T. (2006). *Handbook on restorative justice programmes.* Vienna, Austria: United Nations Office on Drugs and Crime. Retrieved November 17, 2007, from www.unodc.org/pdf/criminal_justice/06-56290_Ebook.pdf.

Dauer, E. A. (2002). Alternatives to litigation for health care conflicts and claims: Alternative dispute resolution in medicine. *Hematology-Oncology Clinics of North America, 16*(6), 1415–1431.

Davies, B., & Harré, R. (1990). Positioning: The discursive production of selves. *Journal for the Theory of Social Behaviour, 20*(1), 43–63.

Davies, B., & Harré, R. (1999). Positioning and personhood. In R. Harré & L. van Langenhøve (Eds.), *Positioning theory* (pp. 32–52). Oxford, U.K.: Blackwell.

Delgado, R., & Stefancic, J. (Eds.). (2000). *Critical race theory: The cutting edge* (2nd ed.). Philadelphia: Temple University Press.

Derrida, J. (1976). *Of grammatology* (G. C. Spivak, Trans.). Baltimore, MD: Johns Hopkins University Press.

Derrida, J. (1994, Autumn). The deconstruction of actuality: An interview with Jacques Derrida. *Radical Philosophy, 68*, 28–41.

Drewery, W. (2004). Conferencing in schools: Punishment, restorative justice, and the productive importance of the process of conversation. *Journal of Community and Applied Social Psychology, 14*, 332–344.

Drewery, W. (2005). Why we should watch what we say: Position calls, everyday speech and the production of relational subjectivity. *Theory & Psychology, 15*(3), 305–324.

Drewery, W., & Winslade, J. (2005). Developing restorative practices in schools: Some reflections. *New Zealand Journal of Counselling, 26*(1), 16–31.

Duncan, R. (2007). *A judge's guide to divorce: Uncommon advice from the bench.* Berkeley, CA: Nolo.

Durie, E. (2000). Peace in customary terms. In W. Tie (Ed.), *Just peace? Peacemaking and peacebuilding for the new millennium: Conference proceedings 24–28 April* (pp. 94–97). Auckland, NZ: Massey University.

Durie Hall, D. (1999). Restorative justice: A Maori perspective. In J. Consedine & H. Bowen (Eds.), *Restorative justice: Contemporary themes and practice* (pp. 25–35). Lyttleton, NZ: Ploughshares.

Eddy, B. (2006). *High conflict people in legal disputes.* Penticton, BC: Janis.

Elton, K. (2007, October 24–27). *Restorative discipline in schools: Creating caring climates.* Presentation at the Association for Conflict Resolution conference, Phoenix, AZ.

Fairclough, N. (1992). *Discourse and social change.* Cambridge, U.K.: Polity Press.

Fisher, R., & Ury, W. (1981). *Getting to yes: Negotiating agreement without giving in.* London: Penguin.

Folger, J. P., & Bush, R.A.B. (1994). Ideology, orientations to conflict, and mediation discourse. In J. P. Folger & T. S. Jones (Eds.),

New directions in mediation: Communication research and perspectives (pp. 3–25). Thousand Oaks, CA: Sage.

Folger, J. P., & Bush, R.A.B. (2001). Transformative mediation and third party intervention: Ten hallmarks of transformative mediation. In J. P. Folger & R.A.B. Bush (Eds.), *Designing mediation: Approaches to training and practice within a transformative framework* (pp. 20–36). New York: Institute for the Study of Conflict Transformation.

Foucault, M. (1972). *The order of things: An archaeology of the human sciences.* New York: Pantheon Books.

Foucault, M. (1977). What is an author? In D. F. Bouchard (Ed. & Trans.), *Language, counter-memory, practice* (pp. 124–127). Ithaca, NY: Cornell University Press.

Foucault, M. (1978). *The history of sexuality: Vol. 1. An introduction* (R. Hurley, Trans.). New York: Vintage Books.

Foucault, M. (1980). *Power/knowledge: Selected interviews and other writings.* New York: Pantheon Books.

Foucault, M. (2000). *Essential works of Foucault, 1954–1984: Vol. 3. Power* (J. Faubion, Ed., & R. Hurley, Trans.). New York: New Press.

Franks, P. (2003). Employment mediation in New Zealand. *ADR Bulletin, 6*(1), 4–7.

Gavrielides, T. (2005). Some meta-theoretical questions for restorative justice. *Ratio Juris, 18*(1), 84–106.

Gee, J. P. (1999). *An introduction to discourse analysis: Theory and method.* New York: Routledge.

Geertz, C. (1983). *Local knowledge: Further essays in interpretive anthropology.* New York: Basic Books.

Geertz, C. (1995). *After the fact.* Cambridge, MA: Harvard University Press.

Gerardi, D. (2003). Conversations that matter: The road to patient safety. *Progress in Cardiovascular Nursing, 18*(1), 63–64.

Gerardi, D. (2004). Using mediation techniques to manage conflict and create healthy work environments. *AACN Clinical Issues, 15*(2), 182–195, 296–298.

Gergen, K. J. (1990). Therapeutic professions and the diffusion of deficit. *Journal of Mind and behavior, 11*(3–4), 353–368.

Gerritsen, J. (2001). Holding different conversations: A restorative justice approach to school discipline. *Education Gazette, 80*(4), 1–2.

Hare-Mustin, R. T. (1994). Discourses in the mirrored room: A postmodern analysis of therapy. *Family Process, 33,* 19–34.

Harré, R., & van Langenhøve, L., (1999). Reflexive positioning: Autobiography. In R. Harré & L. van Langenhøve (Eds.), *Positioning theory* (pp. 60–73). Oxford, U.K.: Blackwell.

Hayes, H., & Daley, K. (2003). Youth justice conferencing and reoffending. *Justice Quarterly, 2*(4), 725–764.

Hill Collins, P. (1991). *Black feminist thought: Knowledge consciousness and the politics of empowerment.* New York: Routledge.

Houk, C. S., & Moidel, B. S. (2003, Spring). A practical innovation whose time has come. *ACResolution*, pp. 30–31.

Hyndman, M., Thorsborne, M., & Wood, S. (1996). *Community accountability conferencing* (Trial report for the Queensland Department of Education). Brisbane, Australia: Queensland Department of Education.

Image-e-nation. (2004–2007). *Apology verses.* Retrieved February 24, 2007, from www.imag-e-nation.com/sorry_verses_poems_quotes.htm.

Ivey, A. (1986). *Developmental therapy: Theory into practice.* San Francisco: Jossey-Bass.

James, W. (1983). *The principles of psychology* (G. A. Miller, Ed.). Cambridge, MA: Harvard University Press. (Original work published 1890.)

Jenkins, A. (2006). Shame, realization and restitution: The ethics of restorative practice. *Australia and New Zealand Journal of Family Therapy, 27*(3), 153–162.

Karp, D. (2002). The offender/community encounter: Stakeholder involvement in the Vermont reparative boards. In D. Karp & T. Clear (Eds.), *What is restorative justice? Case studies of restorative justice and community supervision* (pp. 61–87). Thousand Oaks, CA: Sage.

Kerfoot, K. (2007). Patient satisfaction and high-reliability organizations: What's the connection? *Nursing Economics, 25*(2), 119–120.

Kristeva, J. (1986). *The Kristeva reader* (T. Moi, Ed.). Oxford, U.K.: Blackwell.

Lacan, J. (1977). *Écrits: A selection* (A. Sheridan, Trans.). New York: Norton. (Original work published 1966.)

Lazare, A. (2006). Apology in medical practice. *Journal of the American Medical Association, 296*(11), 1401–1404.

Linehan, C., & McCarthy, J. (2000). Positioning in practice: Understanding participation in the social world. *Journal for the Theory of Social Behaviour, 30*(4), 435–453.

Lyotard, J.-F. (1984). *The postmodern condition: A report on knowledge* (G. Bennington & B. Massumi, Trans.). Minneapolis: University of Minnesota Press. (Original work published 1979.)

Maalouf, A. (2000). *On identity.* New York: Routledge.

Macfarlane, A. H. (2000). The value of Maori ecologies in special education. In K. Ryba (Ed.), *Learners with special needs* (pp. 77–98.) Palmerston North, NZ: Dunmore Press.

MacRae, A., & Zehr, H. (2004). *The little book of restorative conferences New Zealand style: A hopeful approach when youth cause harm.* Intercourse, PA: Good Books.

Marcus, L. J., Dorn, B. C., Kritek, P. B., Miller, V. G., & Wyatt, J. B. (1995). *Renegotiating health care: Resolving conflict to build collaboration.* San Francisco: Jossey-Bass.

Marcus, L. J., & Roover, J. E. (2003, Spring). Healing the conflicts that divide us. *ACResolution,* pp. 16–19.

Maxwell, G., & Morris, A. (1993). *Family participation, cultural diversity and victim involvement in youth justice: A New Zealand experiment.* Wellington, NZ: Victoria University.

Maxwell, G., & Morris, A. (2006). Youth justice in New Zealand: Restorative justice in practice? *Journal of Social Issues, 62*(2), 239–258.

McElrea, F.W.M. (1996). Education, discipline and restorative justice. *Butterworths Family Law Journal,* pp. 91–93.

McGarrell, E. F., & Hipple, N. K. (2007). Family group conferencing and re-offending among first-time juvenile offenders: The Indianapolis experiment. *Justice Quarterly, 24*(2), 221–246.

McGrath, J. (2002). School restorative conferencing. *Child Care in Practice, 8*(3), 187–200.

Mead, H. M. (2003). *Tikanga Māori: Living by Māori values.* Wellington, NZ: Huia Ministry of Education. (2003). *A report on stand-downs, suspensions, exclusions and expulsions.* Wellington, NZ: Ministry of Education.

Mirsky, L. (2003). *Family group conferencing worldwide: Parts 1, 2, and 3.* International Institute for Restorative Practices. Retrieved February 20, 2004, from www.iirp.org.

Monk, G., Winslade, J., Crocket, K., & Epston, D. (1997). *Narrative therapy in practice: The archaeology of hope.* San Francisco: Jossey-Bass.

Monk, G., Winslade, J., & Sinclair, S. (2008). *New horizons in multicultural counseling.* Thousand Oaks, CA: Sage.

Morris, A., & Maxwell, G. (1998). Restorative justice in New Zealand: Family group conferences as a case study. *Western Criminology Review, 1*(1), 1–18.

Morris, A., & Maxwell, G. (Eds.). (2001). *Restorative justice for juveniles: Conferencing, mediation and circles.* Oxford: Hart.

Morrison, B., Blood, P., & Thorsborne, M. (2005). Practicing restorative justice in school communities: The challenge of culture change. *Public Organization Review, 5,* 335–357.

Myerhoff, B. (1982). Life history among the elderly: Performance, visibility and remembering. In J. Ruby (Ed.), *A crack in the mirror:*

Reflexive perspectives in anthropology (pp. 99–117). Philadelphia: University of Pennsylvania Press.

Myerhoff, B. (1986). Life not death in Venice. In V. Turner & E. Bruner (Eds.), *The anthropology of experience* (pp. 261–286). Urbana: University of Illinois Press.

Nash, J. (2004, March 13). *Restorative justice and restorative conferencing: Engaging youth, families and communities in resolutions.* Paper presented at the Association for Dispute Resolution Northern California annual conference, San Francisco.

Ousky, R. D., & Webb, S. G. (2006). *The collaborative way to divorce.* New York: Hudson Street Press.

Pape, T. (1999). A systems approach to resolving OR conflict—operating room. *AORN Journal, 69*(3), 551–566.

Parker, I. (1992). *Discourse dynamics: Critical analysis for social and individual psychology.* New York: Routledge.

Pennell, J. (2006). Restorative practices and child welfare: Toward an inclusive civil society. *Journal of Social Issues, 62*(2), 259–279.

Pfifferling, J. (1997, November-December). Managing the unmanageable: The disruptive physician. *Family Practice Management,* pp. 77–92.

Pranis, K. (2005). *The little book of circle processes: A new/old approach to peacemaking.* Intercourse, PA: Good Books.

Restorative Practices Development Team. (2003). *Restorative practices in schools: A resource.* Hamilton, NZ: University of Waikato, School of Education.

Rosaldo, R. (1993). *Culture and truth: The remaking of social analysis.* Boston: Beacon Press.

Rosaldo, R. (1994). Cultural citizenship and educational democracy. *Cultural Anthropology, 9*(3), 402–411.

Roussos, P. (2006, Winter). Who owns the process? *The Collaborative Review* (Journal of the International Academy of Collaborative Professionals), pp. 24–26.

Said, E. W. (1994). *Orientalism.* New York: Vintage Books.

Schwartz, R. W., & Pogge, C. (2000). Physician leadership is essential to the survival of teaching hospitals. *American Journal of Surgery, 179*(6), 462–468.

Shaw, G. (2007). Restorative practices in Australian schools: Changing relationships, changing culture. *Conflict Resolution Quarterly, 25*(1), 127–135.

Shotter, J. (1993). Bakhtin and Vygotsky: Internalization as a boundary phenomenon. *New Ideas in Psychology, 11*(3), 379–390.

Silverstein, O., & Rashbaum, B. (1995). *The courage to raise good men.* New York: Penguin Books.

Skiba, R., Reynolds, C. R., Graham, S., Sheras, P., Close Conoley, J., & Garcia-Vazquez, E. (2006). *Are zero tolerance policies effective in the schools? An evidentiary review and recommendations* (A Report by the American Psychological Association Zero Tolerance Task Force). Retrieved December 5, 2007, from www.apa.org/releases/ZTTFReportBODRevisions5-15.pdf.

Stuart, B. (1997). Sentencing circles: Making "real differences." In J. Macfarlane (Ed.), *Rethinking disputes: The mediation alternative* (pp. 201–232). London: Cavendish.

Taonui, R. (2007). Tribal organization. In *Te ara: The Encyclopedia of New Zealand* (updated 20-Sep-2007). Retrieved December 14, 2007, from www.TeAra.govt.nz/NewZealanders/MaoriNewZealanders/TribalOrganisation/en.

Tesler, P., & Thompson, P. (2006). *Collaborative divorce: The revolutionary new way to restructure your family, resolve legal issues, and move on with your life.* New York: Harper Collins.

Thorsborne, M. (1999a, July). *Beyond punishment—Workplace conferencing: An effective organisational response to incidents of workplace bullying.* Paper presented at the conference of the Beyond Bullying Association, "Responding to Professional Abuse," University of Queensland, Brisbane.

Thorsborne, M. (1999b). Community conferencing in schools. In A. Morris & G. Maxwell (Eds.), *Youth justice in focus: Proceedings of an Australasian conference.* Wellington, NZ: Institute of Criminology.

Tillich, P. (1987). *The essential Tillich: An anthology of the writings of Paul Tillich* (F. Forrester Church, Ed.). Chicago: University of Chicago Press.

Triggs, S. (2005). *New Zealand court-referred restorative justice pilot: Two year follow-up of reoffending* (Report to the New Zealand Ministry of Justice). Retrieved November 16, 2007, from www.justice.govt.nz/pubs/reports/2005/nz-court-referred-restorative-justice-pilot-2-year-follow-up/index.html.

Turner, W. A. (1960). Karakia. *Te Ao Hou, 8*(4), 47–48.

Umbreit, M. (1994). *Victim meets offender: The impact of restorative justice in mediation.* Monsey, NY: Criminal Justice Press.

Ury, W. (2007). *The power of a positive no: How to say no and still get to yes.* New York: Bantam Books.

von Thaden, T. L., & Hoppes, M. (2005, September 20–22). *Measuring a just culture in healthcare professionals: Initial survey results.* Paper presented at the "Safety Across High-Consequence Industries" conference, St. Louis, MO.

Vygotsky, L. (1986). *Thought and language* (A. Kozulin, Trans.). Cambridge, MA: MIT Press.

Wachtel, J. (2007). *Healing in our land: Jamaica hosts international conference on restorative justice.* Restorative Practices E-Forum, International Institute for Restorative Practices. Retrieved November 16, 2007, from www.realjustice.org/library/jamaicarj.html.

Weick, K. E., & Sutcliffe, K. M. (2001). *Managing the unexpected: Assuring high performance in an age of complexity.* San Francisco: Jossey-Bass.

White, M. (1989). The externalizing of the problem and the re-authoring of lives and relationships. *Selected papers* (pp. 5–28). Adelaide, Australia: Dulwich Centre Publications.

White, M. (1992). Deconstruction and therapy. In D. Epston & M. White (Eds.), *Experience, contradiction, narrative, and imagination* (pp. 109–152). Adelaide, Australia: Dulwich Centre.

White, M. (2000). Re-engaging with history: The absent but implicit. In M. White, *Reflections on narrative practice: Essays & interviews* (pp. 35–38). Adelaide, Australia: Dulwich Centre.

White, M. (2004). *Narrative practice and exotic lives: Resurrecting diversity in everyday life.* Adelaide, Australia: Dulwich Centre.

White, M. (2007). *Maps of narrative practice.* New York: Norton.

White, M., & Epston, D. (1990). *Narrative means to therapeutic ends.* New York: Norton.

Winslade, J. (2003). *Discursive positioning in theory and practice: A case for narrative mediation.* Unpublished PhD dissertation, University of Waikato.

Winslade, J., Drewery, W., & Hooper, S. (2000). *Restorative conferencing in schools: Draft manual.* Wellington, NZ: Ministry of Education.

Winslade, J., & Monk, G. (2000). *Narrative mediation: A new approach to conflict resolution.* San Francisco: Jossey-Bass.

Wittgenstein, L. (1958). *Philosophical investigations.* Oxford, U.K.: Blackwell.

Zammit, L. (2001, October 10–13). *Restorative justice: Building schools' capacities.* Paper presented at the Association for Conflict Resolution Conference, Toronto,

Zammit, L., & Lockhart, A. (2001). *Restorative justice: A manual for teachers, school administrators, police, court personnel, community organizations, and concerned citizens.* Toronto: National Strategy on Community Safety & Crime Prevention.

Zehr, H. (1990). *Changing lenses.* Scottdale, PA: Herald Press.

Zehr, H. (2002). *The little book of restorative justice.* Intercourse, PA: Good Books.

About the Authors

John Winslade is a professor at California State University-San Bernardino, where he is coordinator of the Educational Counseling Program. He also teaches part-time at the University of Waikato in New Zealand, where he was previously director of counselor education. He also regularly teaches mediation at California State University-Dominguez Hills and in the conflict resolution certificate program of the Conrad Grebel University College at the University of Waterloo. His academic work has focused on the application of social constructionist and narrative ideas to conflict resolution and counseling. He is interested in the novel modes of practice that these ideas open up and in the extent to which they constitute responses to new developments in our conditions of life in the twenty-first century. In 2000, he coauthored, with Gerald Monk, *Narrative Mediation: A New Approach to Conflict Resolution*. He has also coauthored five books on narrative counseling.

John has taught narrative mediation workshops in the United States, Canada, Britain, Denmark, Sweden, The Netherlands, Australia, New Zealand, Cyprus, and Israel. Through the sponsorship of the Fred J. Hansen Institute for World Peace, he has also been involved in bi-communal peace-building work in Cyprus. He received his PhD degree from the University of Waikato in 2003.

Gerald Monk is a professor in the Department of Counseling and School Psychology and a faculty member in the International Security and Conflict Resolution program at San Diego State University. He teaches a range of conflict resolution and mediation courses at SDSU as well as multicultural counseling, group work, and narrative therapy courses at the graduate level.

He is also an active presenter and forum participant at the Joan B. Kroc Institute for Peace & Justice at the University of San Diego. Gerald received his PhD degree from the University of Waikato in 1999. Gerald worked as a psychologist and mediator in New Zealand for fifteen years prior to moving to the United States in 2000. He is presently a licensed marriage and family therapist in California and a mediator and trainer in collaborative divorce practices, specializing in mediation in health care. He has coauthored five books on narrative mediation, narrative therapy, and multicultural counseling. Most recently, Gerald has taught numerous workshops on narrative mediation in the U.K., Ireland, Denmark, Austria, Cyprus, Iceland, Russia, Nepal, New Zealand, Canada, Mexico, and the United States.

Alison Cotter has worked as a mediator with the Department of Labour in Hamilton, New Zealand, since 2000. Her work involves mediating employment relationship problems between employers, employees, and unions, ranging from issues in ongoing relationships or collective bargaining negotiations to personal grievances. Alison developed a keen interest in narrative approaches to mediation while studying for her MEd degree, which she earned at the University of Waikato, New Zealand, in the 1990s. She continues to incorporate narrative approaches into her mediation practice. Prior to working full-time in the mediation field, she worked for many years as a lecturer, facilitator, and manager in the tertiary education sector.

Allan Holmgren has served as consultant to many Scandinavian organizations in crisis and conflict. He received his magister artium degree (similar to a PhD degree) in psychology from Copenhagen University in 1981 and was director for a private psychiatric institution from 1982 to 1989. In 1990, he founded DISPUK (the Danish Institute for Supervision, Personnel, Development & Consultation). He also serves as an adjunct professor in coaching and leadership at the Copenhagen Business School. Allan is married to Anette, a clinical psychologist and narrative therapist, and has four children and two grandchildren.

Chip Rose is a board-certified family law specialist who practices mediation and collaborative practice in the family law field in Santa Cruz, California. He earned his JD degree from the University of California, Berkeley. Chip has been a pioneer in the development of client-centered dispute resolution theory and practice since 1980. He is recognized both nationally and internationally for his contributions to the fields of mediation and collaborative practice. He recently authored the chapter "Mediating Financial Issues" for the 2004 compendium *Divorce and Family Mediation* (edited by Folberg, Milne, and Salem). In addition to his private practice, he serves as an adjunct faculty member teaching basic and advanced dispute resolution theory and techniques at the Strauss Institute for Dispute Resolution, Pepperdine University School of Law.

Index

A

Accreditation Council for Graduate Medical Education (ACGME), 245

Action, landscape of, 193

Adair, V., 223

Addressivity, 56

African American cultural tradition, 72

Agency, positions of, 97–98

Agreement: reaching, 31; recording more than, 36–37

Alternative story: construction of, through asking questions, 32–33; example of construction of, 33–35; example of opening, in conversation, 30–31; identifying openings to, 26–31, 79–86; starting points for opening, 27–29

American Psychological Association, 225

Amstutz, L. S., 217, 220, 221

Ancient Greeks, 6

Anderson, C., 247

Andrews, R., 174–175

Apology conversations: facilitating, 267–268; and preparing for apology meeting, 268–270; and recovering from breakdown in communications, 270–271; using negotiating protocol in, 271–274; and working with people who exhibit high-conflict patterns of behavior, 274–275

Appiah, K. A., 105

Argentina, 219

Arizona, 223

Attachment theory, 76

Australia, 219, 223

Authority, forms of, 52

B

Background stories, 4, 5; and background cultural narratives, 124–125; and deconstructing background cultural narratives, 125–128

Baker, K. M., 248

Bakhtin, M., 44, 46–47, 55, 56, 69

Bazemore, G., 217

Belgium, 219

Benhabib, S., 5, 105

Biggs, M., 174–175

Billig, M., 64

Binary opposition, 9

Blood, P., 220–222

Bloodmothering, 72
Border identities, 106–108
Borderline patterns of
   relating, 277
Bosnia, 105
Boulton, J., 223
Bowlby, J., 76
Bowling metaphor, 140
Braithwaite, J., 225, 228
Bruner, J., 2, 87, 105, 133,
   169, 193
Burman, E., 64, 100
Bush, R.A.B., 2, 31, 32, 51,
   201, 284

C
California, 220
Calling, 45
Cameron, N., 135
Canada, 117, 218–220, 222, 223
Charter airplane services meta-
   phor, 149–151
Chavez, S., 107–108
Children, dependent, 162–163
Chouliaraki, L., 64, 66
Cloke, K., 266
Close Conoley, J., 225
Cobb, S., 4, 54, 55, 68, 86
Cold War, 243
Collaborative divorce, 148–154;
   hearing children's voices in,
   162–163; managing cultural
   projections in, 157–159; nar-
   rative strategies for establish-
   ing client goals and vision
   in, 154–165; one-coach or
   one-mediator model for,
   152–154; and preparing

couple and team for adversity in process, 155–157;
   reflections on, 165; team
   mechanics in, 151–152; team
   metaphor for, 149–151;
   using narrative letters in,
   163–165; using reflecting
   team in, 159–162
Collaborative law, 146–148
Community group confer-
   ence, 219
Community justice forums, 219
Community reparative boards,
   219
Complexity, culture and,
   104–105
Conflict: consequences of,
   in health care, 244–245;
   culture and, 243–257; discourses of, 82–83; escalation
   of, in legal system, 132–134;
   mapping effects of, 14–15;
   personalities, 274; understanding of power in,
   109–113; viewing, as
   restraint, 18
Consciousness, landscape of, 193
Constructionist vision, 48,
   103–105; and border identities, 106–108; culture and
   complexity in, 104–105;
   culture as narrative in, 105;
   mediator's stance from perspective of, 113–118; and
   multiple identity narratives,
   106; and race, 108–109;
   summary of principles in,
   120–121; view of power in,

110–112; and working with
cultural narrative, 123–128
Conversation(s), 21; example
of discursive positioning in,
24–26; example of opening
alternative story in, 30–31;
outsider witness in, 172–173;
positioning in multiple,
46–48; positioning people in
different, 53–54; repositioning, 61–63
"Cookie cutter" perspective,
102
Coontz, S., 131
Cormier, R. B., 218, 219,
222, 223
Cotter, A., 185, 288
Counterstory, 17
Critical discourse analysis, 64
Crocket, K., 115
Cultural essentialism. *See*
Essentialism
Cultural narratives: background, 124–125; and con-
structionist vision, 103–105;
discourse and mediation in,
118–120; and governmen-
tality, 112–113; and liberal-
humanist vision, 100–103,
122–123; mediator's stance
from constructionist per-
spective in, 113–118; practice example of working
with, 121–128; and summary
of constructionist principles,
120–121; and understand-
ings of power in conflict,
109–113

Cultural nature, 99
Culture, 21; and complexity,
104; concept of, 99; of lawyers, 134–136; as narrative,
105
Curling metaphor, 140
Czech Republic, 219

D

Daley, K., 223
Dallas–Fort Worth, Texas, 152
Dandurand, Y., 217, 219
D'Antonio, L. L., 247
Dauer, E. A., 245
Davies, B., viii, 21, 43, 48
Deconstruction, 9–11,
286–287; and deconstruct-
ing background cultural
narratives, 125–128; and
working with cultural narra-
tives in mediation, 115–118
Deficit discourse, 228
Definitional ceremony, 170
Delgado, R., 109
Démocratie à l'avenir, 286–287
Denmark, 166, 219
Derrida, J., 9, 10, 115, 286
*Diagnostic and Statistical Manual
of Mental Disorders* (DSM),
274
Dialogue, 44
Difference, moment of, 31
Differing circumstances,
141–142
Disciplinary power, 78
Discourse, 5
Discourse production, 44

Discourse theory, 5; and discursive positioning, 20; terminology of, 5

Discursive positioning: addressing problem of first speaker in, 54–56; example of, in conversation, 24–25; listening for, 20–26; and making sense of interaction, 40–43; repositioning exercise for, 61–63. *See also* Positioning theory

Discursive positioning, through conversation, 64–98; and arranging for further discussion, 93–95; and constructing joint story around new opening, 86–88; and inviting answer from position within new story, 90–91; and listening for connections with wider discursive context, 69; and moving from subjunctive to indicative, 92–93; and positioning as first speaker, 68; and positioning in relation to discourses of conflict, 82–83; and positioning in relation to legal discourse, 67–68; and positioning in story of cooperation, 83–86; and positioning parties as agents, 88; positioning questions for, 65; positioning through summarizing in, 87–88; scenario for, 65–66; seizing opening in, 89–90; and summary of movement of discursive positioning, 95–98; and understanding positioning and mediatory authority, 71–72

Discursive positions: negotiating, 40–63; shifting, 49–50, 97

Disputant, role of, 48

Divorce mediation, 138–146; differences as circumstances in, 141–142; and divorce as violation of culturally sanctioned narratives, 130–131; and dominant discourses of marriage and divorce, 129–137; facilitative orientation in, 139–146; and leading from behind, 139–141; legal system and, 131–137; managing cultural projections in, 157–159; and mutual self-interest, 144–146; and narrative strategies for establishing client goals and vision, 154–165; preparing couple and team for adversity in process of, 155–157; reflections on, 165; strategic metaphor for, 142–144; using reflecting team in, 159–162

Dixon, R., 223

Documenting progress, 35–39; example of letter, 37–39; letter form for, 37; and recording more than agreement, 36–37

Dominating discourses, 119–120, 124

Dorn, B. C., 243

Double listening, 7–12, 80–82;
and deconstruction, 9–11;
Ury's "positive no" as exam-
ple of, 11–12
Double-voiced utterance, 47
Drewery, W., viii, x, 53, 54, 220,
222, 225
DSM. *See Diagnostic and Statisti-
cal Manual of Mental Disorders*
(DSM)
Duncan, R., 134
Durie, E., 202
Durie Hall, D., 218

E

Eddy, B., 274–275, 277–280
Elton, K., 220, 221, 223
Employment mediation,
185–214; and achieving
breakthrough (Rosa's story),
212–213; and concluding
joint meeting (story of Ruby
and Phoebe), 188–192; and
developing counterstory
(Rosa's story), 209–210;
and growing story in later
meeting (story of Ruby and
Phoebe), 196–199; and holding separate meetings with
each party (story of Ruby
and Phoebe), 187–188; and
introducing mediation process (Rosa's story), 202–203;
and inviting further developments in alternative story
(story of Ruby and Phoebe),
193–195; and mapping
effects of problem (Rosa's
story), 205–206; and

negotiating shared story
(Rosa's story), 210–212; and
opening alternative story
(Rosa's story), 207–209;
and opening counterstory
(story of Ruby and Phoebe),
192–193; reaching agree-
ment in (story of Ruby and
Phoebe), 195–196; reflec-
tions on, 213; and story
of Rosa and school board,
199–213; and story of Ruby
and Phoebe, 187–199; types
of, 186–187; and unravel-
ing problem story (Board's
story), 206–207; and unraveling problem story (Rosa's
story), 203–205
Employment Relations Act
(New Zealand; 2000), 185,
186, 188, 203, 206
England, 219
Enlightenment, 52
Entitlement: Alan's claims of,
76; and movement of dis-
cursive positioning, 95–97;
Theresa's claims of, 72–74
Epston, D., viii, 35, 84, 115, 163
Essentialism, 6–7, 9; cultural,
102–103; and essentializing
logic, 42
Expertise, positioning and,
51–53
Externalizing conversation,
12–14; building, 13; example
of, 15–16; and examples of
questions using externalizing
language, 13–14; and map-
ping effects of conflict, 14–15

F

Facilitative orientation, 139–146; and differences as circumstances, 141–142; and leading from behind, 139–141; and mutual self-interest, 144–146; strategic metaphor for, 142–144
Fairclough, N., 64, 66
Family group conference process, 218, 222
Family group decision making, 219
Family law, changes in practice of, 136–137
Family unity meetings, 219
Finland, 219
First speaker: addressing problem of, 54–56; lessening effect of power of, 56–57; positioning as, 68
Fisher, R., 18, 21
Folger, J. P., ix, 2, 31, 32, 51, 201, 284
Foucault, M., 5, 43, 44, 52, 56, 68, 72, 78, 108, 111–113, 118
Framing, 18
Franks, P., 185, 186

G

Garcia-Vazquez, E., 225
Gavrielides, T., 219
Gee, J. P., 47
Geertz, C., 101, 102, 200
Gerardi, D., 245, 246
Gergen, K. J., 228
Gerritsen, J., 220
Governmentality, 112–113

Graham, S., 225
Griffiths, C. T., 217, 219

H

Hare-Mustin, R. T., 115
Harré, R., viii, 21, 43, 48
Hayes, H., 223
Healing, 226–227
Health care: conflict resolution in, 242–281; conflict with patients and families in, 246–247; consequences of conflict in, 244–245; culture and conflict in, 243–257; current restraints on implementing conflict resolution programs in, 245–246; and discursive shifts in relations between doctors and nurses, 248–250; internal institutional demands for conflict resolution skills in, 245; and obstacles to more just culture in medicine, 250; promotion of just culture in, 250–251; recent changes in culture of, 243–244
Health care, narrative mediation protocol for, 258–281; and exploring possible system changes (stage four), 266–281; and follow-through (stage three), 266; and meeting with health care personnel, 259–260; and meeting with patient and family, 258–259; and multiparty or joint session (stage two), 260–266; and separate sessions (stage one), 258–260

Health care professionals:
and causes of conflict with
patients and families and
how medical teams can
respond, 254–257; conflict
and conflict resolution
between, 247–248; and discursive shifts in relations
between doctors and nurses,
248–250; and roles for mediators and ombuds in health
care system, 251–257
Heteroglossia, 47
High-conflict personality,
274–275; helpful strategies
for working with, 277–279;
problem with essentializing
people as, 275–276; working
with people who exhibit,
274–275; and working with
professionals who exhibit
difficult relational patterns,
281; and working with specific problematic patterns of
relating, 276–280
Hill Collins, P., 72
Hipple, N. K., 223
Hispanic, 108
Hispanic culture, 103
Holmgren, A., 166, 176,
183, 288
Hong Kong, 219
Hoppes, M., 251
Houk, C. S., xi, 245
Hui, 218
Human nature, 99
Humanist tradition, 48
Hungary, 219
Hyndman, M., 219, 220
Hysterical behavior patterns, 277

I

"I" statements, 273
Identity: border, 106–108; mul-
tiple, 106
Image-e-nation, 267
Indianapolis, Indiana, 223
Individual, primacy of, 101–102
Institute of Medicine, 245
Integration, 7–8
Internalizing language, 229
Ireland, 219, 220
Ivey, A., 103
Iwi, 203, 205, 208, 210, 212

J

Jamaica, 219
James, W., 174
Japan, 219
Jenkins, A., 221
Just culture, 250–251

K

Karakia, 201, 202, 213
Karp, D., 219
Kerfoot, K., 251
Kirkeby, O. F., 174
Knowledge, professional,
114–115
Kristeva, J., 47
Kritek, P. B., 243

L

Lacan, J., 103
Landscape: of action, 193; of
consciousness, 193
Lazare, A., 264, 268
Legal discourse, 67–68
Legal system: and changes in
practice of family law,

Legal system (continued) 136–137; and conflict escalation, 132–134; and culture of attorneys, 134–136; divorce and, 131–137

Liberal-humanist vision, 100–103; and cultural essentialism, 102–103; primacy of individual in, 101–102; view of power in, 109–110; and working with cultural narrative, 122–123

Linehan, C., 44

Lockhart, A., 220

London, Ontario, 140

Los Angeles, California, 171

Losotho, 219

Lyotard, J.-F., 114

M

Maalouf, A., 105

Macfarlane, A. H., x, 218

MacRae, A., x, 218

Mana, 201, 202, 205, 209, 210, 212, 213

Maori culture, 199–202, 208, 211, 213, 214

Maori population, 218

Marae, 199–200

Marcus, L. J., 243–245

Marriage, dominant discourse of, 129–137

Matua Whangai movement, 218

Maxwell, G., 218, 219, 222

McCarthy, J., 44

McElrea, F.W.M., x, 220

McGarrell, E. F., 223

McGrath, J., 220, 223

Mead, H. M., 200

Meaning: making, 116; narrative, 9; surplus, 9

Mediation: discourse and, 118–120; use of positioning theory in, 58–61; working with cultural narratives in, 99–128

Mediation conversation, 66–95; constructing joint story around new opening in, 86–88; and developing conflict story (Alan's perspective), 74–76; and developing conflict story (Theresa's perspective), 70–71; engaging in double listening in, 80–82; and fashioning narrative of joint care, 91–95; initial statements in, 68–70; opening exchanges in, 67–68; opening space for alternate story in, 79–86; persisting with story of cooperation in, 88–91; and positioning in story of cooperation (Alan's response), 84–86; and positioning in story of cooperation (Theresa's response), 83–84

Mediators: and position parties, 50–57; role of, 48; understanding authority of, 71–72

Memorandum of understanding, 195

Metaphor, 174

Miller, V. G., 243

Minneapolis, Minnesota, 146

Mirsky, L., 219, 223

Moidel, B. S., 245
Monk, G., 2, 43, 48, 72, 84, 87, 109, 115, 163, 193
Morris, A., 218, 219, 222
Morrison, B., 220–222
Mullet, J. H., 217, 220, 221
Multiparty or joint session (health care setting): beginning, 261–262; conflict scenario for, 260–261; and hearing Matt's story, 262–263; and listening to Dr. Spooner's story, 264–265; and negotiating shared story, 265–266
Multiplicity, 105
Myerhoff, B., 166, 170–172

N

Naming, 14, 32
Narcissistic behavior patterns, 277
Narcissistic pattern of relating, 279; helpful strategies for, 279–280
Narrative, 4
Narrative(s), 7; closure, 55; culture as, 105; letters, 163–165; multiple, 8; multiple identity, 106
Narrative mediation: and conflict resolution in health care, 242–281; in divorce mediation and collaborative practice, 129–165; and employment mediation, 185–214; hallmark eight of, 31–35; hallmark five of, 16–20; hallmark four of, 12–14; hallmark nine of, 35–39; hallmark one of, 5–6; hallmark six of, 20–26; hallmark three of, 7–12; hallmark two of, 6–7; and negotiating discursive positions, 40–63; nine hallmarks of, 1–39; and outsider-witness practices in organizational disputes, 166–184; and restorative conferencing in schools, 215–241; and tracing discursive positioning through conversation, 64–98; and working with cultural narratives, 99–128
Narrative restorative conferencing: and adopting respectful language, 227–228; and articulating hope, 233–234; and avoiding deficit discourse, 228; and avoiding totalizing language, 228–229; developing alternative story for, 238–240; exhibit of, 230–231; and making arrangements before conference, 233; mapping counterstory for, 232; mapping effects of problem for, 231, 235–236; and mapping exceptions to problem story, 237–238; method for, 229–240; principles of, 227–229; and using externalizing language, 234–235. *See also* Restorative conferencing in schools

Nash, J., 220
Native Americans, 104
Netherlands, 219
Neutral coach model, 152
New Zealand, 185, 199, 203, 214, 218–221; Department of Labour, 185, 186, 213; Education Review Office, 203, 208; Employee Relations Authority, 185, 199, 206, 211, 213; Ministry of Education, 207, 220, 221
Nigeria, 105
No-fault divorce, 131
North America, 100, 123, 131, 135, 137, 220, 251–252
North Carolina, 223
Norway, 166, 219
Notes, taking, 36

O
One-coach model, 152–154
O'Regan, Tipene, 214
Organizations: high reliability, 251; individual identity narratives within, 168; and organizational identity narratives, 168–170; and outsider-witness practices in disputes in, 166–184; principles of narrative mediation in, 167–170
Orientalism, 42
Othermothering, 72
Ousky, R. D., 136
Outside-in approach, 6
Outsider-witness practices: and conducting final plenary session, 182–183; conducting workshop using, 179–182; example of workshop using, 176–183; and holding initial consultation, 177–178; idea of, 170–176; and interviewing participants, 178–179; in organizational disputes, 166–184; and principles of narrative mediation in organizations, 167–170; reflections on, 183–184; and structure for outsider-witness conversation, 172–173

P
Pakeha, 208
Pape, T., 244, 245
Papua New Guinea, 219
Paradigmatic approach, 2
Parker, I., 64
Pennell, J., 223
Personality disorder, 274
Pfifferling, J., 245
Positioning, 21; understanding, 71–72. See also Discursive positioning; Positioning theory
Positioning theory, 21, 22; definition of, 43–45; and how mediators position parties, 50–57; and how position calls function, 45–49; positioning and expertise in, 51–53; positioning and self in, 48; positioning and social roles in, 48–49; positioning in multiple conversations in, 46–48; and positioning people in different conversations, 53–54; and problem of first speaker,

54–56; use of, in mediation, 58–61

Positions, 21; shifts in, 97

"Positive no," 11–12

Poststructuralist analysis, 54–55

Power: in conflict, 109–113; constructionist view of, 110–112; and governmentality, 112–113; liberal-humanist view of, 109–110; and professional knowledge, 114–115; relations, 6, 7, 44, 52, 54, 55; structuralist view of, 110

Power/knowledge, 72

Pranis, K., 221

Preconstructed space, 66

Problem: defining, 17; viewing, as restraint, 16–20

Professional knowledge, power and, 114–115

Progress, documenting. *See* Documenting progress

Projections, cultural, 157–159

Protected apology, 264

Q

Queensland, Australia, 220

Questions, construction of alternative story through asking, 32–33

R

Race, 108–109

Rashbaum, B., 85

Reductionist vision, 104

Reflecting team, 159–162; and rules for reflecting team members, 161–162

Rejoinder, 46

Relating: borderline pattern of, 277–279; narcissistic pattern of, 279–280; and working with professionals who exhibit difficult relational patterns, 281

Relational conditions, 22

Relationship story, re-authoring, 31–35

Repetition, 44

Repositioning, 184

Response, primacy of anticipated, 56

Restorative chat, 221

Restorative conferencing, 216

Restorative conferencing in schools, 215–241; and addressing need for relationship healing, 226–227; evidence of effectiveness in, 222–223; and increasing number of voices in conversation, 224; and indigenous practices, 218; and integration of offender back into community, 224–226; narrative method for, 229–240; principles of, 223–227; and principles of narrative restorative conferencing, 227–229; and rapid international growth, 218–222; reflections on, 240–241; and restorative justice, 216–223. *See also* Narrative restorative conferencing

Restorative conversations, 221

Restorative discipline, 220

Restorative interview, 221

Restorative justice, 117

Restorative Practices Develop-
ment Team, 220, 221, 232
Restraint, viewing problem
story as, 16–20
Restructuring, 167
Retributive justice, 116
Reynolds, C. R., 225
Ritual conversations, 170
Roover, J. E., 243, 245
Rorty, R., 174–175
Rosa and the school board,
story of, 199–213
Rosaldo, R., 105
Rose, C., 129, 139, 288
Roussos, P., xi, 149–151
Ruby and Phoebe, story of,
187–199
Runbeck, M. L., 267

S

Said, E. W., 42, 105
San Diego Family Law
Group, 151
San Francisco, California, 148
Schwartz, R. W., xi, 244
Scotland, 219
Seidel, M., 174–175
Self: constructionist vision
of, 48; positioning and, 48;
story of needs of, 144
Self-awareness, 172
Self-interest, 144–146
Sentencing circle, 218
Settlement orientation, 51
Shaw, G., 222
Sheras, P., 225
Shotter, J., 46, 56
Silverstein, O., 85
Sinclair, S., xii, 109

Skiba, R., 225
Social constructionism, 14–15
Social norms, 44
Social practice, 118
Social roles, positioning and,
48–49
Solomon, L., 152, 153
South Africa, 219
Southern California, 247
St. Joseph, Missouri, 223
Stefancic, J., 109
Stories: absent but implicit, 10;
assumption that people live
their lives through, 3–6
Story, 4
Story of hope, 10–11; access-
ing, 17–18; example of
accessing, 18–20
Stream of consciousness, 174
Structuralist approach, 110
Stuart, B., 136, 146, 218
Subjective positioning, concept
of, 43
Subjectivity, intertextual, 47
Surplus meaning, 9
Surprise, moments of, 116
Sutcliffe, K. M., 251
Sweden, 166, 219

T

Talking circles, 223
Taonga, 212
Taonui, R., 200
Television talk shows, 78
Tesler, P., 133
Thailand, 219
Thompson, P., ix, 133, 148
Thorsborne, M., x, 219–222
Thrownness, 103

Tillich, P., 103
To Err is Human: Building a Safer Health System (Institute of Medicine), 245
Totalizing language, 228–229
Traces, 69
Transformative approach, 2
Triggs, S., 219
Truancy mediation, 221
Turner, W. A., 201
Tyson, M., 40–42

U
Umbreit, M., 217
Understanding, shifts in, 32
United Kingdom, 220, 223
United Nations, 117
United States, 117, 219; hospitals in, 245
University of Waikato (New Zealand), 232
Ury, W., 11, 18, 21, 243
Utah, 221, 223
Utterances, 44–48

V
Value positions, 11
van Langenhøve, L., 21
Venice Beach (Los Angeles, California), 171
Victim-offender mediations, 117, 223
Voices, corridor of, 46–47

von Thaden, T. L., 251
Vygotsky, L., 31

W
Wachtel, J., 219
Wales, 219
Webb, S. G., 136, 143, 146
Weick, K. E., 251
West African cultures, 72
Western culture, 6, 23, 101, 123, 131
Whanau, 200, 203, 205, 208, 210
White, M., viii, x, 10, 13, 28–29, 35, 84, 87, 115, 163, 170, 172, 173, 182, 184, 193, 227
Winslade, J., 2, 43, 48, 72, 84, 87, 109, 115, 116, 163, 193, 220–222
Wittgenstein, L., 32, 174
Wood, S., 219
Writing, 35–39
Wyatt, J. B., 243

Y
Yugoslavia, 105

Z
Zammit, L., 220, 223
Zehr, H., 216, 218, 226, 227
Zen Buddhism, 139
Zero tolerance, 225